The Spirit of Churchill

The Spirit of Churchill

Deborah Davis Brezina

Murfreesboro, TN

The Spirit of Churchill

Published by Avalon Press.

For information contact us at:
Avalon Press
111 West College Street
Murfreesboro, TN 37130
www.avalonpress.net
www.churchillbook.com

ISBN: 0-9779505-0-6

Printed in the United States of America

General Acknowledgements

The author expresses profound appreciation to the Master, Fellows, and Scholars of Churchill College, Cambridge, for their generous permission in the abundant use of photographs from the Baroness Spencer-Churchill Papers.

The author gratefully acknowledges Curtis Brown, Ltd. of London for their kind permission in the reproduction of photographs from The Broadwater Collection.

The use of the 1940 David Low cartoon is granted by the Centre for the Study of Cartoons and Caricature, University of Kent, and reproduced by permission of Solo Syndication, London.

Photographs from the Imperial War Museum, London, are reproduced by permission of its Trustees.

The photograph of Mr. Churchill delivering The Sinews of Peace is kindly lent for reproduction by The Winston Churchill Memorial and Library in the United States at Westminster College, Fulton, Missouri.

The facsimile of the 1941 FDR letter to Churchill is most graciously supplied by Mr. Allen Packwood, Director of The Churchill Archives Centre, Cambridge.

The photographs of the Bouchain Tapestry of Blenheim Palace and the map at Chartwell of the Normandy landings of D-Day are reproduced by kind permission of Mr. Jeremy Whitaker, MCSD, Hampshire, England.

Cover: The author is most grateful to the Office of Rights and Reproductions at the National Portrait Gallery, The Smithsonian Institution, for their generosity in permitting the reproduction of the 1946 Douglas Chandor portrait in oil of Sir Winston Churchill in RAF Commodore uniform.

Back cover: The Spencer-Churchill Crest is reproduced by the gracious courtesy of the 11th Duke of Marlborough. Its use is endorsed by generous permission of Mr. John Forster, Librarian of Blenheim Palace, Oxfordshire, England through Jarrolds Publishing, Whitefriars, Norwich.

DEDICATION

To Cliff and Betty Davis,
worthy members of the Greatest Generation,
who taught me to love and honor God, family, and country

ACKNOWLEDGEMENTS

In the days and weeks immediately following September 11, 2001, there seemed to be no telecast or broadcast, no newspaper or magazine that did not mention the name of Winston Churchill. Our nation had been violated by the barbarism of a new dark age. The Free World had been shaken to its core. It seemed as if the gatekeepers of information looked for guidance, inspiration, and hope to the memory of one man who rallied a nation in peril to battle the forces that threatened to strike it down. It was then I decided that more than anything else, I wanted to inspire and encourage young people and adults by the heroic example of Sir Winston Churchill—a man who never gave up, who had indomitable courage to stand alone for what he believed was right, and who considered only victory in the face of defeat. While on a research trip to the United Kingdom in February of 2002, my husband Mark and I met Mr. John Forster, Librarian of Blenheim Palace, who by the gracious permission of the 11th Duke of Marlborough, not only opened the magnificent doors of "England's Versailles," but opened the portal to people and places that would change my life. I shall never be able to repay my debt to him, for he sent me to Cambridge to meet the man who pointed me toward the horizon of a new world. Allen Packwood, Director of the Churchill Archives Centre and generous friend, has been with me every step of the way. His life and work on both sides of the Atlantic truly defines "the special relationship" shared by Britain and America. I am a grateful beneficiary of his "open door policy," a policy not without risk. Allen takes those risks because, first and foremost, he believes as much in "the cause" as he believes in helping others. He has been editor, instructor, and mentor. Without him, this book would not have been possible.

I am eternally grateful to friends and family members who lovingly gave their time and attention to my dream. To my parents, to whom the book is dedicated, you modeled selfless sacrifice and unconditional love. Thank you for setting me free to think and be. To my children, Michael, Bonnie, and Zach, thank you for providing me with an unparalleled support system. I love you. I am thankful beyond measure to Sherry Garner Earl, who, for long hours, scrutinized the manuscript with her vast store of historical knowledge and keen eye to detail. Her advice is always sought. Her views are always cherished. Her counsel is tried and true. **Sherry** is synonymous with *friend*. To the Brezina clan, I am honored to be part of you. At the top of the list is Malcolm Zurek, proud heir of a distinguished World War II veteran, and a brother-in-law who is truly a brother, and Ben Brezina, nephew and fellow-laborer, who I am supremely honored to have traveled with on so many journeys. I am deeply obligated to The Honorable Helen Marie Taylor and G. William "Bill" Thomas, tireless champions of the cause of freedom and true patriots whom I have the honor and privilege to call friends. Their unselfish support and encouragement has both inspired and sustained me time and again. They have added a dimension to my life that is unmatched.

For three decades, I have been blessed by the support of dear friends, Philip and Cherie Wentzell. Their unconditional love and unyielding prayers have been an undeserved living gift. With gratefulness and love to my mentor, Eunie Smith, whose unshakable confidence and immeasurable guidance is inextricably woven into the fabric of my life. I am grateful beyond words to Lana and Claiborne Thornton, two of the truest foul-weather friends anyone could have. Always available and generous with their valuable time and sound advice, they have truly walked all the way with me. I am forever indebted to a master of mentoring, Jeff Myers, the embodiment of bold spirit and brilliant insight, who always has time for me. A true Churchillian, his forward-looking eye to the future is coupled with a dynamism that is a privilege to experience. I owe Jeff for the title of the book which truly pulled it all together. I am so thankful to Christian Hidalgo, publisher and friend, who never wavered in his belief in me or this effort. His talent, creativity, and commitment to excellence are beautiful things to behold. I am a grateful recipient of his prodigious labors. To Anne Jaeger, whose encouragement is surpassed only by her editing expertise, I am truly thankful. Her vital constructive criticism was always balanced with genuine concern for this project. She has been a faithful friend. My heartfelt gratitude is extended to Mike Fitzgerald, dedicated Churchillian, World War II devotee, and true friend. For what he has meant to our son, I have a lifetime of thanks. For what he has meant to this effort, I am forever in his debt. I am continually blessed by the unwavering friendship of Craig Metz who always seeks my best and seizes every opportunity to help me reach higher and higher. I am privileged to know him. To my friend, Aaron Yarborough, whose computer skills are second only to his servant's heart, thank you for your years of patience, understanding, and emergency house calls. You made it possible. My warm thanks to Becky Norton Dunlop, whose stalwart defense of the principles of liberty and the values that sustain our nation, is a ceaseless example of what it means to be an American. I am honored she calls me friend.

I shall never cease to be grateful to Jack Kemp, apogee of Churchill aficionados, who generously took a personal interest in this project and this aspiring author. I am always awed by his boundless optimism, contagious energy, and unforgettable passion for human freedom and all things Churchill. I shall be forever thankful for the commitment to liberty by a genuine national treasure, Zell Miller. His life of service, love of country, and courageous stands has truly made him a man for all seasons. Finally, and most important of all, to my husband Mark, whose unshakable confidence, love, and support made this dream a reality. Wonderfully wise, steadfast and sure, walking through life with him has made all the difference.

CONTENTS

Foreword	*Jack Kemp*	i
Introduction	*Allen Packwood*	iii
Prologue		v
Vox Anglorum		xi
One	The Way Ahead	1
Two	Then and Now	17
Three	Reconnaissance	31
Four	Wolf at the Door	41
Five	In the Wilderness	49
Six	Vindicated Prophet	67
Seven	"Very Well, Alone!"	83
Eight	Fire Over England	99
Nine	English Bulldog	115
Ten	To Make Men Free	135
Eleven	Into the Breach	147
Twelve	The Noblest Work	163
Thirteen	On the Ramparts	195
Fourteen	For Liberty	217
Fifteen	Back to the Future	237
Sixteen	A Fixed Point	251
Seventeen	Forge and Anvil	269
A Rendezvous		291
Addendum		295

FOREWORD

Many figures throughout the long march of humanity have been deemed "great" but few have remained in the collective conscience of those who came after. In times of supreme crisis, great leaders counter pessimism and fear with hope and resolve. The quality and character of their leadership is key to the survival of their people. Such leaders transcend time and bend history to their will. Great Russian novelist Leo Tolstoy once posed an intriguing question: Do the times create the leader, or does the leader create the times? When considering the life and legacy of Sir Winston Churchill, the answer to both questions is *yes.*

Rarely has a man and a moment been so wonderfully wedded than in May 1940 when Winston Churchill became Prime Minister of Great Britain. His were the most dangerous of times in which the fate of the world hung in the balance. His uncertain days seemed to be waiting for a certain kind of leader, a leader with an unmatched spirit of courage and conviction. With unwavering assurance, he believed destiny had saved him for that moment in history. As history looks back, it is assured as well, for without his leadership, the fate of his nation and the world would have taken a markedly different course. As world events continue to unfold, it is evident the redoubtable Mr. Churchill is still the man of the moment.

The Spirit of Churchill is a stirring call to this present generation to reclaim the noble heritage of those who preserved our freedom. Author Deborah Brezina brings to life Winston Churchill. She challenges and inspires by the heroic example of a man who never gave up, who only considered victory in the face of defeat, and who had indomitable determination to stand alone for what he believed was right.

The Spirit of Churchill causes the reader to think about issues of integrity and character as it presents Winston Churchill as the consummate historical model of conviction and courage in the face of impossible odds. In entertaining narrative style, Debbie recounts the forces in his life that helped Winston Churchill become the bold and brilliant leader he was—truly one of the most pivotal figures of the

20th century. Her account of his life and times is inspirational, refreshing, dramatic, and moving.

The Spirit of Churchill literally takes the reader through the major events of the Second World War and presents a leader who left no room for compromise in the defense of liberty, a leader who understood he had to take a stand regardless of the consequences. Churchill never changed from being Churchill: consistency of character, consistency of aim, consistency of will. His stubborn quality of unchangeableness brought steadiness to an unsteady world. He could be reviled but not ignored, scorned but not silenced, even in the lonely times deemed his "wilderness years."

The Spirit of Churchill illustrates the continuing relevance of the Anglo-American Alliance and special relationship between the leaders of the United States and Great Britain. It stresses a vital truth: what one believes matters. In 1940, it mattered to the whole world. In the 21st century, it still does. As the Free World stands fast in the global war against terrorism, we could do no better than to capture the man and his moment. This book does it.

John F. Kennedy once said of Winston Churchill that he marshaled the English language and sent it into battle. Thankfully, for those of us who have come after, he did. The history of the 20th century was, in great part, the narrator of his life. The history of the 21st century is, in great part, a measure of his legacy.

Winston Churchill carved a path of duty and honor in defense of freedom. His spirit won the heart of the British people. Their blood, toil, tears, and sweat won Britain its finest hour. He left the world a heritage of hope time cannot dim. Courage, conviction, optimism, devotion to family, duty to country, reliance on history, adherence to tradition, love of liberty, and romantic reverence for the crown and throne of England is the spirit of Churchill. But, his spirit does not—it cannot—belong to England alone, it belongs to freedom-loving people everywhere.

Jack Kemp
November 1, 2005
Washington, D.C.

INTRODUCTION

My role, as Director of the Churchill Archives Centre, is to preserve the raw material of history and ensure it is accessible for this and future generations. It is vitally important that each new generation be aware of its history and be able to assess and interpret contemporary events in the light of what has come before.

Winston Churchill had a lifelong passion for history. This must have been instilled in him as a young child, while playing in the grounds of Blenheim Palace, imbibing the historical legacy of his illustrious ancestor, John Churchill, 1st Duke of Marlborough. Throughout his long life, he enjoyed visiting battlefields, refighting the great issues of the past, and reconstructing great historical narratives.

Yet he also believed in the power of history to inform the present. He wrote about the life of the 1st Duke of Marlborough against the backdrop of the rise of Nazism in Germany. In his book he described the role of a Churchill in leading a coalition of states against a mighty European despot. It was then John Churchill versus Louis XIV's France. In his *History of the English Speaking Peoples*, begun in the 1930s but finished and published against the backdrop of the emerging Cold War, he stressed the development of the shared laws and values that would enable Britain and the United States to stand together.

It seems to me this book by Deborah Brezina takes those Churchillian values and seeks to apply them to a new generation. The author believes passionately in the ability of the past to inform the present, and the importance of the example of great men. Churchill wrote of his *History of the English Speaking Peoples* that it was very much a "personal view." *The Spirit of Churchill* is a personal view—on the nature of leadership, the lessons of history, and the strengths of the relationship between the United States and the United Kingdom—and one that will help keep discussion of the past alive in the present.

The power of Debbie's book comes from her deep passion and enthusiasm for her subject and from her desire to illustrate to the youth of the day that current challenges and problems should not be viewed in isolation. This is also a political book—when talking about Churchill how could it be otherwise—and sets out very firmly a particular view of recent history. Others may want to challenge Debbie's interpretation, but the very purpose of a book like this should be to stimulate debate. I have no doubt this work will be an invaluable learning tool. It will educate people about the key events of the twentieth century and get them thinking about the relevance and interpretation of those events for the twenty-first.

Sir Winston Churchill was passionate about the importance of learning history. The history he enjoyed was the history of great people and great events. He believed that individuals could make a difference, and he carried this conviction into his public and political life. He also wrote history, and wrote it to shed light on the problems of his own time. This book is very much in that Churchillian tradition.

Allen Packwood
Churchill Archives Centre
29 September 2005

PROLOGUE

On September 11, 2001, America entered a new world war. President George W. Bush will no doubt be remembered as a wartime Commander-in-Chief. His greatest challenge came less than a year after his oath of office. In the years since the horrific attack on America, her leader has demonstrated at every turn the courage of his convictions and the upholding of the values of America and of Western civilization itself.

At this time in history perhaps it is fitting to pause and reflect upon another wartime leader—a leader whose times and circumstances were very different, yet in the fundamentals and consequences for the future, amazingly similar. Each leader was given the duty of rallying his respective nation, and each possessed the resolve and courage to see it through. Times change, but the transcendent values which ultimately preserve the temporal foundations of successful civilizations do not. They must be, with vigilance, carefully guarded by each new generation. This is the mantle of leaders who have a rendezvous with history, and those with whom history keeps that rendezvous. The leader to whom freedom-loving peoples in any era should hearken is, of course, the indefatigable Winston Churchill.

So much has been written about him and said of him that to capture his essence and significance is like trying to empty the English Channel with a teacup. He still speaks. His spirit—the courage of his convictions and the boldness to stand alone for the right—still stirs the hearts and minds of every generation. He is still the giant who seems to buttress the 20th century itself as he stands astride it from its very center.

From his recognition of the danger of Hitler in the 1930s, to his recognition of the danger of communism and its "iron curtain" in the 1940s, the wisdom and farsightedness of Winston Churchill is unsurpassed, even though he often paid a heavy political price. Many times he was considered an anachronism, out of time and place. Yet, in the days following September 11, no higher compliment was sought by any world leader than to be described as "Churchillian."

Winston Churchill once said, "There is no history, only biography." The word *biography* literally means "to write a life," and Churchill's life has certainly been chronicled by renowned scholars. His worthy admonition to "study history! study history!" serves as a reliable guide, for when one studies a biography of the great man, the history of his era comes to life. Seldom has a public person been, at the same time, held in such esteem and such affection. For so many, the passing of time has not changed this.

It has been said we live in "an unheroic time" when great leaders have been replaced by administrators and bureaucrats, heroes seemingly found only within the telling of the great histories of the past, or worse, relegated to the remoteness of textbooks. Therefore, many young people today have difficulty in relating to Winston Churchill. Perhaps it is because we are six decades removed from the times in which he performed his most crucial role in helping preserve the civilization they so enjoy. Or perhaps it is because all this generation knows is peace, progress, and prosperity. For whatever the reasons, they—and we—need to remember this giant of the past who, as have few others, helped to shape the present. A true Renaissance man, he was warrior, journalist, war correspondent, politician, author, painter, sportsman, historian, orator, innovator, scholar, and statesman.

In his classic wit, Mr. Churchill once remarked, "History shall be kind to me, for I intend to write it." From *Marlborough, His Life and Times*, to his panoramic works, *A History of the English-Speaking Peoples* and *The Second World War*, his prolific writings have contributed much to the illustrious record of the history of his nation. His eloquent speeches—especially the ones during World War II—are without equal. Not only do they embody the essence of that era, they possess a quality that is both timeless and transcendent. It is, therefore, not surprising he received the Nobel Prize in Literature as much for his majestic spoken words as for his scholarship and historical élan. The greatest men and women of history *knew* their history. And when a people know their past and understand its importance to their future, they are never caught unaware by present dangers. It is no surprise such a man of history was so well acquainted with the study of it. Fittingly, he is one of modern history's favorite subjects!

In this age of relativism and post-modernism, the lines between good and evil and right and wrong are often blurred. *Truth* has become only "individual" or "personal" or declared as not existing at all. The clarity of spoken words is often vital to define differences and give meaning to the real world in times of crises. When Ronald Reagan used the term "Evil Empire," it was a shot across the bow of the Soviet ship of state and presaged the fall of the Berlin Wall, the collapse of the Soviet Union, and birthed the democracy movement in Eastern Europe and beyond. In 1989, Vaclev Havel, leader of the Czech resistance, declared his opposition to oppression by his bold declaration that *"what we need is truth!"* His courageous cry helped bring communism down in the Eastern Bloc. When President George W. Bush defined the war on terrorism in the aftermath of September 11, he unashamedly declared this would be a struggle between "good and evil." His words galvanized and mobilized his countrymen for the days and months ahead.

Men like Churchill never truly die, for they lived for something higher and greater than themselves. It is they, as examples of courage and valor against all odds, who history holds securely for generations yet unborn. With clarity of vision, of purpose, and of communication, such leaders impart strength, resolve, and the will to persevere. *Winston Churchill was clear on fascism, Ronald Reagan was clear on communism, and George W. Bush is clear on terrorism.* These are defining moments in history. For by such clarity, leaders define the times, frame the issues, and make clear the challenges. The result: hope for the future.

As the mid-point of the 20th century approached and the darkness of totalitarianism threatened to engulf the globe, the world went to war. By implacable resolve and steadfast determination, the darkness was dispelled by the gleaming light of freedom. A half-century later, the world knows the nations under the grip of that darkness were indeed saved. A half-century later, as the darkness of terrorism threatens civilization, the world must, as never before, remember *how* these nations were restored. In the "Fighting Forties" victory was won by the courage of millions coupled with the vision of leaders who knew how to stay the course, where that course would take them, and why history had placed them there. No less is required from responsible statesmen who have risen to lead in the dawn of the volatile years of a new millennium—the 21st century. As the civilized world stands once more against a hateful enemy, liberty-loving men and women have need of principled leaders and steady statesmen. As never before, statesmen of strong fiber are not only essential, they are indispensable if the cause of peace, freedom, and civilization is to prevail.

On March 3, 2004, in the rush hour of a normal workweek, bombs ripped through four commuter trains in Madrid. Just a week before its national elections, Spain was hit hard by Islamic terrorists. The death toll was 132 innocent men, women, and children. Many believe in the aftermath, terrorists altered an election and set a different course for a nation. In the wake of al Qaeda bombings in Madrid, the comprehensive war against global terrorism by democratic nations seemed in jeopardy. "This is not Europe's first experience with appeasement." Italy's *Corriere de la Sera* warned, "The spirit of Munich is again blowing across Europe."[3]

On June 7, 2005, in the heart of London, the worst strike of terror on British soil since the Second World War shattered a summer morning. Within hours, the resolve of the British people was evident. A phrase used countless times during the Blitz of six decades before was heard again: "London can take it!" Dazed and bloodied Britons who survived blasts on three London subway trains and one double-decker bus seemed to speak with a single voice: "If that's all they can do to us, we'll make it!" The British nation took it in stride and carried on: "We won't give in to terror—no matter the cost!" The world again witnessed the spirit of Churchill.

Because the long tradition of democracy runs deep in the history and psyche of Great Britain, the question becomes: Does Britain have the spirit of Churchill or did Churchill have the spirit of Britain? At the celebration of Sir Winston's 80th birthday, this question was posed. In characteristic wit and wisdom the Lion of England aptly replied, *"It was the nation who had the lion's heart. I had the luck to be called upon to give the roar."*

Many today are naïve about human nature, differences between good and evil, and the lessons of history. Many were so in Churchill's day. Many today believe nothing is worth fighting for because terrorists can be appeased. Many thought so in Churchill's day. The Free World has a choice to either learn or not learn the lessons of history. Each choice comes with consequences. In the days and years to come, the world will choose the "spirit of Munich" or the spirit of Churchill.

You ask what is our aim? I can answer in one word: Victory—victory at all costs, victory is spite of all terror, victory however long and hard that road may be. For without victory, there is no survival.
Rt. Hon. Winston Churchill
First Speech to Parliament as Prime Minister
May 13, 1940

Vox Anglorum
"Voice of the English"

Arm yourselves and be ye men of valour and be in readiness for the conflict. For it is better for us to perish in battle than to look upon the outrage of our nation and our altar.
Mr. Churchill's 1ˢᵗ BBC Broadcast as Prime Minister, May 19, 1940

During the darkest days of World War II across the Nazi-occupied countries of Europe, all seemed lost. Yet there was a glimmer of hope—a lifeline of freedom—albeit only a voice. But what a voice! Many evenings, thousands of conquered Europeans huddled around secreted-away and often makeshift radios as they awaited a broadcast from the BBC across the English Channel.

In occupied Holland, young Anne Frank wrote in her diary: "We listen to German radio for entertainment, but we listen to the BBC for hope." Periodically, the BBC broadcast would feature remarks by the wartime Prime Minister of Great Britain, Winston Churchill. From across the channel, his statements were to give hope and encouragement to all under the heel of tyranny—a hope of freedom and a will to not give up the fight.

Six decades later, it is as if we can hear the collective and hushed voices of those freedom-loving people in occupied Austria, Czechoslovakia, Poland, Holland, Belgium, Denmark, Norway, and France who waited patiently for the broadcast to begin. As the static seemed endless in anticipation, they seem to whisper with one voice, "Quiet please! Mr. Churchill's going to speak!"

Well, Mr. Churchill *did* speak. And with a voice not only of resonance, but of confidence, conviction, and courage. Whether he addressed a small gathering on a street corner, his peers in the House of Commons, or a world broadcast by the BBC, his message never changed, only the grandeur of his words. As we reflect upon his times and ours, let him speak.

Chapter 1

THE WAY AHEAD

We are a free people because a man named Winston Churchill lived.
The Spectator, London, 1965

The epic battles of the Second World War have long faded from the memories of many, but the story of sacrifice made by millions of young men and women must never leave the minds of free people everywhere. When call of country came, ordinary young men willingly left the comfort and security of family and home to fight and die on foreign fields. It was the phenomenon of an age, the definition of an era. When homelands were viciously attacked, Allied armies and navies, comprised mostly of civilians, raised themselves up to defeat one of the greatest professional armies in history. Ordinary young men and women suspended their lives to serve their nations and the world—teachers, salesmen, engineers, doctors, lawyers, nurses, longshoremen, truck drivers, farmers, secretaries, bankers, professors, telephone operators, miners, railroad workers, firemen, and policemen—all declared as one voice: *"We are determined no one and no country will take our freedom away! It is ours—the blood of our forefathers earned it. It is our heritage, our birthright, and we are going to fight to the death if need be to preserve it!"*
The history of those days reminds the present world what is worth living for, fighting for, and dying for. The saga, still unfinished, is of survival of life, legacy, and liberty. The never-ending story will live as long as courage, duty, honor, and faith. It will never become old or outdated. Ordinary, yet unique, men and women from every culture and creed will forever rise and rise again to fight against all who seek to destroy civilization. The kind of men and women who will forever guard *the way ahead.*[1]
Because memory is to an individual as history is to a civilization, the historical memory of a nation and its people are essential to its continuance. Faded from the collective memory of many are the

major battles of the American War for Independence. Still, who can forget the Minutemen? Colonial farmers, merchants, blacksmiths, and teachers who, never trained to fight, picked up muskets, fired shots heard 'round the world, and changed all of history. Protecting the memory of heroes is a prime duty. Guardians of the past speak with careful admonition: *"Be careful. Do not forget. Remember."*

One of those guardians was Abraham Lincoln. Custodian of an immortal presidency spent in the shadow of war, he was seldom far from the sound of cannon or the fury of gunfire. In ghostly imagery, he reminded a country that forgetfulness is fostered by "the silent artillery of time." As if removed by a distanced bombardment muffled from the conscience of a people, the passing of years too often leaves ingratitude for those who protected the blessings and made possible the benefits of liberty. Mr. Lincoln's unforgettable phrase proclaims the past indispensable, the present meaningful, and the future hopeful. In the 21st century and beyond, guardians of the past are needed to defend against the silent artillery of time.

It has been well said that great men and great nations supply the themes for great history.[2] Winston Spencer Churchill was legend in his own time. With the passing of years, his legacy grows only greater.

His long-view of history and his realistic understanding of the true nature of mankind became part of the strength of his leadership and secret to his greatness. By countering force and fear with faith and freedom, his time of tyrants and darkness became a season of trust and light. Winston Churchill built a permanent bridge between those days—and the present.[3] We know him. Or at least we think we know him. Certainly, we would very much like to have known him! Seen now only in portraits, he is as familiar as a family photograph. There shall never be another like him. He shall never be forgotten. He is history with a human face.

In a remarkable sense, Winston Churchill occupies the present day, the present hour, the present moment. He is relevant and real in the 21st century. His spirit of courage still calls. His spirit of resolve still reverberates. Time cannot dim it. History cannot obscure it. He imparts lessons of leadership because the Free World will always need men and women of conviction and courage.

At the opening of the Churchill Museum in London, Allen Packwood, Director of the Churchill Archives Centre at Cambridge University, reminded those in the present how those from the past point the way ahead:

> *As we entered a new century, we inevitably looked back to the last century for defining moments and defining characters. In the aftermath of September 11, leaders on both sides of the Atlantic looked for examples of strong leadership, they looked back to the last great moments of world crisis, and they used Churchill as role model and example.*[4]

Men and women who are giants of the past, the ordinary who became extraordinary, were confronted with all of life's ups and downs, highs and lows, victories and defeats. In times of great pressure and difficulty the true character of these individuals was revealed by their response to the crises in their lives. When Winston Churchill was squeezed by difficult circumstances, out came determination. When confronted with defeat, he countered with doggedness. He would not leave his post—his beloved country—in its hour of greatest need, for he knew he had to stand up to a bully and a tyrant. When tested to the fullest, he had the defiance and will to not only endure, but also to win.

Building blocks of character shaped Winston Churchill into a statesman of vision and principle. Application of character shaped him into a lion-hearted leader. His life provides lessons for success for all who desire to be ready when circumstances confront and destiny calls. His character qualities provide a model for all who desire to lead: vision, conviction, courage, determination, optimism, endurance, and responsibility.

Vision—Ability to See and Understand What is Ahead

Winston Churchill could see beyond the ordinary sight of his contemporaries. He did not only look, he saw. Because he knew he had a purpose and a destiny, he saw beyond difficulty, disaster, and defeat. Because he knew history, he visualized victory. In the era in which he lived, Winston Churchill recognized danger and opportunity earlier than other statesmen. He had farsightedness—a unique ability to foresee what could and did happen. He understood evil and evil people while many of his contemporaries were foolish and naïve. He saw this at an early age when he wrote of his encounters with radical Islam in the Sudan War of 1898. He knew this during the time when much of Europe did not see the evil of Adolf Hitler, and his contemporaries tried to work out differences with a malevolent tyrant. He was sure of this before the end of the Second World War when he warned the world of the goals of communism. Winston Churchill anticipated what lay ahead. His reward for such invaluable service to his nation and the world was to be shunned and dismissed again and again. In these moments of discouragement his attitude was *"Never give up!"* He hoped time would reveal the larger picture to the world. He was a true visionary—sometimes impractical, frequently idealistic, but always quixotic. This visionary history-maker is not unreachable, dusty or dead; he is important to the 21st century and beyond:

> *Vision, in most politicians, is a plan to cope with yesterday's headlines. Churchill, with the knowledge of the historian and the valor of a soldier, not only dared to predict what people did not want to hear—the advent of two World Wars as well as the Cold War—but also offered the plans to prevent them. That foresight and the courage to act on it distinguish Churchill.[5]*

Conviction—Steadfast Belief in a Cause or a Goal

Whatever may be said of Winston Churchill, there is no doubt he was a man of conviction. Stout-hearted and strong-minded, he often stood alone for what he believed was right. And right or wrong, he knew what he believed. Exasperating? Often. Off-putting? Frequently. Admirable? Always. More often than not, his convictions went against the rest of the world. Many thought he was wrong, but in the end he was right. It is hard enough for one man to stand against the conventional wisdom of his own country, but to stand against that of a continent takes unwavering conviction. The English word *believe* is derived from two words, *by-live*. And *believe* is Winston Churchill in purest form, for what he believed, he lived by. A solid, unyielding boulder, he could be pushed and pulled but nothing was going to move him. He is a model for those who succeed in life. He is a model for those who take the risk of standing by their convictions. It is as if he can be heard to say, *"I will make my own way. When I know I am right, I will go against my own peers if I must. I will stick to my principles no matter what!"*

With apposite imagery, historian and author Mark Helprin described the essence of statesmen who hold fast unchangeable principles. His words capture the essence of Churchill:

> *Principles are eternal. They stem not from our resolution or lack of it, but from elsewhere, where in patient and infinite ranks they simply wait to be called…Things such as courage and honor are the moral equivalent of certain laws written throughout the universe. They can be neglected but they can not be lost. They can be thrown down but they cannot be broken…No matter what people may say in times of prosperity and peace, all men and women hunger for acts of integrity and courage. They hunger for a statesman magnetized by the truth—unable to put his interests before that of his nation.*[6]

Courage—Boldness to Act on What One Believes

The name *Churchill* has almost become synonymous with the word *courage*. There is little doubt Winston Churchill possessed boldness to act on what he believed, audacity to confront an opponent with the confidence of ultimate success, and defiance to respond to danger without thought of retreat. He was a man of action. In that dangerous summer of 1940, Britain's pugnacious Prime Minister called upon perhaps his most important character quality—his resolve to not fear. He was not afraid of people who wanted to destroy him, his country, and his way of life. When told to give in by Hitler, he looked him square in the eye and did not back down. He transferred his courage to the British people. He stood and they stood. He stepped out with valor, they marched into history.

Winston Churchill had another kind of courage, the courage to go beyond the expectations of his parents and his peers. He had money, social position, an illustrious name, and a secure place in the hierarchy of the British classes. He had no need to take chances or to do or say anything controversial. He could coast through life safely. He did not. Throughout his life, he demonstrated a disregard for either his personal or political safety. There is something marvelous about someone who takes risks with life when he does not have to. It is courageous. It was Churchill:

> *Courage for some sudden act may be in the heat of battle, we all respect. But there is that still rarer courage which can sustain repeated disappointment, unexpected failure, and shattering defeat. Winston Churchill had that too, and had need of it, not for a day, but for weeks and months and years.*[7]

Determination—Resolve to Persist in Spite of Challenges, Circumstances, Difficulties or Defeats

Every great war leader has dark moments, those critical moments in the heat of the conflict when many tell him the war may be lost because he is doing or would do the wrong thing. Great leaders stand firm in dark moments. They persevere when others speak harshly of them. They do not lose sight of the ultimate goal no matter who or what comes against them. They remain firmly committed to completing the task. They are steadfast and sturdy.

Because he realized present struggles were essential for future achievement, Winston Churchill willed to withstand prolonged hardship, difficulty, and strain. He stayed focused on the objective and expended the necessary resolve to see a crisis through. Passionately tenacious, he symbolized the determination of the British people. Through sheer rhetoric and force of personality, he exhorted a nation to believe that victory was attainable. He galvanized the mood of his country into fiery, dogged defiance: *"We shall not flag or fail!"*[8]

In that summer of all summers in 1940, German planes roared up the Thames and loudspeakers in Germany blared a triumphant message: *Bomben auf Engelland!* or "bombs on England!" Winston Churchill recounted, *"The odds were great, our margins small, the stakes infinite."* Yet he was determined to prevail. An RAF captain remembered, *"Above all, it was an exhilarating period. We had purpose and pride, and Churchill gave them to us. We all waited for his voice on the radio. Everybody in the air as well as on the ground relied on this one man."*[9] The young soldier and sailor had full confidence in him. They knew he would make sure they would have what they needed to fight to victory. They knew England would never waver. They knew because of Churchill.

A silhouette style photograph taken July of 1940 captures the uncompromising resolve of Britain's wartime Prime Minister. Standing on the rocky southern coast of England is Winston Churchill. Atop a bunker, leaning on a cane with cigar firmly clenched in his teeth, he looks out across the Channel toward Nazi-occupied Europe. A row of helmeted British soldiers stands in the trench just below him. They are looking up and smiling, all grateful and proud to have him there. Determination in the face of destruction. Defiance in the face of defeat. Resolute, ready, regardless:

> *He kept England in the war. He exemplified her resourcefulness. He kept her fighting after defeats, impervious to anything but persistence. It was heroic. But, it was not bravado, for Churchill's knowledge of history fortified his confidence. He was leading a nation committed to its sense of the past. And in this, he preserved its future.*[10]

Optimism—Confident and Cheerful Belief for the Best Possible Outcome

General Eisenhower once observed the power of outlook by noting optimism and pessimism are equally infectious. The conscious choice of either view affects people and circumstances in a given situation. Pessimism is a gutless choice. Optimism takes courage and will. How fortunate for England to have had an ebullient optimist for Prime Minister during her most critical days in a thousand years. He was infectious. May the world never be cured!

Winston Churchill had the ability to look at the negative and see positive. He had unshakable optimism. He chose to act with assurance of a good outcome and never failed to encourage others along the way. He cheered the people as much as the people cheered him.[11] His moments of pessimism were rare, and during the war never public. He once left the residence in haste without his trademark cigar. Keenly aware of how he affected the British public, an aide was dispatched to bring one with the order: "they expect to see it."[12]

Unrelenting optimism served Winston Churchill well, for who better to lead his nation from the absolute hopelessness of a Dunkirk or the certain doom of a Battle of Britain? Only a man who knew how to rise from the depths of despair! Who better to stir the heart of a people in time of national peril? Only a leader who was everywhere! Old Winny in the shelters, on the ships, and in the streets. Old Winny with the armies, in the air, and on the airwaves. At a time when the world expected Britain to surrender, Old Winny expected to win. He refused to give up, give out, or give in! His spirit brought to the present a hope for the future:

> *If the human race wishes to have a prolonged and indefinite period of material prosperity, they have only got to behave in a peaceful and helpful way towards one another...Thus we may by patience, courage, and in orderly progression reach the shelter of a calmer and kindlier age...Withhold no sacrifice, grudge no toil, seek no sordid gain, fear no foe. All will be well.[13]*

Endurance—To Continue Under Pain and Hardship without being Overcome

The long life of Winston Churchill was characterized by the ebb and flow of positive and negative forces. Faced with impossible odds within and without himself, he refused to surrender. He often suffered. He always endured. Forced to deal with parental neglect and rejection by the father he worshiped, he never lost the ability to love. Fighting attacks of dark depression he called "the black dog," he kept his spirits up with optimism and strength of will. Foundering many times as a student, he delighted in the beauty of the English language and ultimately elevated its written and spoken influence to heights seldom seen in history. Fated with a debilitating stutter and a lisp never fully lost, he became one of history's most eloquent orators once described as "the Demosthenes^ of the West."[14] In victories and defeats he conquered himself. By victories and defeats he conquered his times. An admiring young photographer once told the octogenarian of his desire to photograph the great man on his 100th birthday. Without reservation, Churchill replied, "I don't see why not, young man. You look reasonably fit."[15]

Winston Churchill exemplified the quality ever associated with those who call themselves British—stamina. In times of extreme pressure, Mr. Churchill called upon this inward drive and power. He remained firm under suffering. He outlasted his challenges. He did not perish. He saw the race to the end. His fellow brave Britons endured with him. They did not worry, for through the darkest night they knew he would be there in the morning. To them Sir Winston spoke words of gratitude and pride, words which provide a fitting epitaph for the man himself: *"You have drawn from the heart of suffering itself the means of inspiration and survival, and of a victory won not only for ourselves, but for all."* [16]

Responsibility—Will to Preserve the Trust and Guard the Duty One has been Given

The way ahead depends on the responsibility of leaders. In Mr. Churchill's words, *"...the moment when Honor points the path of Duty..."*[17] Destiny handed Winston Churchill a great task. His responsibility to that task was tested by time. His lasting achievement was revealed by history.

Winston Churchill lived out what has become the British standard for responsibility to obligation: *England Expects Every Man Will Do His Duty*. This call of duty was memorably commanded by Lord Nelson at the Battle of Trafalgar[B] where the odds were great, the margins small, and the stakes infinite. As one of history's greatest naval battles was about to commence, Britain's immortal Admiral ordered signal flags to flash a message of inspiration to every ship in the British fleet. Nelson's call from his flagship *Victory* typified patriotism and perseverance. It has become part of the British psyche and is remembered as simply, *England Expects…* As did Nelson, Churchill had the will to preserve the trust and guard the duty given him by those who had gone before. As was Nelson, Churchill was grateful to his countrymen for their obligation to it.[C]

The indelible image evoked by mere mention of the name CHURCHILL served the consummate bearer of the name well time and again. Winston Churchill's unquestionable responsibility to the call of duty helped him see and foresee the peril posed to his world. His accountability to the charge he was given pointed toward the promise of its future. Lord Nelson's last words were, "Thank God I have done my duty." As Mr. Churchill reflected on Germany's surrender in 1945, Britain's greatest sailor could hardly have been far from the mind and heart of Britain's greatest wartime Prime Minister:

We were weary and worn, impoverished but undaunted, and now triumphant. We had a moment that was sublime. We gave thanks to God for the noblest of all His blessings, the sense that we had done our duty.[18]

A genuine leader finds a way to overcome the impossible. With all its difficulties and dangers, he assures others as he takes them along the unseen course ahead. He is able to make decisions quickly and effectively with the self-confidence to shut the door and not return the way he came. A leader does not linger over a decision. He knows what to do and does it. He is decisive.

A leader who lasts the passage of time possesses integrity. A great leader maintains honor and trust. He has an undivided loyalty to truth. No leader can be faultless, but he can be blameless. He will make mistakes, but his desire to do the right thing holds fast his purity of purpose: *"There is a helpful guide to nations facing difficult choices. This guide is called honor."[19]*

A true leader never changes his core values. He is not driven by the opinions of others. He never woos a high percentage of the people and is most misunderstood during times of conflict and pressure. A genuine leader is often lonely, but seldom desolate. While his greatest disappointments come from those he is leading, he remains confident in who he is and what he is called to do. A true leader keeps coming at his challenges—coming and coming again.

The young member of Parliament, Mr. Winston Churchill, as he appeared at the time of his election in 1900, as Conservative member from Oldham, aged just 25.
(Churchill Archives Centre; Baroness Spencer-Churchill Papers)

11

A leader who lives throughout history has the imperishable spark of inspiration. The passion in his life draws others like a flame. When he catches fire, people come to watch him burn. The root of the English word *passion* is "suffering." A great leader is willing to suffer for his calling and his cause. His dedication and devotion are awe-inspiring. The English word *inspire* means literally "to breathe."

In history, a leader who inspires is an undying ember which needs only the breath of challenge and opportunity to bring the fire alive again in the hearts and minds of those who discover him. An inspirational leader has characteristics others desire in themselves. He has the ability to motivate others to identify with him. He moves them to become more than they are at that moment. They seem to believe: *"If it's possible for him, it's possible for me!"* An inspirational leader fills others with the power and energy of his example. He causes others to see the mission of his life. He influences others to reach heights they never believed they could reach.

The image of Winston Churchill is *inspiration*. He passionately animated ideas and ideals. He inspired hope in a people who purposed to survive bomb upon bomb, horror upon horror. He gave life to a nation facing death. When his Island witnessed France fall in a matter of days, Paris in just hours, it's as if he inspired his country to say: *"If Old Winny can stand against insurmountable odds, we can hold out against anything! If Old Winny refuses to be defeated, we will be victorious!"*

For any individual, the chance for historic greatness is a combination of character and circumstance. Character demands each person answer his call to duty with responsibility for decisions and actions. Circumstances require each individual be prepared to take hold of every opportunity. When circumstances presented themselves, greatness seized Winston Churchill. In *Never Give In*, author Stephen Mansfield sums up his legacy:

> *It could be said that when the final chapter of human history is written and Churchill is remembered from that distance, his greatest gift to succeeding generations may be found to have been the very issue of teaching men the price of greatness.*[20]

Winston Churchill bequeathed to history a bold spirit. He had the ability to see things others could not see. He knew where to go when others did not know and dared to take them there. He had vision to say it could be done, courage to make it happen, and determination to stick it out when the going was tough. Winston Churchill had the undivided heart of a leader of integrity and inspiration. A bona fide hero in his day, his spirit is vitally needed for tumultuous times.

Holding trademark cigar, Prime Minister Winston Churchill waves to well-wishers outside 10 Downing Street.
(Churchill Archives Centre; Baroness Spencer-Churchill Papers)

Mr. Churchill lives on. We hear his spirit in the voices of leaders who continue on his path. We see his spirit in individuals who live out integrity of character. We desire his spirit as a model of courage and conviction. We cherish his spirit in the lives of leaders who inspire passion for just causes. As the values of the Free World are once again challenged by great forces of darkness, Western civilization must stand now as it did then. Stand it must. Stand it shall. For it has great shoulders upon which to stand.

Sir Winston's father once reflected on the character of leaders. Lord Randolph Churchill could scarcely have known he was poignantly and prophetically describing his progeny:

> *Real leaders of men do not come forward offering to lead. They show the way. And when it has been found to lead to victory, they accept as a matter of course the allegiance of those who have followed.*[21]

In the darkest days of 1940, the lights of liberty were all but extinguished. Across a continent, all hope of freedom seemed lost. The vision of victory was but a faint flicker until a voice traveled across the rugged and rocky coasts of the English Channel. "The Voice" promised blood, toil, tears, and sweat. The man gave leadership, inspiration, and hope. Winston Spencer Churchill marked for his time—and the world—the way ahead.

> *He was a man. Take him for all in all.*
> *We shall not look upon his like again.*
> *Hamlet*, Act 1, Scene 2

A. Demosthenes is considered the greatest orator of ancient Greece. According to Plutarch, ancient Greek historian and biographer, Demosthenes stuttered in his youth and improved his speech by practicing with pebbles in his mouth. Throughout his life he espoused the democratic principles upon which the immortal legacy of Greece would rest.

B. Lord Nelson twice stopped Napoleon in his ambition to bring England to her knees. After his subjugation of Western Europe, Bonaparte, in an effort to dominate the globe, conquered Egypt on his quest to take India. It was Nelson alone—with help from the British fleet—who stood in his way. After the Battle of the Nile, Napoleon escaped to the Continent to plot the invasion of the "Island just across that ditch which one can jump whenever one is bold enough to try." The little Corporal and his ambition to subjugate the seas was finished on October 21, 1805, at the Battle of Trafalgar by the raw courage of just one man—Nelson.

C. After the war, as a gift in recognition of his victory, Churchill was given Nelson's Prayer Book by a descendant of the Admiral's daughter by Lady Hamilton.

Chapter 2

THEN AND NOW

Qui desiderat pacem, praeparet bellum—
Let him who desires peace, prepare for war.
Flavius Vegetius AD 4ᵗʰ century

When Winston Churchill took the reins of power in May of 1940, he understood much more was at stake for England than green rolling hills dotted with wooly sheep or patchwork quilt meadows criss-crossed with ancient hedgerows. Winston Churchill understood men would not fight to the death for a mere piece of geography, no matter how special that geography may be. Because he knew what Britain was at her core, he knew men would fight for what mattered most. He knew what she had given the world—liberty, justice, and the rule of law. Winston Churchill knew if Britain was subjugated by Germany's Fuehrer, what would be left would not be Britain, but an island off the northern coast of Europe, conquered and controlled as the rest of the continent. In those first critical days when he became Prime Minister, his lifelong world and life view was communicated to his War Cabinet in one strong sentence: *"If we do not fight, there will be no British victory!"*[1] From this instant history lesson, his advisers instinctively saw the whole picture. They did not just nod approvingly. They responded with a thunder of pounding fists on the conference table![1] At that moment, Britain's leadership was united, purposed, and determined:

> *It took a certain kind of genius to see situations early, when Churchill saw them. It took an amazing persistence and courage to advance against the forces Churchill faced. But what he saw was not subjective or mysterious. It was the difference between tyranny and free government, the distinction upon which Churchill built his political life. If we cannot see this we cannot see anything. If we cannot honor those who see this in time to save our freedom, we cannot honor anyone.*[2]

It is often difficult for those who live in the present to realize their times may be historic. As history reveals the past, it teaches how present days can quickly become monumental times. September 1, 1939 and September 11, 2001 were two such days. In the aftermath of these September mornings, the world was forever changed. In 1939, Adolf Hitler had a definite view of the world. So did Winston Churchill. As the clash resounded between the adverse views, the world entered into a struggle for life or death. In 2001, two views of the world were again seen in operation across the globe. As history over half a century ago has validated, one view *will* prevail:

> **All great statesmen have a central idea or insight.**
> **Churchill's was that the distinction between liberty**
> **and tyranny, between civilization and barbarism,**
> **is real and substantial.**[3]

A world and life view is a philosophy of life. It is a vision *of* the world and *for* the world. It demonstrates how one *sees* the world and how one *approaches* the world. When wedded to a figure of power and influence, a worldview can affect all of history for good or for ill. The record of mankind is a chronicle of opposing struggles between ideas, beliefs, and powerful forces. The circumstances and challenges mankind has faced clearly illustrate all world and life views are *not* equal. The inevitable collision of philosophies and ideologies become the points and counterpoints of history.

After the fall of the Berlin Wall in 1989 and the breakup of the Eastern Bloc in 1991, many astute geopolitical observers noted that the tense balance of power during the four decades of the Cold War had tended to stabilize the dangers posed by rogue states. In 1993, just two years after the collapse of the Soviet Union, Dr. Samuel Huntington of Harvard University predicted the end of the Cold War would bring new dangers and a threat to world stability. He termed this "a clash of civilizations." Dr. Huntington warned of a coming conflict between the worldviews of the two major civilizations in the East and the West: the Islamic world and the Western world. He further stated the world is divided not so much by geographical boundaries as by differences in ultimate beliefs—in world and life views.[4] Dr. Huntington predicted a clash, initiated by the former, was soon to come:

> *After World War II, the West began to retreat, the colonial empires disappeared and the first Arab nationalism, then Islamic fundamentalism, manifested themselves... The centuries—old military interaction between the West and Islam is unlikely to decline. It could become more virulent... On both sides the interaction between Islam and the West is seen as a clash of civilizations.*[5]

Many believe there is moral equivalence between America and her terrorist enemies. Those who think this should consider a statement Winston Churchill once made in another context: *"Such people are unable to choose between the fire brigade and the fire."* If civilization is to survive, civilization must have men and women who know the difference.[6]

Winston Churchill knew the difference. His refusal to appease the evil of his day has lessons for the present. His fighting spirit never allowed him to back away from speaking truth:

> *Churchill did not denounce the Nazi Empire merely as a threat, actual or potential. Nor did he speak of it as a depraved but possibly useful ally. He excoriated it as a wicked and nihilistic thing.*[7]

Winston Churchill recognized the dangers of war-driven fascism as well as war-driven fanaticism. In *The River War*, young Churchill tells the riveting story of the British re-conquest of the Sudan at the end of the 19th century. Making his mark as a young army officer in the Sudan War of 1898, he not only rode in the last classic cavalry charge in British military history, his first-hand account of his experiences fighting forces of militant Islam is considered "a penetrating analysis of fanaticism."[8] His observations were as real then as now. His dramatic parallels between two fierce warrior classes provide a succinct analysis of two worldviews and the rules of war: "Britain's ruthless decency and her opponent's ruthless indecency."[9]

In 1896, young Churchill joined Lord Kitchener's campaign to regain Khartoum from the fanatical followers of Mohammed Ahmed, a messianic Muslim with a hundred thousand loyal adherents.[A] Ahmed proclaimed himself the Mahdi, "the messiah" or "guided one." The Mahdi considered himself "the Second Prophet of Islam who would come to lead a crusade to conquer Egypt and wipe out the infidels."[10] Standing in his way was the garrison at Khartoum and British General Charles "Chinese" Gordon.[B] Churchill described Gordon as "a type without comparison with few likenesses in history…who brought true civilization to the Sudan."[11] With few supplies and little troops, Gordon's forces held the isolated city for almost a year before they were besieged and massacred. The general's body was mutilated and his head paraded through Muslim villages in triumph. To the Mahdi, the sacking of Khartoum was the beginning of *jihad*, or "holy war." A decade later, General Kitchener's forces avenged the atrocities at Khartoum.

Winston Churchill understood that Western culture and civilization holds fast an idea of justice and moderation that protects human rights. He understood barbarism destroys civil and just order, freedom and prosperity. The war young Churchill fought then is not unlike the war facing the world now. Then, as now, victory must be won against an enemy who values nothing more than the complete annihilation of all who hold another view of humanity. The growth of worldwide terrorism is genuine. It is global, well-financed, and driven by religion. It is a clear and present danger. As such, it is an ongoing threat to all nations who believe in liberty, democracy, and the rule of law. For those engaged in the pitched battles in the 21st century against terrorist forces driven by religious fanaticism, the reflections offered by Winston Churchill over a century ago are insightful, instructive, and important:

That religion, which above all others, was founded and propagated by the sword—the tenets and principles of which are incentives to slaughter and which in three continents had produced fighting breeds of men—stimulates a wild and merciless fanaticism. . .The desert tribes proclaimed they fought for the glory of God. But although the force of fanatical passion is far greater than that exerted by any philosophical belief, its function is just the same. It gives men something which they think is sublime to fight for, and this serves them as an excuse for wars which it is desirable to begin for different reasons. . .Fanaticism is not a cause of war. It is the means which helps savage peoples to fight.[12]

Winston Churchill in 1896. The 21 year-old Subaltern in the 4th Queen's Own Hussars strikes a regal pose two years before riding in the last cavalry charge in British military history. (The Broadwater Collection)

Over a century later on the first anniversary of the Iraq War of Liberation, President George W. Bush issued remarks which revealed his understanding of the two views of the world in operation and the stakes for the victor and the vanquished:

> *There is a dividing line in our world. Not a dividing line between nations or cultures or religions, but between two visions of justice and the value of life. . .There is no neutral ground—no neutral ground—in the fight between civilization and terror. . .*[13]

In 2003, Prime Minster Tony Blair acknowledged the clash of civilizations as he defended the joint policies of Britain and America in regards to preemptive action, solidarity of purpose, and undaunted leadership in the global war on terror:

> *What is happening now is very simple. It is the battle of seminal importance for the early 21st century and it will define relations between the Muslim world and the West. It will have far-reaching implications for the future conduct of American and Western democracy . . . If I had the same decision to make again I would do the same thing. . .Global terrorism is the threat of the 21st century and Britain should be right in there with it . . . It is the only leadership I can offer—it is the only leadership worth having.*[14]

As the years unfold, history will look back to this time of terror and war. History will judge the leadership of America's President and Britain's Prime Minister. History will record that these statesmen understood the profound difference between the use of force in liberation and the use of force for conquest. History will see they acted off the same script as did their 20th century predecessors who steadied a shaken world. George W. Bush and Tony Blair affixed their mission of fighting terrorism to their mission of bringing liberty to all who cry out for it.[c] As the modern purveyors of freedom and democracy, Bush and Blair comprehend the world of the 21st century. They understand that totalitarians are merely terrorists who got their way. As such, their sense of duty to history drives them to cling to no other ideology except freedom. As did their predecessors, Bush and Blair have faith in ordinary and decent folk to decide their future regardless of any nation in which they live. They know the United States, Great Britain, and the Free World must fight not only for its liberty, but for the liberty of those who may not agree liberty must be defended:

> *...Through world war and Cold War we learned that idealism—if it is to do any good in this world—requires common purpose, national strength, and moral courage. And now our generation has need of these qualities, for great responsibilities fall again on the great democracies...In our conflict with terror and tyranny, we have an unmatched advantage, the appeal of freedom to all mankind.*[15]

At the midpoint of the first decade of the 21st century, forces for freedom liberated the nations of Afghanistan and Iraq, hope began to spread, and democracy took root in the rocky ground of the world's most troubled region. In 2005, as the clouds of war began to disperse over the horizon of the Middle East, glimpses of liberty and independence came into view. As the cause of freedom advanced across the globe, some leaders of Old Europe and the Middle East began to rethink the uncompromised and courageous stands by the modern-day representatives of the Anglo-American Alliance.

In 2003 at the liberation of Iraq, a message of optimism and hope was given to nations struck to the heart by fanatical terrorist forces not unlike those faced by a young Winston Churchill. President George W. Bush looked past the barbarities of his time and of a time long past. America's leader proclaimed a power stronger than hate, an ideology higher than destruction, and a true promise for mankind, the transformational power of liberty:

> *The stakes in the Middle East could not be higher. We are told that Islam is incompatible with a democratic culture. Yet, one-half the world's Muslims are contributing members within democratic societies. People throughout the Middle East share a high civilization, a religion of personal responsibility, and a need for freedom as deep as our own. It is not realism to suppose that one-fifth of humanity is unsuited to liberty. It is pessimism and condescension and we should have none of it. We will help the Iraqi people establish a peaceful and democratic country in the heart of the Middle East.[16]*

It has been speculated had Winston Churchill been in power in the 1930s, the world may well have avoided the Second World War. In time, Sir Winston would refer to the great conflict of the 1940s as "the unnecessary war." His description confronts modern times and speaks to the necessity of peace through strength. At the onset of the War in Iraq, Winston S. Churchill was asked what he believed his grandfather's position would be on the global threat to peace and freedom in the 21st century:

> *My grandfather referred to the Second World War as "the unnecessary war" because he believed that had the coalition that won the First World War held together and acted early instead of appeasing tyranny and totalitarianism, they could have stopped Hitler in his tracks without firing a shot…Here we are together facing a group of mighty foes who seek our ruin; here we are together defending all that free men hold dear.[17]*

Peace through weakness did not win the Second World War. Peace through weakness did not bring down the Berlin Wall, take down communism, or dismantle the iron curtain. Peace through weakness will not win the War on Terror. Peace through strength saved Great Britain and the West in the "Fighting Forties." Peace through strength brought down communism five decades later. Peace through strength brought forth a free Afghanistan and Iraq. Peace through strength established a beachhead of liberty and democracy in the cradle of civilization. Affirming this path to peace, President George W. Bush addressed the United Nations:

> *For decades, the circle of liberty and security and development has been expanding in our world. . . Now we have the historic chance to widen the circle even further, to fight radicalism and terror with justice and dignity, to achieve a true peace founded on human freedom…Liberty is the path to both a safer and better world…When it comes to the desire for liberty and justice, there is no clash of civilizations.[18]*

Each era must tear down its own evils. Every generation must face threats posed to its existence. In our day comparisons are inevitable among fascism, communism, and terrorism. Each deadly disease directly attacks the bloodstream of Western civilization. Each cripples all who do not adhere to its tenets. Each must be fought on two fronts: militarily with no outcome acceptable but victory and ideologically with the virtues and values of the West.

From fascism and communism in the 20th century to terrorism in the 21st century, civilization has been preserved by leaders who refused to deal with virulent ideologies from a posture of appeasement. Responsible leaders refused to placate, manage, or co-exist with destructive tyrannies; they just purposed to defeat them. This is the spirit of Churchill.

Heroes will always captivate the world, especially heroes who fight for causes that seem hopeless and battles that seem lost. The world not only clamors for fictional heroes who capture the romantic imagery of good over evil, no-hope contests, and impossible quests, but historical heroes who built a better world. Deathless heroes who dared to dream *possible* dreams. Persevering heroes who might be beaten, but are never defeated. Winston Churchill was such a hero, ageless, invincible, unchanging. In all phases of his remarkable life, his spirit embodied the root meaning of the word *conquer:* "to win past winning, to vanquish past vanquishing."

Our world faces a different enemy than it did a half-century ago. It does not face an iron curtain or a Berlin Wall. It does not face a nation or axis of nations. It faces a stateless enemy with no borders. A stateless enemy of vicious barbarians with no regard for human life—even their own. A stateless enemy consumed with hatred of humanity—hatred unparalleled in human history—focused and formidable, determined and deadly. To combat it, the world needs the spirit of Churchill.

In a day when belief in evil was hardly in fashion, a three-part tale about good versus evil became a worldwide phenomenon when the saga was made into three fantastic films, *The Lord of the Rings*. Author J.R.R. Tolkien[D] set his epic allegory in Middle Earth, the midpoint between life and death, heaven and hell. Middle Earth, the place where all of earth's inhabitants dwell, and the biggest battlefield in the Universe. Tolkien's trilogy depicts a titanic struggle between choices and portrays the unstoppable consequences of those choices. Tolkien's vivid battles between physical forces are eclipsed only by the intense battles in the realm of the cosmic. His characters struggle for the hearts and minds of all inhabitants of Middle Earth. His message is an imperative to fight evil as many times as necessary to defeat it. Ancient yet contemporary, Tolkien's tale is a timeless story for then and now. In the final installment crafted for the silver screen, the King of Gondor gives a stirring speech in the moments preceding the final battle for Middle Earth. The words ring with truth. They speak not only to a mythical world, they speaks to ours:

A day may come when the courage of men fails,
When we forsake our friends and break all bonds of fellowship.
But it is not this day...
An hour of wolves and shattered shields,
When the age of men comes crashing down.

But it is not this day...
This day we fight!
By all you hold dear on this good earth,
I bid you stand, men of the West![19]

During his first week as Prime Minister in May of 1940, Winston Churchill stood defiantly against not only the forces of evil, but the voices of appeasement. France had fallen, the army of Great Britain was struggling to evacuate from Dunkirk, and Germany was calling for surrender. As Mr. Churchill addressed his anxious War Cabinet, he hearkened back to what he knew best—the truisms of history. His words still ring true to 21st century ears as the nations of the world face the terror of an implacable foe and are faced with the choice to resolve or give in: *"Nations which went down fighting rose again— but those which surrender tamely are finished."*[20]

Winston Churchill served and saved his nation not only out of ideology, but out of a sense of duty—his sense of oneness with his country and its history. He served and saved his nation in a spirit of determination to preserve for posterity the past, present, and future. His admonitions have no expiration date:

> *I must warn you that there still is a lot to do and that you must be prepared for further efforts of mind and body and further sacrifices to great causes....After all, Europe has only to arise and stand in their own majesty, faithfulness, and virtue to confront all forms of tyranny, ancient or modern.*[21]

If a nation desires peace it must insure its freedom. To insure its freedom it must prepare for war. In war it must fight to victory. As in 1940, the Free World today stands on a precipice. It will stay the course or go the way of civilizations studied only in history books. To preserve the Free World, it will take brave men and women who continue to sacrifice for the freedom of others they will never know. It will take blood, toil, tears, and sweat. Sometimes it will take all.

In the months and years to come, America and her allies must seek to preserve the values that have sustained all we have come to cherish. Great comfort and encouragement may be found in those who have carved out a well-worn path that marks the way. Individuals who lived—and often died—for something higher and greater than themselves capture the collective imagination of those who live today and those who will live in all the tomorrows yet to come. Their heroic qualities make them seem larger than life, and in a real sense, perhaps they were. They transcend time because, although they lived in the temporal world, they did not live by temporal principles. They are never out of time or place, for they held to the transcendent values which will never pass away. This is why they still fascinate. This is why they still inspire each new generation yet unborn.

Why do some nations stand resolved in the face of terror and others do not? The Spirit of Churchill. What will it take to win the War on Terror? The Spirit of Churchill.

A   Within the Islamic forces of Churchill's day there arose a class of highly skilled Arabian swordsmen. The Dervishes became a strong and effective movement in the region. With amazing precision, each could artfully swirl his sword above his head. Each came to be known as "a whirling Dervish."

B   Charles George Gordon became a national hero for his exploits in China and his gallant, but ill-fated defense of Khartoum, the capital of Sudan. A distinguished officer in the Crimean War of the mid-1800s, he defended Shanghai and earned the sobriquet "Chinese." As Governor of Sudan in 1873, he crushed rebellion and suppressed slavery. After his death, Gordon's Bible was presented to Queen Victoria and is prominently displayed in a specially designed glass case in the Queen's apartments at Windsor Castle.

C   On June 28, 2004, the handover of power from the Coalition Government to the newly-installed Iraqi Prime Minister took place in a modest ceremony. While at a summit meeting in Istanbul, Turkey, President Bush received word at the moment of transfer. Seated next to him was Prime Minister Blair. Cameras recorded the moment as Mr. Bush wrote a brief message, handed it to Mr. Blair, and whispered the news. The two leaders quietly shook hands. The message on the paper said: "Let freedom ring."

D   John Ronald Reuel (J.R.R.) Tolkien is considered a major scholar of the English language. He was a Professor of Anglo-Saxon or Old and Middle English at Oxford University. Best remembered for a three-part epic set in a pre-historic era, he used the ancient Anglo-Saxon expression "Middle Earth" to describe his version of the world. Tolkien is considered one of the world's foremost authorities on the epic Saxon poem, *Beowulf*, from where he derived many of the names given to his people and places in *The Lord of the Rings*.

Chapter 3

RECONNAISSANCE

*How the English-speaking peoples through unwisdom, carelessness,
and good nature allowed the wicked to rearm.*
Winston Churchill
Theme of "The Gathering Storm"
The Second World War, Volume I

Despots know no era. Tyranny is found in any age. Yet those voices which deliver a clarion call to stand against the threats to civilized men and women endure because they bring light out of the midst of darkness. But sometimes those voices go unheeded, and in our weaker moments, often derided. One would do well to understand that in a temporal world, it is those voices which proclaim the self-evident truths of a transcendent order that are vital for the preservation of all that is held dear—liberty, justice, the rule of law—those principles which comprise the very foundation of civilization itself. Each new age produces new evils which challenge and confront the present generation. This is why the study of the past is so vital to the stability of the future. This is the tried-and-true formula for a continuing hope.

Questions are still asked in history classes across America a half-century after the Second World War. Who or what was responsible for Adolf Hitler's rise to power? How could a seemingly civilized world produce such a monster? How could the world stand by to witness millions elevate him to the heights of power and then follow him with blind euphoric fervor?

At the beginning of the 21st century, as one considers the vast terrorist network and its allies that spans the globe and resides on every continent, one again asks these same questions. But these questions must not be the focus, for tyrants will always do what tyrants do—rise and fall. It is better to ask: What are the elements that give rise to those individuals who have the courage and fortitude to stand against such evil?

Discernment. Wisdom. Knowledge. One of the most important parts of any war effort is the gathering of intelligence information. Not even the special forces of the United States military go into a situation without it. Before the Allies came ashore on the beaches of Normandy on D-DAY, their greatest weapons of courage and valor were buttressed by the information gathered beforehand, secured by the ability to recognize what was true and what was false.

This is why history is the most vital tool, for it puts the present time in focus and serves the future as a most reliable guide.[A] Its messages are clear and distinct for all those who heed its admonitions: *"For if the trumpet does not sound a clear call, who will get ready for battle?"*[1] Civilization is dependent upon those who can distinguish between the forces of right and wrong, good and evil. A story was once told of a member of the German Parliament of 1933 who was asked decades later about the rise of Hitler and fascism. In attempting to explain the dilemma many had in dealing with this new political movement, he quietly but fervently replied, "We could not tell if it [Nazism] was a force for good with a few bad effects, or a force for evil with a few good effects. We could not tell! We could not tell!"[2]

Sound reconnaissance[B] was the critical element present on September 11, 2001. Before Flight 93 crashed in the Pennsylvania countryside, as that aircraft headed toward its intended target, something changed over those skies. The courageous few who thwarted the suicide-bombers on that ill-fated flight were no different than other brave Americans on the hijacked planes which plummeted into the Twin Towers and the Pentagon on that infamous day. Somehow during Flight 93 they were able to gain the *correct* information regarding their intended fate at the hands of the maniacal terrorists. Proper knowledge and accurate information made all the difference between pacifism and heroism. Courageous individuals, especially those like Todd Beamer, altered the maniacal goal of the fanatics on Flight 93. These brave Americans—and all the others who perished that day—will always be remembered. Mr. Beamer's immortal "Let's roll!" stands as the epitome of self-sacrifice and duty to country.

In many respects the 1930s were no different than any other era, for the basic essence of mankind does not change. Just as today, there were many then who did not understand the times in which they lived. But fortunately, there were a few who did. The fate of nations and the freedoms of men and women rested upon those who not only understood what was at stake, but also had the conviction and determination to stand against the darkness that threatened to engulf the globe. Even a few possessed the courage to stand alone against the whole world if necessary. One of these lone voices was Winston Churchill. In 1948, three years after World War II, he published his first-hand account of the events leading up to the rise of Adolf Hitler. He chronicles, in detail, through six lengthy volumes, an invaluable record of what transpired over those five history-altering years. Within the pages of those volumes, Mr. Churchill reflected on what his nation and the world had just accomplished by ridding the world of one of the most heinous regimes in its history. His recognition of the causes and effects of why tyranny becomes a force and how it is defeated serves as a warning to future generations:

> *It is my purpose, as one who lived and acted in these days, to show how easily the tragedy of the Second World War could have been prevented;* **how the malice of the wicked was reinforced by the weakness of the virtuous;** *how the structure and habits of democratic states often lack those elements of persistence and conviction which can alone give security to humble masses...We shall see how the counsels of prudence and restraint may become the prime agents of mortal danger;* **how the middle course adopted from desires for safety and a quiet life may be found to lead directly to the bulls-eye of disaster;** [c] *and how absolute is the need of a broad path of international action pursued by many states in common across the years irrespective of the ebb and flow of national politics.*[3]

The era of the 1930s was one of the most critical periods of the 20th century. It was a time in man's history when civilization was about to be tested as it had few times before. The outcome of the approaching world conflict was by no means certain. But one thing *was* certain. Truth and loyalty, honor and duty, courage and liberty *had* to prevail. And prevail they did because of the vision and resolve of one man who inspired his nation to hold them as closely as life itself. Winston Churchill's *reconnaissance*—his ability to recognize, survey, examine, and determine the scope of the situation—coupled with his knowledge of the required resources and manpower was vital to the strategy necessary for victory. Yet, all the knowledge, information, and resources would have fallen short of the goal of preserving the freedom, peace, and stability of the civilized world without the determination to persevere to the end. In this, Winston Churchill was invaluable.

Determined not to stand in "the bulls-eye of disaster," Prime Minister Churchill undertakes some target practice.
(Churchill Archives Centre; Baroness Spencer-Churchill Papers)

But, reconnaissance can work both ways. Knowledge and information is just as important to those who seek to destroy the values of the civilized world as it is to those who seek to preserve them. No doubt, prior to September 11, 2001, there were many months, if not years, of planning by the terrorist forces who had enough correct information to coordinate and carry out one of the most horrible crimes in history and the worst attack on American soil ever conceived. Their reconnaissance proved deadly.

In 1930s Germany the Nazis had a powerful secret weapon, a weapon that was crucial to the lightning speed in which the Third Reich engulfed the European continent. That secret weapon was *information*. During the years leading up to the Nazi invasions, a vast network of spies had been carefully placed, a network which infiltrated the nations of Europe and beyond. Whether it was "students" in Norway sending home geography assignments, "engineers" in France telegraphing the home office with mathematical equations, "weathercasters" in Spain reporting rainfall statistics, or German "archeologists" in Egypt surveying sites for research, great mountains of mail poured into Germany—ordinary mail which contained all kinds of information disguised as mundane facts. The now famous weather forecast regarding Hitler's invasion of Poland ᴰ gave the world a clue as to Germany's reliance on its intricate network of stealth reconnaissance: *"There will be no rain in Poland in September of 1939."*[4] The message referred to the fact there would be ineffectual resistance by Poland to invasion—all would be clear for a Nazi conquest. There *would* be "rain" over Poland, but it would not be from nature. It would come as a deluge of fire and death.

The invasion of Poland by Germany, in the early hours of September 1, 1939, was the spark that ignited the Second World War. The unlawful and unforeseen invasion by the Nazi forces of the Third Reich brought Great Britain and France into the fight and was the culmination of months and years of Adolf Hitler's plans to dominate Europe. The German leader's lust for power had not been satisfied with his taking of Austria and Czechoslovakia. As he made hollow promises to Poland, Britain, and France, he was planning to continue his conquests. His strategy included a vast information infrastructure, crucial to his swift success in the invasion and occupation of nation after nation.

Because of careful reconnaissance, the Nazi network knew of back roads and river crossings unknown to most of the Polish citizenry.

Nazi tanks and armaments were unstoppable as they rolled over Poland. On that terrible September morning, a sea of tanks and ground forces crossed the whole of the Polish frontier as the mighty *Luftwaffe* [E] commanded the skies above. Because of the sheer magnitude of the invasion, there was no force available to stand against it.

Only weeks later, the Nazi war machine rolled into Norway. The invasion and occupation was so swift and complete that by the time citizens returned with bayonets and pitchforks, German military bands were marching through the streets of Oslo. Next was Holland. Invasion of the land of windmills and dikes was achieved with little effort. Because of detailed and precise information, Nazi parachutists knew the way to every backwater and spillway throughout the Lowlands. It was all over before any Dutchman even knew there had been an invasion. And in France, the network of Nazi reconnaissance provided the key in breaking down the supposed walls and fortifications which had for centuries protected the largest of the European countries. The Nazis' knowledge of the vast communication systems of France was achieved through their complete infiltration and resulted in the total breakdown of French morale. German tanks and soldiers clogged all roads of escape so that thousands of refugees lost all hope. This scenario of success would be repeated in the months ahead throughout Europe and beyond.

As Hitler's henchmen drew geopolitical lines across the Eastern Hemisphere, the map of Europe began to be transformed into a map of Germany. Conscripted workers in the occupied countries became virtual slave labor for the Nazi war machine: Czechs, Poles, Austrians, Frenchmen, Norwegians, Danes, and Dutchmen. The conquests were complete. Back in Berlin, the Nazi propaganda machine lost no time in informing the staggering and subjugated countries of the effects of resisting the might of the Third Reich. Now as then, people soon lose the will to resist when they can be convinced that resistance of any kind is too late.

The formula was seemingly unbreakable: the quick, decisive, and paralyzing action by the Nazi juggernaut, followed by celebration in

Berlin. The icing on the cake was provided by the knowledge that these quick victories provided lucrative results, as all the goods, raw materials, industries, banks, and labor resources of the conquered countries were handed over intact to Adolf Hitler. The Nazis' famous exultant cry of *"Today we own Germany! Tomorrow the world!"* no longer seemed hollow. Hitler's dreams of conquest began to take shape with grim reality.

What Adolf Hitler failed to recognize in 1940—as did Osama bin Laden in 2001—were the unseen factors that overcome even the power of tyranny and terror. Each of these madmen underestimated the indomitable human spirit—that spark of celestial fire[F] which is given to men and women who understand that they are created in the image of God and who understand the difference between good and evil. These tyrants did not count on the tenacity of ordinary people the world over who would fight to the last breath to protect and defend their families and homes and the very ground on which they were born.

Even as Hitler's hostages were tortured and prisoners executed, each day unknown hands eliminated another sentry, derailed another train, sabotaged another telephone line, and planted another explosive. The forces of terror no longer faced a purely defensive war. Day after day on a thousand fronts, a force for freedom, both from the underground movements in the occupied countries and the advancing Allied armies, continued to gain momentum. Unstoppable. Unrelenting. Unconquerable. A force which would never rest until liberty, decency, and security were restored to all free peoples. A force which was inspired by the resolve and by the words of leaders who more than rose to the occasion.

During the darkest days of World War II, those who valued liberty over life itself never wavered. These unknown and unsung heroes and heroines made sure Adolf Hitler would be proved wrong when he took for granted that the territories he had once overwhelmed and conquered would remain so. Those brave freedom fighters became part of another vast network—an underground network honeycombed throughout the conquered countries. This network relied on their own reconnaissance. They understood a crucial truth—that the gathering of correct information alone was of little importance without the courage and determination to persevere in the fight for freedom.

There is a story about a leader of the German resistance who likened their situation to a colony of ants he had once observed emptying a sugar bowl. He watched a line of the ever-moving, untiring, constantly focused ants which went about the task until it was completed. He watched the ants form a long line which stretched from the sugar bowl, across the table, down the table leg, across the floor, and under the wall. Each tiny ant carried a particle of sugar to the nest and tirelessly returned for another. It took several hours but the bowl was emptied. The leader remarked, "They might stop some of us, but they cannot stop us all. It may take a long time, but the job *will* be done."[5]

At the dawn of the 21st century, civilization is being tested again. If it is to prevail, it will be because those who lead recognize the values and principles upon which it rests must be, and will be, preserved no matter the cost. The spirit of Churchill lives on in those people and nations who resolve to stand triumphantly in the face of terror. Civilization will prevail because all those who love freedom will never give up until the job is done.

A   *"I have no way of judging the future but by the past."* Patrick Henry, Liberty Speech, Richmond, Virginia, 1775

B   *Old French:* "to recognize"

C   The following two famous quotes on the folly of seeking security over freedom are applicable here. *"And you all know security is mortals' chiefest enemy."* William Shakespeare, *Macbeth*, Act III, Scene v. *" Those who would trade their liberty for security deserve neither."* Benjamin Franklin

D   The country of Poland was mainly an agrarian society. Comprised mostly of rural roads known to become quite muddy during the rainy harvest season, it was believed that such conditions would make an invasion by tanks and motorized vehicles extremely difficult and would aid in slowing down the enemy. Many held an almost quaint view that Poland's famed cavalry units would "run rings 'round the enemy" in such a conflict. But the Polish autumn of 1939 brought an unusual dry spell and with it, sun-baked roads which made concrete-like conditions for the tanks and trucks of the Nazi forces. The now-famous weather forecast gave the green light to the invasion, which proved the key in the amazing swiftness of the conquering of Poland.

E   The *Luftwaffe* was the mighty air armada of Germany masterminded by former airline executive and Hitler henchman, Hermann Goring. The literal meaning of *Luftwaffe* is "air weapon."

F   "Do not forget to entertain that spark of celestial fire called conscience." (from *110 Rules of Civility and Decent Behaviour*, by George Washington)

Chapter 4

WOLF AT THE DOOR

If Hitler invaded Hell, I would make at least a favourable
reference to the Devil in the House of Commons.
Rt. Hon. Winston Churchill, Speech to Parliament, 1941

The decade of the 1920s was a time of uncertainty and instability within the nations of Europe. Even before the end of World War I, the situation for Germany was especially desperate. The Treaty of Versailles, which ended "the war to end all wars," was a document containing the punitive measures that left Germany little with which to rebuild. The treaty gave control of Germany to the Allied powers, with its self-determination laid out by the nations to which it surrendered. Germany would not be allowed to even enter into negotiations with other nations. Its armed forces were reduced to a mere, hollow status. All foreign holdings were confiscated, and its manufacturing and industry were curtailed. The immediate post-war years saw a drastic decline in the German economy and the Germany currency—the mark. But the most punitive measure of all was the "war guilt clause" in Article 231 of the treaty, which stated, "Germany is responsible for all damage and loss to the Allies." Subsequently, 20 billion gold marks were required as payment to the victorious nations. This left the country virtually bankrupt and provoked bitter indignation throughout the land. Marshal Foch of France, Supreme Allied Commander in World War I, said prophetically upon hearing of the signing of The Treaty of Versailles: "This is not peace. It is an armistice for twenty years."[1] He had it right-almost to the day.

By the early 1920s, one out of three German workers were unemployed. The country was severely weakened both economically and politically. Before the war, four German marks were equal to one U.S. dollar. By the war's end, it took 7,000 marks to equal one dollar. The result was runaway inflation at a higher rate than any other European nation. Germany's Parliament (the *Reichstag*) was fractured. Many factions vied for control and the power to govern. During this critical period in Germany's history, a new political party was formed—the

41

National Socialist German Workers Party. Likened to underworld conspirators, this new faction would soon be known as Nazis. A young veteran with a radical hunger for change and a fanatical belief in German supremacy joined this fringe group. By 1921, he was its leader. His name was Adolf Hitler.

By 1923, Hitler was ready for a situation he could use to seize power. He hated communists and democratists, considering himself the alternative between the two. He hated democracy because its philosophy is rooted in the idea that all men are equal. He believed that this could not exist because of the "pureness of the Aryan race" which was "superior" and could never be equal to any other race of men. He believed communism was the greatest threat to Nazism because it was rooted in Marxist philosophy, and he believed Marxism was controlled by the Jews, the "very incarnation of evil." Winston Churchill drew the connection well between the dangerous philosophies which were brewing in the 1930s:

> **As Fascism sprang from Communism, so Nazism developed from Fascism. Thus were set on foot those kindred movements which were destined soon to plunge the world into even more hideous strife.** [2]

Typical of Hitler was his double-mindedness. While he hated the communists, he employed the tactics of the Marxist revolutionaries. Using their methods, he soon found himself arrested for staging a bloody riot. His first "stormtroopers"[A] had created the incident, and in the melee believed their leader was killed. At his trial, Herr Hitler gave a stirring defense and emerged as a hero and martyr. While in Landsberg Prison in the mid-1920s, he penned *Mein Kampf* (My Struggle) which railed on about his hatred of the Jews, the evils of Marxism, his racial purity theories, his contempt for the democratic system, and a call for future political action. But not in the written word would he find success beyond his wildest dreams. His writings would have never given him mass appeal, for they revealed a crackpot mentality. His appeal would manifest itself in spoken words. Few have ever come upon the scene—either good or bad—with the fantastic oratorical skills possessed by Adolf Hitler. Upon his release, he was calling himself by a new name, *Der Fuehrer* (The Leader), and he was planning a new strategy.

Hitler now realized that the path to power lay not in violent revolt, but in political takeover. He cunningly used the communists' propensity for street violence to contrast with his seemingly measured and diplomatic approach. Hitler brilliantly used conflict to gain power. The two main forces which threatened the old order were the German communists and the National Socialists (Nazis). Hitler decided to masquerade as the leader of the one who did not threaten an overthrow of the government. He began to express his vision for a great national revival and unapologetically claimed that he had the solution for Germany's woes. But for the terrible fate which awaited Germany and the world, the solution he promised was he himself.

This period in history seems to be the one in which the times did seem to create the leader. Germany was in total despair and, coupled with the loss of national pride and crushing economic conditions, she awaited a savior. Adolf Hitler's messianic visions seemed the perfect match. Technology seemed to be ready, too. Hitler was the first politician in history to use the airplane as a campaign tool.[3] This new venue allowed him to be in several cities on the same day. The airplane, first used as a weapon in the First World War, would later become the great tool of terror over the skies of Europe, giving Germany the assurance of invincibility.

With his mesmerizing speeches and his campaign slogan of "The Fuehrer and Germany," Hitler's popularity and that of the Nazi Party spread like wildfire. His message was simple—only *he* could save Germany. But the old line political leaders, the aristocrats whose bloodlines could be traced to Saxon times, opposed this new upstart. In an effort to hold the "rabble-rouser" at bay, the old guard persuaded 85-year old Paul von Hindenburg, the great father-figure of the German nation, to run for President. Hindenburg, the soldier-patriot and symbol of honor, was persuaded by duty alone, for he could not bear to hand the reins of power in Germany to "that Bohemian corporal."[B]

By the time of the elections of 1932, even in the depths of depression, the National Socialist Party with Hitler at its helm, had captured

1/3 of the vote and 230 out of the 608 seats in the *Reichstag*. Hitler was at a crossroads. He could not muster enough votes to gain outright control of the government, yet his strong showing prevented any other political party from gaining control. By November, his Nazi party was in trouble. The middle class voters wanted him to take any position offered, and his stormtroopers wanted to seize the power outright. His right-hand man, Major Gregor Strasser resigned because of Hitler's "all or nothing" strategy. Hitler was lampooned in cartoons and derided in *The Munich Post*. His opponents could not achieve control either, so they knew they had to deal with him. He was rescued by former Chancellor Franz Von Papen's desire to get even with a political opponent. In a backroom deal, a coalition agreed to make Adolf Hitler Chancellor of Germany, with the leader of the old line military, Von Papen, the Vice-Chancellor. Even though Hitler had to accept less power than he wanted, he secured for himself the Chancellorship—legally. He was now the *legitimate* ruler of Germany. Armed with the full authority of the state behind him, Adolf Hitler proceeded with the total overthrow of what had been Germany. All other parties other than the National Socialists were suppressed.

Von Papen was supposed to hold the real power, for he was aligned with the ailing President Hindenburg and believed that "we can control that tramp from Vienna." Little did they know it would take forces aligned from around the globe to stop him. The leader of a heretofore fringe faction was now poised to pounce on the world. Hitler was later to boast that this third major empire of Germany would "last a thousand years." One of his henchmen, who was to become world-famous as the master of propaganda, Joseph Goebbels, wrote of this triumphant coup in his diary: "It is a dream, a victory!"[4] The Third Reich[c] was born.

One month after Hitler gained power, the Reichstag Building was set on fire. Convenient timing, for the new chancellor had predicted that there would be a communist plot to overthrow the new government. No one has ever proven that it was a Nazi ploy, but there seems little doubt as to the perpetrators. Panic ensued, and before the night was over the Parliament house was ablaze. Hitler brilliantly and swiftly used this crisis to his advantage. Once again he used violence and fraud to gain for himself power. Hitler and his close associates drafted a set of decrees and had them approved "for the safety of the German people." These came under the title of "The Enabling Act," which was to remain the constitutional basis of Hitler's dictatorship—written by him, enforced by him. These new laws swept away all vestiges of democratic freedoms—speech, assembly, freedom from indiscriminate arrest, and the like. But, most importantly, these laws allowed Hitler's Nazi party structure to issue decrees independent of the *Reichstag* and placed him, as its leader, in total control. Adolf Hitler was now the sole and arbitrary ruler of Germany.

Hitler completely transformed the political landscape. The new Chancellor deputized his stormtroopers, the elite *SS*[D] which became the police in every town and city. The jails could not hold all those arrested, so new facilities were created, *das Konzentrations' zelten*, the concentration camps. A solemn ceremony was performed at the great national cathedral and burial place of Frederick the Great.[5] Hitler was seen as a dignified leader who represented the latest in the long line of glorious German statesmen. He had the people firmly in his hand. He crushed all opposition parties and voices declaring "democracy does not work—Germany must unite behind one party, one Fuehrer." By May of 1933, the "Nazification" of Germany was complete. Hitler's portrait was everywhere. City streets as well as newborn babies bore his name.[6] Within weeks, book-burnings began as an initiative from his young followers who desired to eradicate all that was "un-German." Soon, it would not be only books that would burn.

By the end of 1933, the Nazis clearly had the momentum in German politics and the government. The only threat to the absolute power of Adolf Hitler remained in the military. Germany's armed forces were still fiercely loyal to President von Hindenburg and could crush the Nazi stormtroopers at his command. Understanding full well the situation called for conciliation, Chancellor Hitler cleverly masked his motives by proposing a merger. With cold cunning, he appeared as rational politician and not the insurgent. He promised all resistance by "the radicals" within his own faction would be controlled. The old guard resisted, but due to the failing health of the President, they proposed their support of Hitler as sole leader in Germany at the death of Hindenburg *if* he would "take care" of the leaders of the stormtroopers. Hitler agreed. His ***coup de grace*** struck on the night of June 30, 1934. All friendships and ties were easily sacrificed to the ultimate power within his grasp. Hitler personally led what is known today as "the blood purge" or "the night of the long knives." The most militant leaders of his *SA*, (Brownshirts) were Captain Ernst Rohm and his lieutenants. In one night, they were rounded up and brutally murdered—shot, stabbed, and hanged.[E] His former friends who had risen with him to power like Rohm and Major Strasser were his personal victims. The editor of ***The Munich Post***, his harshest critic in the press, was shot in the head along with his wife as they slept in their beds.[7]

There was no mercy. Hitler kept his end of the deal. He proved his capability—even if he had to eradicate those who had helped him climb to power. One month later on August 2, President Hindenburg was dead. The last restraint to total Nazi control was gone. The old leader was no more, a new leader was raised up. With no one remaining who would dare to question his motives, Hitler combined the offices of President and Chancellor into one. That very day, the army swore allegiance—not to Germany, not to her laws—but to Adolf Hitler. His "New Germany" was awash in patriotism and propaganda and he was her Caesar. Spectacular military parades patterned after the glittering pageantry associated with the legions of ancient Rome filled the streets of German cities. Within eighteen months, Adolf Hitler was the single, arbitrary dictator of a totalitarian Nazi state. The nation had fallen under his spell.

To the outside world, Germany's transformation was welcomed and Adolf Hitler was just the strong leader needed to restore his nation. With his political and military transformation complete, during the next few years he would transform Germany economically, socially, and even spiritually. The majority of churches and church leaders became united in a "state church" which supported Germany's new leader. A few brave pastors resisted Hitler. Men like Dietrich Bonhoffer and Martin Niemoller will always be remembered as pastors willing to give their lives rather than support the Third Reich and *Der Fuehrer*. Hitler masterminded dozens of public works programs which put thousands back into the labor force. The famous and then state-of-the-art highway system, the Autobahn, was built by the new government. A great achievement, it connected all parts of Germany and was an important link to national unification. Hitler's gigantic re-armament program served the dual purpose of putting the masses back to work and built an arsenal that would challenge the nations of the world. Germany's new leader could do no wrong. The German people seem to say, "I don't care what he does as long as I have my bread and sausage." Even former British Prime Minister Lloyd George came to tea. Praising the new Chancellor, he proclaimed: "You have done great things for Germany. You have restored her honour and gained for her equal rights in the world."[8]

The meteoric rise of Adolf Hitler is attributable to the desperate need for a strong leader in post World War I Germany, coupled with his unequalled ability to exploit and then shape events to his own ends. The son of Hitler's foreign press officer was interviewed years later and asked about the secret to the Fuehrer's astonishing success in captivating his countrymen. He stated: "He had that ability to make people stop thinking critically and to simply emote—the ability derived from his readiness to throw himself totally open, to appear bare and naked before his audience, to tear open his heart and display it. He had an actor's ability to become charged with energy and raw emotion. He mesmerized his audience."[9]

Hitler's favorite nickname was "the wolf," and it certainly fit in myriad ways, including the name he chose for his country hideaway, "the wolf's lair." As he promised "peace for Germany and the world," he was preparing a war to conquer Europe as "a great empire for the master race."[10] Publicly he posed as a man of peace, but privately to his inner circle he revealed his true plans. After five years in power, he felt the time had come to shed his "sheep's clothing" as the restorer of Germany and peacemaker to his neighboring countries. The wolf was on the prowl.

^A The *Sturmabteilung*, or SA; the brownshirted "Nazi militia"

^B Adolf Hitler, an Austrian, served four years as a private and then as a corporal on the Western front during World War I.

^C Reich means "empire" yet some sources indicate that the actual term is not fully translatable because it holds a mystic connotation. The First Reich was from 962-1806 and was part of the Holy Roman Empire. The Second Reich was established by Otto Bismarck in 1871 and lasted a generation (approximately 30 years). Hitler's Third Reich was to last 1,000 years and was to be more enduring than Christendom. It lasted but a dozen horrendous and horrific years.

^D *Schutzstaffel* "defense detatchment." The *SS* was the elite, black-shirted special guard, ruthless and brutal. It was the most feared and hated of all Nazi appendages.

^E The destruction of Rohn's brown shirts allowed the alternative *SS* under Heinrich Himmler to become more powerful.

Chapter 5

IN THE WILDERNESS

Never give in—never, never, never, never. In nothing great or small, large or petty, never give in except to convictions of humour and good sense. Never yield to force; never yield to the apparently overwhelming might of the enemy.
Prime Minister Churchill At Harrow School
(his old private school) October, 1941

Winston Churchill knew what it was like to stand alone. In a few years his beloved nation would know the same. In the early 1930s, Churchill found himself facing political oblivion. These were his "wilderness years" and they were to last most of the decade. But he would not be down for long. He couldn't, for his firm belief in his "destiny" would not let him.

There were many influences that shaped the life of Winston Leonard Spencer Churchill: his never-wavering admiration and respect for his harsh father, Lord Randolph Churchill; his adulation of his beautiful, vivacious, and distant mother, the American-born Lady Randolph Churchill, *nee* Jennie Jerome; and the lifelong affection he held for Mrs. Everest, his nanny, who had filled the long hours of separation from his absent parents with her unconditional love. But, most important and unquestionable, was the influence which grew from his deep love and devotion to "Clemmie," Clementine Churchill, *nee* Hozier, his beloved wife and lifelong partner.

Yet there was one influence that cannot be discounted, for it served as a truly formative focus in his life. It was not a person, but a place. A place, yes, but really a presence, for its influence was vital in shaping him as a young politician and providing a strong center throughout his long life. It was an ever present symbol of what he believed to be his life's destiny, especially during the time when he would find himself at the center of the world stage. It is what is known as "the Blenheim Factor," so named for the place of his birth—magnificent Blenheim Palace^ near Oxford, England. He once stated, *"At Blenheim, I took two very important decisions: to be born and to marry. I am happily content with the decisions I took on both occasions."*[1]

Observing British Army maneuvers in 1910, Mr. Churchill, in regimental uniform of the Oxfordshire Hussars, stands alongside his wife, Clementine.
(Churchill Archives Centre; Baroness Spencer-Churchill Papers)

No doubt, Winston Churchill considered the circumstances of his birth no accident, for he came into this world at the home of his most famous ancestor. He always considered himself to be "a great visitor of Blenheim," most likely because he was born there during a visit by his parents on November 30, 1874. It was probably not his mother's choice that her first-born son be delivered unexpectedly at the home of her husband's parents. But a fall from her horse in her seventh month of pregnancy, coupled with a ride on a rickety wagon from the site of a country weekend shooting, became a factor in the course of her son's life. The doctor, who was rushed to the palace to deliver Lady Churchill's son, required a fee of 25 guineas, which is a bit more than 25 pounds sterling.[2] Just 25 years later, young British soldier Winston Churchill was captured by the Boers during the war between the Dutch and the English. Following a daring escape and subsequent lone stand against a contingent of Dutch troops—from a stranded troop train, young Winston held off armed soldiers with only a pistol. A reward of 25 pounds was issued for his capture "dead or alive." Noticing the discrepancy, in classic Churchillian wit, he remarked: "my value has obviously gone down."[3]

Young Winston spent many happy times at the place of his birth. His love of the military, formed early in life, was noticed here. On his many visits as a young boy to the palace, he would often play with his young cousin, the 9th Duke of Marlborough. Here, in the corridors off the fabulous Great Hall, young Winston would play "French and English" (much like the American counterpart, "Cowboys and Indians"). A glimpse into his future character quality of defiant determination was present even then as he set the rules of play, never contested by his playmates: "Rule #1: Winston is always the General of the English," Rule #2: "There will be no other promotions."[4]

During Churchill's early years as a young and struggling politician, it was his visits to Blenheim that would be remembered by him with fondness as his most thrilling of experiences. At Blenheim, he would be in the company of the brightest minds of the day and privy to the crucial decisions made by those gathered there. The most influential decision-makers in Britain were invited to the palace for a country house party to discuss the business of one of the most powerful nations on earth. There in the Long Library, he would take part in these conversations. It was during those times that he would form his important and lifelong political connections.[5]

Yet, such an influence on Winston Churchill could have hardly come from just a place, even one as grand as "England's Versailles."[6] Rather, it encompassed an attitude of responsibility and a style of leadership which, he believed, was imparted to him by his greatest and most illustrious ancestor, Sir John Churchill, the 1st Duke of Marlborough. For Winston Churchill, Blenheim Palace epitomized the achievement of the British nation. Its land was given as a grant by Queen Anne to Sir John Churchill, after she bestowed upon him the title of Duke in 1704 following his monumental victory over the forces of the most powerful monarch at that time in Europe, King Louis XIV of France. The fabulous palace was built for the Duke and his Duchess by a grateful nation. England's victory at the Battle of Blenheim ended French domination in world history and set the stage for the eventual rise of the mighty British Empire. John Forster, Librarian of Blenheim Palace, explains it this way:

> *The Churchill style was formed in part by young Winston being the grandson of a Duke. His early experience at Blenheim contributed immensely to his confidence. He was born here and considered himself to be 'a great visitor' of his ancestral home. For Churchill, Blenheim epitomized the achievement and destiny of the nation and ultimately his responsibility to that sacred trust.*

It was to Blenheim Palace that Churchill would return during his difficult times out of power, as if he desired to keep faith with his family and his ancestry. The ancient Roman roads that cut through the estate imbue the land with a historical significance that would not have been lost on Churchill. He is buried but one mile away in the Bladon Churchyard, a site he chose himself. As one takes in the vista from the rear of the palace, his grave is positioned in a direct line through the middle of the palace and "connects" with the great commemorative Column of Victory which depicts the First Duke and stands in the magnificent courtyard.[6]

The decade of the 1930s would be a time when Churchill would find himself out of the circles of power. It would be one of the most difficult periods in his life. *"In the twinkling of an eye, I found myself without a seat, without a party, without an appendix."*[c] As he began to prepare for "the new young giants" in Parliament, he did what he always did in times of political exile, he turned to painting and writing. He began to paint, in his words, "with audacity" and to write the commanding biography of his most distinguished ancestor entitled, *Marlborough, His Life and Times.* It would not take long for art to imitate life. The more

Churchill delved into the life of the Duke, the more he felt he saw parallels with his own life and calling. It was the Duke alone who had saved England—and half of Europe—from the ambitions and the expanding power of "The Sun King," Louis XIV of France. As he observed the political landscape, perhaps he took to heart the words of Shakespeare, "the past is prologue," and reasoned that a similar challenge awaited another Churchill.[7] He believed that a similar crisis was looming which threatened Europe at the present time through the dangerous ambitions of Adolf Hitler. While writing this biography, he also painted a giant canvas from one of four magnificent tapestries which hang today in Second State Room of the palace. The images woven into these stunning works of art recount the valiant Duke crushing the French army. Churchill was most intrigued by the Bouchain tapestry which shows the Duke on his famous white steed, his "Hanoverian Grey," outmaneuvering the enemy. Perhaps he saw in it the magnificence of victory or the challenges which faced his nation. For whatever reasons, Churchill painted his canvas from this tapestry in 1933, the same year that Hitler came to power in Germany.[8]

Always seeing parallels between the past and the present, Winston Churchill saw within this panel from the Bouchain Tapestry, the call for unwavering leadership to combat the rise of a continental tyrant. Intrigued by the dog with the hooves of a horse, Churchill painted a canvas depicting the glorious victory of the 1st Duke of Marlborough. (Jeremy Whitaker, MCSD; use endorsed by Blenheim Palace)

If anyone in public life felt he was ready for the challenges that awaited, it was Winston Churchill. His lineage, his ancestry, and his early life experiences provided the raw materials—he now awaited the refiner's fire. He would have one of the longest, most interesting and distinguished careers in British politics. His life of inspiration did not just happen; it was a result of one failure, one setback, one pivotal decision after another. It was what he did with his failures that made him into the leader he became. Failure forged in him a steely resolve to never give up in any venture.

As a young boy he had been an average student at Harrow School. Yet he desired to attend Britain's most prestigious military academy—Sandhurst—the English equivalent of West Point. After two tries, it required a tutor to aid him in passing the entrance exam on his third attempt. His hard work and determination paid off. He graduated from this pinnacle of institutions eighth in his class of 150.[9] An unfortunate event at Sandhurst provides a window into the character of a young, 19-year-old Winston Churchill. His father, Lord Randolph, had given him a family heirloom, a gold watch. While returning to his dormitory from an outing, he accidentally dropped the watch down a deep pool in a nearby stream. After repeatedly diving into the frigid waters in a determined effort to retrieve it, young Winston ran for help. He commandeered twenty-three of his classmates in a major rescue operation. He obtained a fire engine for pumping the water and even took the elaborate method of digging out a new course for the stream. Here he showed enormous leadership, determination, resourcefulness, and dependability. He was successful, but the watch was damaged. He attempted to have it repaired, but by this time, his father found out. Always the harsh critic and never believing much in the son that adored him so, Lord Randolph wrote to his son: "Once again, you have let me down."[10] Young Winston ensued with an apology, stated in the most touching of terms, in a letter which has become known as the "watch letter." Here, we get a glimpse of the admiration and respect he felt for his father. Complete with a detailed description of the rescue procedures, the young man repeatedly endeavors to demonstrate to his father how much their relationship means to him. Even if he was not the most brilliant of academicians, it is obvious from this letter that young Churchill was a son of whom any father could be proud. He ends the letter with the following:

> *...I would rather you had not known about it. I would have paid for its mending and said nothing. But since you know about it—I feel I ought to tell you how it happened in order to show you that I really valued the watch and did my best to make sure of it. I quite realise that I have failed to do so and I am very sorry that it should have happened. But it is not the case with all my things. Everything else you have ever given me is in as good repair as when you gave it first. Please don't judge me entirely on the strength of the watch. I am very, very sorry about it. I am sorry to have written you such a long and stupid letter, but I do hope you will take it in some measure as an explanation.*
>
> *With best love, I remain ever your loving son,*
> *Winston S. Churchill*[1]

Grammar, language, and writing did not come easy to the young man. It may be difficult to reconcile the fact that someone who would one day win the Nobel Prize in Literature and whom history would remember most of all for his spoken words would have had trouble in the language arts. But, that describes Winston Churchill. So, what career did he eventually choose for himself? He chose a career in journalism and writing. Perhaps this is an indication of his ability to take the challenges life gave him and determine to conquer them. Whatever the reasons, after leaving Sandhurst he set out for adventure and at the age of 22 was stationed as a cavalry officer on the northwestern front of India. Two years later, he joined the 21st Lancers in the War of the Sudan. From here, he wrote dispatches for *The Morning Post* and authored his second book, *The River War*, that included his observations on Islamic fundamentalism he encountered first-hand. Then it was off to India again where he resigned his commission to make his first run for a seat in Parliament. He lost. Undeterred, he set out for South Africa and the Boer War[D] as a *Morning Post* correspondent. It was here that he would rise to national prominence as a bona fide hero, following his daring escape from a Boer prison. He returned to England in triumph, and was elected a Conservative Member of Parliament in 1900 at the tender age of 25, just one month shy of his 26th birthday. His convictions were evident in his maiden speech to the House of Commons, February 18, 1901: *"In war with any great power, if we are hated, it will not make us loved; if we are in danger, it will not make us safe. Our enemies are enough to irritate, not enough to overawe."*[12]

Just three years later, he crossed the floor of the House of Commons to join the loyal opposition, the Liberal Party. It paid off for him politically. The Liberal Party became the Liberal Government in the 1906 landslide election victory. He quickly rose to high office, being appointed to Home Secretary[E] just six years later at age 33, following his re-election to a seat in Parliament.[F] He became First Lord of the Admiralty in 1911, just prior to World War I.[13] Here came the first indication of his talent for innovation. In what he saw as a more vital defense strategy for Great Britain, he advocated the transition from coal to oil and provided new battleships with guns which gave them the greatest range and power on the seas. Just two years later he learned to fly. Realizing the importance of this new phenomenon, he pioneered The Royal Naval Air Service which would eventually become the Royal Air Force—the RAF. Winston Churchill was, thereby, one of the founding members of Britain's air power.[14] Always on the cutting edge of science and technology and forward-looking in his desire to aid in the development of the arsenal of Britain, he was farsighted enough to recognize the essential role of new technologies for the advancement of society and the betterment of free men. He mobilized the Royal Navy in 1914 on the eve of World War I. As bloody trench warfare escalated all over the European countryside, the ever-farsighted Churchill devised a "landship," an armored vehicle which would run on caterpillar-type treads.[6] The tank was born. At the tree planting ceremony for Churchill College at Cambridge University, he stated in October, 1959, *"The only way to compete with the new super-powers is with our brains."*

But Winston Churchill was not acquainted with success alone. He also knew failure. In 1915, during the First World War, he was a leading advocate of a naval plan to force British ships through the enemy-held Dardanelles straits[11] with the intention of knocking Turkey out of the war. The British Army Cabinet heeded his strategy but sent a badly planned expedition to the Dardanelles. It was a disaster. The Allied ships could not maneuver between the minefields, so British and Australian forces had to be landed. There were over 200,000 British casualties on the beaches and cliffs at Gallipoli. It was a tragedy of immense proportions. During one fateful campaign there, the Australians needlessly lost thousands of men. Ill-advised to advance due to a miscalculation by the British high command, they were slaughtered by Turkish forces as they charged head-on in what only can be described as a suicide mission. No matter where the blame lies, Winston Churchill accepted the disaster at Gallipoli as his responsibility. He was removed from the Admiralty by the Prime Minister and then chose to resign from the Government. He took an army commission on the Western Front where he commanded a battalion of Royal Scots Fusiliers. He was brought back into the Government by the new Prime Minister, Lloyd George. As Minister of Munitions, Winston Churchill helped to develop good relations with Britain's new ally—the United States of America. After the war, he was serving as Secretary of War and Air and was set for re-election. He lost the elections at Leicester and Westminster in 1922, but won a seat in Parliament at Epping in 1924. Victorious as a Constitutionalist Member, he promptly rejoined the Conservative Party just twenty years after abandoning it.[15] He then published his four-volume *The World in Crisis* and was appointed Chancellor of the Exchequer[1] by Prime Minister Stanley Baldwin. It was little wonder that Mr. Churchill's peers considered him opportunistic.

Winston Churchill was no stranger to controversy. By 1932, he began warning his countrymen about the resurgence of German military power, but Britain refused to listen, trusting in diplomacy and appeasement to take care of the new Chancellor of Germany and his ambitions. Yet he felt compelled to begin speaking out about the situation brewing on the Continent. His assessment of the coming situation became eerily prophetic. He recognized before any others that Nazism would destroy the peace and order of Europe. He realized this as a danger because Hitler had created a powerful psychological weapon: a blending of nationalism and socialism. This was a patriotic socialism that swept the German people into heights of euphoria. He argued for a call to rearm Britain in the face of German militarism. But his constant warnings of "the gathering storm" only alienated him from his Conservative allies in Parliament and the political establishment in general. He seemed unlikely to ever hold high office again. The public considered him eccentric and dismissed him as Winston the warmonger who loves the smell of gunpowder.

But, he never lost his sense of humor or proportion. His quick wit is legendary. A story goes that once a woman, fearful of war and irritated by his warnings, remarked to him after one of his frequent street speeches, "Mr. Churchill, you are a worm." Without a pause, he replied, "Madam, we are all worms, but I do believe that I am a glow-worm!" Another story is remembered from his younger days when he sported a mustache. At luncheon, he was seated next to an outspoken lady who declared, "Young man, I care neither for your mustache nor your opinions." He immediately replied, "Madam, you are as unlikely to come into contact with the one as with the other." Then, there is the story that once, while listening to remarks by a political opponent in the House of Commons, the speaker noticed Mr. Churchill's obvious posture of disagreement. "I see my right honourable friend shaking his head," stated the speaker, "but I am only expressing my opinion." "And I", stated Churchill, "am only shaking my own head." And who has not heard of the famous dinner party exchange between Lady Nancy Astor and Churchill? Lady Astor was a strident foe of Churchill and his "incessant saber-rattling." Often, a hostess would seat them next to each other for the entertainment of the other guests. They did not disappoint. Once, during a heated exchange on a political point, an exasperated Lady Astor blurted out, "Mr. Churchill, if you were my husband, I'd give you poison to drink!" He calmly replied, "Madam, if I were your husband, I'd drink it."

The 1930s were Churchill's "wilderness years." During this difficult time, he was seen as a "political dinosaur" and out of touch with his nation, especially during the time of the abdication of King Edward VIII.[16] A strong monarchist, Churchill was one of only a few who, against public opinion, strongly encouraged the king to not give up the throne. He was also out of touch with mainstream political opinion for his reluctance to grant independence to India, even supporting the imprisonment of Mahatma Gandhi after the Second World War. And, perhaps the position for which he was most disfavored was his vocal and continued advocacy of re-armament while almost every other political leader in post-WWI Britain advocated disarmament. It seemed that Winston Churchill loved war more than peace.

Churchill's dedication to his unpopular positions was generally a source of puzzlement to his peers. Often exasperated, they were no doubt left with the sense that Winston may be wrong, but he's never in doubt! However, Winston Churchill was not totally motivated by politics or the acquisition of power—he had crossed the aisle and crossed back again during his early career. On these very controversial decisions he once stated, *"Anyone can rat, but it takes a certain ingenuity to re-rat."*[17] Like most politicians, he was ambitious. But, it could be said that in the final analysis, he was motivated by ideology over either power or politics: *"Some men change their party for the sake of their principles; others their principles for the sake of their party."* [18] He unapologetically believed in British democracy and saw the British Empire as the best venue for spreading it throughout the world. The driving force of his character and will was by the strength of truth over even ideology. But, more often than not, most people can find truth hard to take. For when truth is confronted, then duty and responsibility are not far behind. Novelist Mark Helprin explains it this way:

Winston Churchill was half-European, half-American—this is why he understood what to do, and saved the West. As a

59

European, he understood power, as an American, he knew
that the only weapon able to combat unchecked power is the
truth. Every word he spoke was rooted in truth. It enabled him
to see when others could not, to speak when others would not,
and to record his times with majesty, elevation, and wit.
He did not live by power. He was at his best when completely
alone—even scorned by all around him with not a hope of
gaining power.[19]

Ironically, he was seemingly unaffected by the ridicule of others
for his lone and unpopular positions. Somehow, these positions
worked *for* him, because this practiced obstinacy put him in good
stead during that time in his life and in the life of his nation when his
strong, unwavering positions were vital to the future of civilization. It
was this exact quality which was the key in gaining the support he
needed to become Prime Minister; support, *not* just from his own
party, the Conservatives, but from the Liberal and Labour Parties, his
opposition in Parliament. There was a quality of character that
Churchill possessed, a quality found in great leaders who can go the
distance through any circumstances. It is the ability to turn any misfortune into success and triumph. Allen Packwood relates a story to illustrate this. In 1931, Churchill was on a visit to the United States and was
run over by a car on the streets of New York City. How different world
history would have been if the future Prime Minister had met his end
there. This incident would be enough to stop anyone from making
future plans. Not Winston Churchill—he was unshaken in his outlook,
turning misfortune into success. He promptly wrote an article about
what it was like to be hit by a car. He titled it: "I Was Conscious
Through It All."[20]

It is not hard to understand the British mindset during the 1930s.
They did not want to hear anything of a possible armed conflict less
than two decades after the end of the First World War. The war-weary
country longed for a continuing peace and rejected Churchill's admonition, *"Do not allow diplomacy to supersede preparedness."*[21] The
sceptered isle had lost the flower of her British manhood during World

War I and no one was ready so soon to sacrifice sons again. But Churchill was motivated by truth, no matter how unpleasant.

He never took the world as it was, but led it in the direction he thought it should go. His grasp of history, his knowledge of the reality of the condition of mankind, and his confidence that truth must ultimately prevail if the world was to remain civilized, were the keys to his understanding of the times. He knew that without true freedom there could never be true peace. And he knew that throughout history securing the freedoms of mankind came with a cost—a cost that almost always involved the taking up of arms: *"I have always been ready to use force in order to defy tyranny or ward off ruin.""*[22]

From his seat in Parliament two years after Hitler came to power he stated the following:

> *We must be aware not only of the importance of self-preservation, but also of the human and the world cause of the preservation of free governments and of Western Civilisation against the ever advancing sources of despotism.*[23]

His wilderness years were the crucible that would forge Winston Churchill into the wartime leader upon which not only his nation, but Western civilization itself would depend. These years prepared him to remain steadfast in his principles. As America now purposes to fight for freedom from the tyranny of terrorism, the spirit of Churchill provides reassurance and hope. How prophetic his words would become. Historian John Keegan once said Churchill did not only **hate** totalitarianism, he **despised** it. He would not just defend Britain against the Nazi onslaught, he would fight on to complete victory. He never tried to appease the forces of despotism for the sake of "peace," for he understood that *freedom* must be the goal, the only triumph for mankind. He was never awed by the might of the enemy. It was this remarkable combination of determination and defiance in the face of overwhelming circumstances that would define him in history.

Throughout the 1930's Churchill meditated constantly upon the European situation and the rearming of Germany and tried desperately to alert Britain to "the gathering storm."[24] To a complacent England and the West his warnings went unheeded. Time and time again he warned of Hitler's aim of world conquest. Time and time again he was greeted with indifference and ridicule. As biographer Norman Rose states: *"Churchill from the outset had detected the deadly peril Hitler's regime posed."*[25]

Winston Churchill remained courageous in the wilderness. Often referred to as "the last lion of England," he demonstrated the qualities of strength and tenacity. The sheer spirit of will was the essence of his calling of leadership. Throughout his life, in times of personal defeat, he always looked ahead to victory. These invaluable characteristics mark the statesman and make possible the only hope for a civilization. The simplicity of his dependence on the truth, stating it without apologies, raised the ire of his opponents and the hopes of a wartime nation:

> *The way out of the wilderness is the truth: recognizing it, stating it, defending it, living by it. Better defeat with the truth in sight than a thousand hollow victories without it. Precisely that conviction is what allowed Winston Churchill his extraordinary relation to victory. And it is this paradox that, exiting this period of forgetfulness, we would do well to remember.*[26]

In 1935, the disarmament clause of the Versailles Treaty[j] was abolished. In less than a year, Hitler re-armed in defiance of the treaty and withdrawn from the League of Nations.[27] His Nazi forces would assure Germany's re-occupation of the Rhineland—the strip of land between Germany and France bordering the Rhine River and the fertile Rhine Valley. This area had been made a demilitarized zone (DMZ). Under no circumstances could either side cross this area armed. Adolf Hitler decided to test the Allies. In direct violation of the treaty, he ordered his army to approach the DMZ. France's resistance consisted of two tanks that did nothing. Hitler's forces crossed into the forbidden zone. No Allied protest followed, save a short statement by the French. Encouraged by his success in the Rhineland, the way was cleared for the Nazis to take Austria.[28]

Churchill's fears were confirmed. That autumn, he warned of the possibility of war. But the desire to avoid the horrors of war was all too paramount. He warned his countrymen from his seat in Parliament, but they did not listen. The cries of "peace! peace!" were too strong. The soothing voice of Prime Minister Neville Chamberlain was the only voice Britain wanted to hear.

Winston Churchill knew the wolf would soon be at the door. The truth of his unheeded warnings was about to become a tragic reality. He understood his times as no one in his position did. He understood, because he knew the history of mankind, and he knew that history confirmed the truth that the nature of men did not change. Therefore, he could not be fooled by Hitler's promises of peace. He knew that true peace could only be achieved by total victory over the enemies of freedom:

> *Winston Churchill was one of the few in all of England and Western Europe who knew that the main purpose of constituted governments was to protect its people and not to avoid war for the sake of peace.*[29]

Churchill authority Allen Packwood sums up the secrets to Churchill's greatness:

> *Winston Churchill was so effective for three reasons: he was controversial, prophetic, and courageous. He possessed the long view of history and he had an unwavering assurance of a destiny. He knew that his nation's role in the world must be preserved at all costs. He believed that a balance of power in Europe and the West was crucial to the stability of a continued peace.*[30]

The Honorable Jack Kemp,[K] former candidate for Vice President of the United States, delivered an acceptance speech in 1990 upon receiving The Winston Churchill Award of the Claremont Institute in Los Angeles. His speech is noted for its moving prose and historical acumen. His remarks characterize the ongoing relevance of Winston Churchill:

Churchill was in fact the earliest advocate of peace through strength . . . What was it that ultimately sustained him over six long decades in public life in triumph and in tragedy, in the First World Crisis, following the Dardanelles, throughout the Wilderness Years, during the War Years, and after his defeat in 1945 . . . I believe the anchor of his being was a deeply held commitment to freedom and democracy, ideas which enoble the long story of Britain, ideas extending forth from Magna Carta to the birth of America's declaration "that all men are created equal." Ideas which he believed were an external promise to transform the world for men and women everywhere.[31]

Far from being an historical figure from six decades ago, Winston Churchill endures. He endures not only for who he was, but for what he **believed.** He is admired as a leader who never lost the courage of his convictions. He was a politician comfortable with who he was, what he believed, and what he knew to be right. So comfortable, that even when he loses his power, he does not change his views. He writes and paints and waits. He waits for the world to come to him. And it did.

In any setback or defeat, Winston Churchill never gave in. All his life experiences readied him for the time his nation and the world would need him most. His optimism, his unyielding belief that his country would prevail against tyranny was one of the secrets of his greatness. His unflagging devotion to truth, his commitment to principle, and his dogged belief that not only he but also his nation had a destiny, prepared him to stand alone against fascism and renew the world's faith in democracy. The wolf was about to meet the lion.

A Blenheim Palace is one of the greatest palaces in the world. With over two hundred rooms, it is home to the 11th Duke of Marlborough and his family and is the birthplace of Sir Winston Churchill. The magnificent palace grounds contain over three thousand acres of gardens, all designed by England's most famous landscape architect, "Capability" Brown.

B *Versailles:* resplendent palace of King Louis XIV just 13 miles outside of Paris. It is possibly the most opulent home in existence, and is best-known for its 24 karat gold furnishings and Great Hall of Mirrors.

C Churchill had just had an operation to remove his appendix. One of the reasons he could not fight the 1922 election effectively was because he was still recovering from surgery.

D The Boers were descendants of the Dutch who settled in South Africa. They had become a colony of the British Empire. This was the war these Dutch descendants fought for their independence from Great Britain. *Boer* literally means "farmer."

E The Home Secretary is the British counterpart to the United States Secretary of State.

F Churchill had been forced to leave his seat in Oldham in 1906. He held a Liberal seat in Manchester, and was then forced to stand for re-election on gaining a Cabinet position. He lost the election and then found a safe Liberal seat in Dundee.

G During his first stint as First Lord of the Admiralty during the First World War (1914-15), Churchill advocated the use of the tank as a possible means of breaking the stalemate on the Western front. It was wildly successful.

H The Dardanelles have been one of the most strategic points on the globe since ancient times. The 40-mile long waterway drains into the Aegean Sea and is the most crucial ferry point for the shortest overland route from Asia and the Near East to Europe. Named for a mythical ancestor of the Trojans, their shores are the site of Troy and were immortalized in Homer's *Iliad*. Alexander the Great crossed there to begin his Asian conquests, and the Romans used this vital waterway for military and commercial purposes. These waters are owned and controlled by the country of Turkey which entered WWI on the side of the Germans, hence the conflict there with the British forces.

I The Chancellor of the Exchequer is the British counterpart to the United States Secretary of the Treasury.

J According to the Versailles Treaty, Germany was allowed to retain this valuable land located on its west bank of the Rhine River, provided that there be no militarization. This stipulation was added to prevent Germany from enacting any revenge upon France, its former enemy during the First World War.

K Mr. Kemp was a former top quarterback in professional football. He served nine terms in the United States House of Representatives from New York, served in the Cabinet of President George H.W. Bush, and was nominee for Vice President of the United States. He co-authored the famous Kemp-Roth tax-cut bill which is considered one of the key initiatives responsible for the era of unprecedented economic growth and prosperity during the 1980's dubbed "the Reagan Revolution."

Chapter 6

VINDICATED PROPHET

We Have Peace in Our Time!
Prime Minister Neville Chamberlain
Holding the "treaty" with Adolf Hitler, 1938

You were given the choice between war and dishonor;
you chose dishonor and you will have war.
Sir Winston Churchill, The War Cabinet Rooms, London, 1944

Adolf Hitler had a simple plan. First, he conspired to unite the German-speaking peoples in a greater Germany. His program of "Germanization"ᴬ was to unite all the conquered countries. Second, he moved to embark upon a war of conquest throughout Europe. He held all military power in Germany—and would hold it until the end of the war. He held all political power in Germany and was now emboldened to begin playing off the rivalries between his neighboring nations.

In the mid-1930s, Winston Churchill kept watch on the situation brewing in Europe. His eloquent description of the unfolding circumstances across the continent as "the gathering storm" captured the developing mood of the times. In 1935, he penned an article which turned out to be quite prophetic. It described the intentions of the new Chancellor of Germany and the direction he was taking his nation. Churchill's warnings were published in *The Strand*:

> *Hitler had long proclaimed that, if he came to power, he would do two things that no one else could do for Germany but himself. First, he would restore Germany to the height of her power in Europe, and secondly, he would cure the cruel unemployment that afflicted the people. His methods are now apparent. Germany was to recover her place in Europe by rearming and the Germans were to be freed from the curse of unemployment by making the armaments...It was not until 1935 that the full terror of this revelation broke upon the careless and imprudent world, and Hitler, casting aside concealment, sprang forth armed to the teeth...[1]*

67

Adolf Hitler made no pretense of his ambitions. Before the close of the decade, he was ready for the dramatic step which would begin his march through the sovereign nations of Europe. In 1936, a series of agreements between Germany and Italy became the Rome-Berlin Axis. In direct violation of the Versailles Treaty, Hitler re-militarized the Rhineland. The strategy of "divide and conquer," used by the Roman Caesars to rule their world, was not lost on the madman who considered himself in direct line to these ancient emperors. He used this tactic to drive a wedge between Russia and the Western powers and to pit faction against faction within the governments he sought to subdue. Only eight days after he assumed supreme command of all German forces, Hitler summoned the Austrian Chancellor with the following threat: *"You don't really believe that you could hold me up for half an hour? Who knows—perhaps I shall be suddenly overnight in Vienna like a spring storm."*[2]

On March 12, 1938, he boldly declared that Austria would be "annexed to the Fatherland." Before a vote was taken in the Austrian Parliament, Nazi troops were in place and Hitler had indeed taken Vienna. Winston Churchill called this "the rape of Austria." The German-Italian alliance now emerged as a powerful threat to the stability of the continent. Churchill stated: *"This has been a good week for the Dictators—one of the best they have ever had."*[3] As tyrants always do, Hitler wanted not only to abolish Austrian independence, but historic Austria as well. He prohibited the use of the term "Austria" and even changed the name of the country of his birth to "Eastmark." Nevertheless, Austria welcomed him with parades and celebrations. The ***Anschluss***[B] was virtually peaceful. It all seemed so easy. He was ready for his next target.

Hitler next set his sights on the section of land occupied by German citizens who resided within the Czech border. The German-speaking Sudetenland of Czechoslovakia was to be taken in "the spirit of unity" and "to free the German minority." His successful ploy of seeking "freedom" for his fellow citizens convinced Britain and France to pressure the government in Prague to annex these lands.

Hitler declared that this would be his last demand: *"This is the last territorial claim I have to make in Europe."[1]* In six months, he would be advancing toward Poland.

Alarmed, British Prime Minister Neville Chamberlain desired to find a peaceful solution to Hitler's aggression. At Chamberlain's behest, delegates came from Europe and Britain to Munich for a conference. On September 30, 1938, a "peace settlement" was reached, called *The Munich Accord.* This agreement among the delegates forced the Czechs to surrender the German-speaking areas. For this, Hitler was to be satisfied and promised that no other aggression would take place. Privately, Hitler was furious. He felt deprived of his first act of conquest. He detested the "democratic solution imposed at Munich." Winston Churchill saw his fears of German aggression begin to manifest and stated in Parliament: *"Germany has completed a programme of aggression, nicely calculated and timed."* And on the frustration he felt on "His Majesty's Government's continual groveling to Germany," he remarked: *"Dear Germany, do destroy us last."[5]* The "March to Prague" began to open British eyes to Hitler's desire for German supremacy. Churchill issued a statement to the London press:

> *Is this the last attack upon a small state or is it to be followed by another? Is this in fact a step in the direction of an attempt to dominate the world by force? The belief that security can be obtained by throwing a small state to the wolves is a fatal delusion.[6]*

Prime Minister Chamberlain flew home to a hero's welcome. As he was driven through cheering crowds, he remarked to Lord Halifax: "all this [Hitler's aggression] will be over in three months."[7] Chamberlain stood on the balcony of 10 Downing Street.[c] The now famous photo was taken of him holding the treaty paper high over his head as he exuberantly proclaimed: *"We not only have peace with honour, but peace in our time!"*

Winston Churchill rose to speak in the House of Commons on October 5, 1938. He addressed Chamberlain's "triumph" at Munich and the complete betrayal of Czechoslovakia by the Western powers. Quietly and solemnly, he lamented the fate of that nation:

> *This is a total, unmitigated disaster that has fatally endangered the safety, even the independence of Britain... We bid farewell to Czechoslovakia as she recedes into darkness as Hitler, instead of snatching his victuals from the table, has been content to have them served to him course by course.*[8]

Then, his eloquent words painted a word picture of the glorious battles long since past which secured the liberties of his Island home and seemed to be designed to prepare his countrymen for the inevitable struggle which lay ahead: *"Do not suppose that this is the end. This is only the beginning of the reckoning. This is only the first step of a bitter cup which will be proffered to us year by year unless we arise again and take our stand for freedom as in the olden time."*[9]

The path to Hitler's dangerous ambitions was paved by the policy of appeasement to which the countries of post-World War I Europe tenaciously clung. Churchill knew that the road to peace pursued even with the best of intentions by Neville Chamberlain would end only in disaster. On several occasions he unapologetically stated his view of appeasement: *"An appeaser is one who continues to feed the crocodile in the hopes that it will eat him last."*[10]

A critical component in the calculus of Winston Churchill was his firm belief in the acknowledgment of the existence of definite forces for good and definite forces for evil. As he surveyed the simmering situation in Europe, his world and life view, rooted in realization that the choice of either would lead to specific consequences, would be put to the ultimate test.

In his post-war work, *The Second World War*, Churchill defended his position of watchman:

> *All this time (1930-1935) the Allies possessed the strength and the right to prevent German rearmament without the loss of a single life... It was necessary to present this new and*

fearful fact which had broken upon the still-unwitting world: Germany under Hitler, and Germany arming.

The Munich Accord made Adolf Hitler more popular than ever. So much so, that the very institutions which were designed to hold civilization together left him unchallenged. He had delivered what he had promised—he had averted war and enhanced the greater Germany. He had revived the German economy and restored German patriotism. The weakness of the leaders in the nations that had the strength to contain him was an integral factor in his ability to sustain his power. Although well-meaning, they erred by seeking to secure peace above all else. It seemed as if the lessons of history were forgotten.[D] Lessons which teach that peace is only achieved by one of two means: either by the external force of armed tyranny, or by a free people willing to secure that peace by the taking up of arms against aggression and oppression.[E] Hitler immediately capitalized on all the opportunities before him. "Peace at any cost" would prove to be far beyond the cost that any era or people should ever have to pay.

At the height of his popularity, Adolf Hitler cast off restraint and unabashedly revealed the driving force behind his ambition—his homicidal anti-Semitism. He set the stage for the persecution and extermination of the Jewish race through the use of the power of words. His semantic destruction through an unprecedented propaganda campaign, spearheaded by his maniacal puppet, Joseph Goebbels, was astonishingly successful. Films were made editing footage of hundreds of rats running through sewers with the voice of Hitler at fever pitch declaring the need to eliminate "the Jewish vermin" to create "a cleaner and better Germany." Time and again he declared that "they are not German, they're Jews." In 1935, Hitler created **The Nuremberg Laws** [F] which over time prevented Jews from making a living, receiving an education, or conducting business outside the Jewish community. These infamous laws officially deprived Jews of all basic civil rights. They even forbid marriage between "Jews and persons of German blood."[11] The social and economic consequences created a mindset that the Jews were not German, and, coupled with his horribly successful propaganda campaign, not even human. **The Nuremberg Laws** were so named for the place where they were drafted, the city of Nuremberg, Germany.[6] Hitler chose this city because it was the host of the notorious and extravagant rallies and parades which celebrated his Third Reich. His decision was symbolic, for he desired to link the "glory" of his regime to his fanatical racial purity policies.

Hitler knew that he could not overtly and physically attack his Jewish countrymen—not outright, at least. He needed a reason, and he was patient. Within the next few years, his plan of Jewish persecution began to take shape. Jewish property was confiscated and declared forfeit to the state. Tens of thousands of Jews were restricted to the ghettos of major cities, the most notorious being the Warsaw Ghetto in Poland. Here, they would languish until they were moved **en masse** to the concentration camps and death camps in preparation for systematic extermination.[12] Many years later Hitler deputy Rudolf Hess[11] openly admitted that "at least 2,500,000 victims were executed and exterminated at Auschwitz alone by gassing and burning, and at least another half million succumbed to starvation and disease, making a total dead of about 3,000,000."[13]

By the fall of 1938, Hitler's opportunity came. One month after the Munich Conference, in November of that year, he had his first chance to openly persecute the Jews. By this time, Jewish emigration from Germany had swelled to half a million. Borders of neighboring countries blocked thousands trying to flee the fury they felt certain would come. Jewish refugees were trapped between countries. They could not go back to Germany and the bordering states feared to take them. The situation was intolerable for months. The spark to ignite the fury came when a young Jewish man living in Paris received word that his family was among the refugees. In his futile efforts to help them, he became desperate. After he received no aid after repeated attempts to negotiate, he shot a German diplomat at the German Consul in Paris. This was November 8, 1938. Word reached Germany in lightning speed, and Hitler made a pubic showing of coming to the personal aid of this formerly obscure bureaucrat. The next night, November 9, spontaneous riots broke out all over Germany spearheaded by the

SS. A thousand synagogues were burned and the shattering of windows destroyed hundreds of Jewish homes and businesses. Hundreds were dragged through the streets and killed. This night would forever be known as "Crystal Night" (*Kristalnaact*) or "night of the broken glass." Germany was changed forever. A former member of Hitler's youth would years later remark, "This was the day Germany lost her innocence."[14]

Hitler's control of the media and education persuaded the people not to worry about what was happening to the Jews. By 1939, his "prophecy" of "the Jewish conspiracy" would come true because he would *make* it come true through systematic genocide. From the ghettos created in Poland and elsewhere, to the placing of hundreds in the concentration camps throughout the Third Reich, to the building of the death camps, the diabolical plan began to take shape. Eventually when the executions in the concentration camps were not efficient enough to eliminate the high numbers desired by the orders of Hitler's twisted henchmen, Heinrich Himmler[i] and Adolf Eichmann,[j] nine death camps were designed and constructed for mass murder that would destroy not hundreds a day, but thousands.[15] Hitler's fanatical "Jewish Question" would be answered by the grisly barbarism of Himmler's "Final Solution." Step by step, the plan to annihilate an entire race was becoming a reality. Winston Churchill's many warnings of the danger posed by Adolf Hitler on so many fronts were tragically coming true. Before the world really grasped what was happening in Germany, Winston Churchill knew of the potential harm to the Jews. In a 1935 trip to Germany with the British delegation, he was to meet the new Chancellor. Mr. Churchill was ushered out when he expressed the desire to have a moment to ask Hitler, "What do you have against the Jews?"[16]

Unknown to the outside world, and only a year and a half after Britain declared war on the Third Reich, the Holocaust had begun in earnest. Winston Churchill understood what was happening in Germany. In *Never Again*, Churchill biographer, Sir Martin Gilbert, recounts Mr. Churchill's forthright proclamation on the plight of the Jews:

None has suffered more cruelly than the Jew the unspeakable evils wrought on the bodies and spirits of men by Hitler and his vile regime. The Jew bore the brunt of the Nazis first onslaught upon the citadels of freedom and human dignity. He has borne and continued to bear a burden that might have seemed to be beyond endurance. He has not allowed it to break his spirit; he has never lost the will to resist. Assuredly in the day of victory the Jew's sufferings and his part in the struggle will not be forgotten. Once again, at the appointed time, he will see vindicated those principles of righteousness which it was the glory of his fathers to proclaim to the world.[17]

> Winston Churchill
> *The Jewish Chronicle*
> November 14, 1941

The history of this era teaches vital lessons. It teaches that there is a difference between good and evil. It teaches that the value of *one* human life must be preserved at all costs if a civilization is to have any meaning or relevance or survival. It also teaches that while peace is always preferred over war, a lasting peace can never be truly achieved unless it ensures *freedom*. That assurance of freedom can only be guaranteed by those willing to provide the sufficient force required in order to sustain its lasting success—those who are ever vigilant and willing to fight and die in its cause.[K] In that sense, when there is presented a choice between peace and freedom, peace can often become the *enemy* of freedom. This was certainly true in 1939 as Neville Chamberlain sought peace at all costs, even the cost of the precious lives of fellow human beings and of the freedom of the nations in his own backyard.

Early in 1939, Hitler demanded the right to build a railway across the entire country of Poland.[L] His next conquest was now obvious—Poland was open to invasion on three sides. Britain and France now fully realized the ambitions of the dictator of Germany. The German people were not alarmed at any negotiations Hitler arranged, for they had come to accept that their leader was accustomed to getting his way. "Peace for our time!" was about to be in shambles.

The British government issued a guarantee of unilateral support to Poland in the event of German aggression. Immediately, Hitler strengthened his alliance with Italy and its fascist dictator, Benito Mussolini. In August of 1939, Hitler struck a deal with Josef Stalin— the *German-Soviet Non-Aggression Pact*. This agreement secretly sought to divide the whole of Eastern Europe and carve up the country of Poland which lay between Germany and Russia. In a private letter revealed years later, Hitler had planned to overthrow the USSR.

Hitler did not want a general war, but one large enough to destroy Poland, not because he wanted to merge the Eastern front, but because the conquest of Poland would clear his path to Eastern domination. He prepared for a quick settlement for peace. And, why shouldn't he? Up to this point, that had been his formula for success. By this strategy, he would have conquest of all Europe. He reasoned that if he could form an alliance with the Soviet Union, Britain and the West would withdraw their support of Poland and dare not start a world war.

Not surprisingly he was stunned, when during the same month, Britain and France held firm in their support of Poland by the signing of a mutual assistance pact. He fully expected the British to hand over Poland as they had Czechoslovakia. Adolf Hitler could not allow this unexpected wall of resistance to stand. At dawn on September 1, 1939, without warning and without declaration of war, the combined air and land forces of the German army crossed the frontiers of Poland. Fifteen hundred German aircraft were unleashed over Polish skies which spread terror far and wide. A valiant stand was made by the small Polish forces, including their famed cavalry regiments which were crushed under the mechanized divisions of the enemy. Stated Churchill, *"It was one of the greatest battles of extermination of all times."*[18] The beautiful *Polonaise*, Poland's national anthem which was written by their great patriot and composer Chopin,[M] was played continuously over Warsaw radio with a declaration that the music would stop only when the city could no longer hold out. The capital of Warsaw[N] was reduced to rubble because the Polish people stood firm against the Nazis. The strains of the *Polonaise* were stilled at last, but not the memory of Polish valor which has gone down in history.[19] By such valiant stands does a nation preserve its honor. Two days later, on September 3, 1939, Britain and France declared war on Germany. World War II had begun.

> *In this solemn hour, it is a consolation to recall and to dwell upon our repeated efforts for peace. All have been ill-starred, but all have been faithful and sincere…Outside, the storms of war may blow and the land may be lashed with the fury of the gales, but in our hearts this Sunday morning, there is peace. Our hands may be active, but our consciences are at rest. This is no question of fighting for Poland. We are fighting to save the whole world from the pestilence of Nazi tyranny and in defence of all that is most sacred to man. This is no war for domination and Imperial aggrandizement, for material gain. It is a war pure in its inherent quality, a war to establish on impregnable rocks the rights of the individual, and it is a war to establish and revive the stature of man!*[20]
>
> Speech to the House of Commons
> September 3, 1939

Chamberlain was left disgraced and broken. He is remembered in history as the man who contributed to "the disaster that befell the world" and whose tragic epitaph became: "the man who could have stopped Hitler."[21] The one man in all England whom Hitler had proved right and in whom the nation would place its trust was called back to office. Sixty-four year old Winston Churchill was named First Lord of the Admiralty and placed in command of all naval forces in Great Britain. By that evening, he was on duty and the British ships at sea flashed the signal: *"Winston is Back…"*[22] Now present were the glimmer of hope and the promise of the strength and resolve that would be a critical force in the days ahead. Mr. Churchill was now poised to take the reins of power as Prime Minister just eight months later. A glowing ember of freedom was kindled in the hearts of the British people—ready to burst forth into flame.

In *Churchill: The Life Triumphant*, the authors vividly describe the temper of those times:

> *It was tragically easy during the 1930s to ignore Churchill and his grave, prescient prophecies of danger. While he spoke of the realities of power, his listeners took shelter behind a self-deluding idealism. When he warned of Nazi Germany's rearming, people retorted that all nations had the right to arm. When he recalled the age-old British policy of maintaining the balance of power, men replied that power politics was the cause of war. Despite Hitler's undisguised ferocity, it was the peaceful Prime Minister* [Chamberlain] *who held the nation's confidence. "Peace in our time" Chamberlain assured a grateful people after handing Czechoslovakia to Hitler in 1938. It was easier to believe the Prime Minister— until that fateful day in 1939 when the Nazi war machine rolled into Poland and peace in our times lay in ruins.*

In his memoirs of the Second World War, Mr. Churchill sources his own book, *In the Aftermath*, where he presented an account of the events in pre-war Europe which had now become amazingly prophetic:

> *I have set down my impressions of the four years which elapsed between Armistice and the change of Government in Britain at the end of 1922. Writing in 1928, I was deeply under the impression of a future catastrophe.*[23]

As the 1930s came to a close, Winston Churchill was no longer in the wilderness. He was a vindicated prophet. Never one to mince words, Churchill later pointedly spelled out his differences with Mr. Chamberlain regarding their respective approaches to Adolf Hitler:

> *This is the deep difference between the Prime Minister and myself throughout these days. The Prime Minister has believed*

in addressing Herr Hitler through the language of sweet reasonableness. I have believed that he was more open to the language of the mailed° fist.[24]

Resolute. Ready. Regardless.
(Churchill Archives Centre; Baroness Spencer-Churchill Papers)

In 1930s Europe, a world and life view mattered desperately. When two views of the history of man and his world came into conflict as they did between Chamberlain and Churchill, the future of the whole world hung in the balance. Churchill foresaw the ability of the West to bring about a true peace for Europe—but only a peace through strength. He knew that the only true path to peace was found in a nation's will to fight to the end if necessary. Winston Churchill knew that it could not just be Britain's leader who should wage war, it would take the will of the British people to stay the course. He knew that it was not just the integrity of Europe that was at stake, but the integrity of free men and women everywhere. In a BBC broadcast following the fall of Poland he declared:

Lift up your hearts! All will come right. Out of the depths of sorrow and sacrifice will be born again the glory of mankind.[25]

Osama bin Laden, the mastermind behind the horrific attacks on America, held a worldview. Ask the families of his victims and their countrymen if what one believes can matter not only to a nation, but to the entire globe. Leaders raised up for such times understand this. In an interview just three months after September 11, 2001, President George W. Bush stated with resolve:

We are in a fight for civilization itself. We are engaged in a just and noble cause—it is the calling of our time—we must succeed so that we never take our freedoms for granted again.

How important it is for a people to have an understanding of the times in which they live. How much more important—even vital—it is that the leaders entrusted with the authority and power to govern possess this understanding as well. It was controversial British author George Orwell[P] who once remarked upon the geopolitical situation in 1930s Europe and England: *"Pacifism is the handmaiden of fascism."* Orwell's statement holds an element of truth. In early 2002, Professor Thomas Sowell of Stanford University paraphrased Orwell by stating: *"Pacifism is the handmaiden of terrorism."*[26] If this be true, all freedom-loving people dare not waver in their determination to stand strong in the belief that peace can only be assured after the cost of freedom has been paid. Just months before Winston Churchill would assume the reins of power as Prime Minister of Great Britain, he delivered a message with prophetic tones. By year's end, the battle of which he spoke would no longer be metaphorical:

Come then: let us to the task, to the battle, to the toil— each to our part, each to our station. There is not a week, nor a day, nor an hour to lose.[27]

Winston Churchill had the ability to predict the future because he used the past as a guide to the present. He had the resolve to affect the times in which he lived. All his life experiences—his triumphs and tragedies, his successes and failures—readied him to rally his nation to face the life and death struggle which lay ahead. Had his warnings been heeded, perhaps Hitler could have been contained. Perhaps the Second World War would have not happened. We shall never know. What we do know is that Winston Churchill changed his times and thereby changed the world. But, before the world could be changed, his nation would have to stand alone against that world.

A   This idea was to make all citizens of the Reich the same in looks, language, and attitude: "How German are you?"

B   *The Anschluss:* "the connection"

C   Located in London, "Number 10 Downing Street" is the official residence of the Prime Minister of Great Britain.

D   "Those who do not learn the lessons of history are condemned to repeat them." George Santayana

E   There was peace throughout the Third Reich; there was peace for 70 years in the Soviet Union; there is peace today in Beijing, China and Havana, Cuba—but there is little freedom.

F   In the infamous Nuremberg Laws of 1935, the criterion for defining a Jew was: "one with at least two Jewish grandparents." The first result of the post-Nuremberg Laws was that all who were "defined" as Jews lost their citizenship. It did not take long for the Jews to lose much more than mere citizenship. The Nuremberg Laws became the standard for all case law in the judicial system of the Third Reich and set precedent in all cases tried in German courts during the following ten years. The Nuremberg Laws set dangerous precedent: first you destroy a person semantically, then it is not difficult to destroy him physically.

G   It was no accident that in 1945, after the war, the Allies chose the same city for the most famous of the post-war trials. Here, a tribunal represented by the victorious Allied nations tried twenty-four of the highest-ranking Nazi war criminals. This trial has remained a powerful symbol of justice and of the principle of "higher law" and will forever be remembered as "The Nuremberg Trials."

H   Rudolf Hess was one of Hitler's most loyal lieutenants. He voluntarily returned to Landsberg Prison during Hitler's time there. Serving as Hitler's secretary, Hess recorded Hitler's dictation of parts of *Mein Kampf*. In *The Second World War*, Churchill recounts the bizarre capture of Rudolf Hess when Hess parachuted into Scotland in 1941, in Hess' words, to attempt to broker a peace settlement between Britain and Germany. The British government held him as a prisoner of war for the duration. He was tried for war crimes at Nuremberg. Hess received a life sentence at Nuremberg and from 1946 on, he was the sole inmate of Spandau Prison. If he held any secrets, he took them to his grave. Rudolf Hess died in 1987 at the age of 93.

I   As a true merchant of death, Himmler wore a distinctive and visible "skull of death" in the center of his uniform cap. He deposed Hermann Goring as the second most powerful man in the Third Reich. Himmler was head of the state network of terror: the hated and feared *SS* and Gestapo. He established the first concentration camp at Dachau. His Waffen-SS became so powerful, it rivaled the German army. Beginning in 1941, he organized the death camps throughout Eastern Europe. In the waning months of the war he tried to secretly negotiate surrender to the Allies. Hitler discovered his "treachery" and ordered his arrest.

He fled. Cowardly to the end, he disguised himself as a private to avoid capture. The British discovered his identity and arrested him. Before he could stand trial, he committed suicide by taking poison.

J Adolf Eichmann was Himmler's top lieutenant in the *SS*. He ordered the identification, capture, and transport of Jews to Auschwitz and other death camps. In 1945, he was captured by U.S. troops. He escaped and fled to Argentina. In 1960, he was arrested near Buenos Aires and taken to Israel. Under the glare of worldwide publicity, he stood trial for war crimes and for his part in the Holocaust. He was hanged.

K *"Eternal vigilance is the price of liberty."* Thomas Jefferson

L Hitler desired to make Poland a model Nazi state. One in five Poles died during World War II. Not surprisingly, the most notorious concentration camps and death camps were located in Poland, a model indeed for ethnic cleansing.

M A beautiful story is told of this famous master composer. When he left his beloved country to travel the world with his celebrated music, he was given a silver cup filled with Polish soil. He kept it until the day he died. The soil was spread over his grave by his friends and family as he was laid to rest in the country of his birth.

N Warsaw, Poland was called "the Paris of the North" because of the beauty of its hundreds of illuminated buildings.

O The term "mailed" refers to the type of medieval armor worn by knights. Hundreds of small links of metal formed a flexible sheath which a knight wore over his clothing to protect him while allowing freedom of movement. This was called "chainmail" and was of much lighter weight than the solid metal armor previously worn. A mail-covered fist would have the same effect as brass knuckles and could do considerable damage in an altercation.

P George Orwell (real name, Eric Blair) was the author of *1984* and *Animal Farm*. He penned *1984* in 1948 (a reversal of the last two digits) which painted a grim, futuristic picture of a technologically advanced world which systematically removed the past and was constantly monitored under the never-ceasing watch of "Big Brother." In *Animal Farm*, he wrote of life in a "utopian" barnyard. The animals revolt against the oppressive Farmer Jones, only to find themselves struggling against the tyranny of several fellow "equal" animals who rose, as elites always do, to power. ("All animals [men] are equal, but some are more equal than others.") Although the book is a satire, it contains a chilling message about the real-life consequences of egalitarian socialism/communism and vividly illustrates the folly of seeking a perfect society which, because of human nature, will never exist in reality. (The word *utopia* was coined by Sir Thomas More and was derived from the Latin. It actually means "no place.")

Chapter 7

"VERY WELL, ALONE!"

It has come to us to stand alone...I have nothing to
offer but blood, toil, tears, and sweat...
Prime Minister Winston Churchill
The House of Commons, May 13, 1940

In early 1940, the storm clouds amassed ominously across the European continent. Britain braced for the next assault by Nazi forces. *"Now at last the slowly gathered, long pent-up fury of the storm broke upon us...Within six weeks we were to find ourselves alone, almost disarmed, with triumphant Germany and Italy at our throats, with the whole of Europe in Hitler's power."[1]* By April, Denmark and Norway fell to the German onslaught. In May, Hitler conquered the Low Countries and had decided to finish off France and Britain before continuing his conquest on the Eastern front. Although he originally had no plans to invade Britain, Hitler ordered preparations for invasion of the Island across the English Channel. Now newly installed as Prime Minister, Winston Churchill encouraged the House of Commons: *"I take up my task with buoyancy and hope. I feel sure that our cause will not be suffered to fail among men."[2]* He later wrote of his attempt to warn the neutral countries which simply answered him with resentment. These neutral countries would soon fall like dominoes.

The Scandinavian countries of Denmark, Norway, Sweden, and Finland held great strategic significance. From its shores off the North Sea to its southern tip, the 1,000 mile Scandinavian Peninsula provided control of a vital gateway to northern Europe. The corridor of waters between the hundreds of islands and the mainland became a vital lifeline to the West. Through these waters passed British ships which carried the raw materials and supplies needed to prepare for the inevitable. Germany was interested, too. The German war industry was dependent upon the abundance of Swedish iron ore. Hitler was not about to pass up Scandinavia's location, geography, and natural resources.

Norway and Sweden desperately tried to stay neutral as they equally feared both Germany and Russia. The Soviet Union's assault on Finland just six months before was not forgotten. Russia had long desired their neighbor. But the Red Army underestimated the valiant Finns who were well-equipped with skis and snowshoes and proved to be aggressive fighters. Finland turned back the Russians who were ill-prepared for the harsh terrain and such determination. Finland became a model for resistance against tyranny. It was here that the "Molotov Cocktail"^A was born. This homemade hand grenade wreaked havoc on Russian tanks and was so-named for the Soviet Foreign Commissar, V. M. Molotov who instigated the invasion.[3] By January of 1940, German plans for a full assault on Denmark and Norway were underway. Norway and Denmark desperately tried to avoid an invasion. In April, these nations allowed the German army into their countries for the protection of Germany's iron ore supply route and to secure the Baltic Sea. By month's end, there was total occupation in two key Scandinavian countries.

The British government was in disarray. Chamberlain knew he could no longer lead a National Government and would have to resign. Winston Churchill was certainly not his first choice as successor. Churchill had been a headache for Chamberlain as evidenced by remarks he once uttered in exasperation, "Winston is public enemy number one in Berlin."[4] He preferred his Foreign Secretary, Lord Halifax. Chamberlain still believed in negotiation as the solution to Adolf Hitler. Hitler believed that Britain was pacifist and decadent. He was convinced that Chamberlain was forced into declaring war and would therefore wage as little of it as possible. On May 9, the office of Prime Minister was Halifax's for the taking. But Lord Halifax wisely realized that he might not have the confidence and support of all political factions and the common people. In a last-moment decision, he declined in favor of Prime Minister Chamberlain's First Lord of the Admiralty. Said Mr. Churchill: *"By the time Lord Halifax had finished [speaking], it was clear that the duty would fall upon me—had in fact fallen upon me."*[5]

The political dynamic in Britain during the 1930s had kept Churchill on the sidelines. He knew his time in "the wilderness" had allowed him to be trusted and mistrusted equally on all sides of the political spectrum, and therefore relatively neutral. He would return to the corridors of power when Herr Hitler left no doubt his dangerous ambitions threatened the very existence of the British nation. It was a time when opposing political factions came together during a national crisis for the sake of the national cause.[B] This is one of the most important aspects of civilized societies based on democratic principles and the rule of law.

The political dynamic which brought Churchill to power is fascinating. Winston Churchill remained a vehement anti-communist throughout his life. After the overthrow of the Czar in 1917 which sparked the Bolshevik Revolution, he once remarked that *"Marxism-Leninism will create a condition of barbarism worse than the Stone Age...Bolshevikism must be strangled in its crib."*[6] But by the 1930s, he came to view fascism as a greater threat than communism because he believed it was changing the balance of power in the West. After all, he reasoned, Russia was self-contained, but now Germany was moving well beyond her borders. So, by the end of the decade, many on the Left supported him because they saw fascism as a great threat and danger from the Right. They knew that they needed "a strong man" to confront the danger to peace and stability, even if that man was from the opposite side of the aisle. Interestingly, many of his own Conservative Party members did not support him. They had never forgiven him for switching parties a quarter century before, viewing him as "a turncoat." But they also knew that Britain needed a war leader with a strong hand and strong convictions to lead the nation. It was also important that this leader be seen as "a man of the people."[7] Winston Churchill was brought to power, in no small measure, by the opposing political parties. He was summoned to Buckingham Palace by the King[C] who asked him to form a new government. The courage of his convictions—even controversial ones—was not lost on his peers.

On May 10, 1940, sixty-five year old Winston Spencer Churchill became Prime Minister of Great Britain. No Prime Minister in history received his seals of office facing such dangers. On this very day, Hitler unleashed his *Blitzkrieg* (lightning war) on the West. At dawn and without warning Hitler's army crossed the borders of The Netherlands in a wall of fire and steel. German U-boats prowled the North Sea and the Nazi Panzer Divisions burst into the Low Countries of Belgium, Holland, and Luxembourg. The Panzers were mammoth tanks and the ultimate in ground weapons. They struck fear in the hearts of all in their path. The distinctive whine of their engines could be heard from miles away and the ground literally shook at their unstoppable approach. They seemed invincible. By daybreak, the 150 mile frontier was aflame. The German forces cut a path of death and destruction as they pushed forward toward France. The Dutch and Belgian armies would surrender within two weeks, still stunned by the invasion. Of that fateful night, Churchill penned the following:

> *On the night of the tenth of May, at the outset of this mighty battle, I acquired the chief power in the State...at last I had the authority to give directions over the whole scene...I felt as if I were walking with Destiny and that all my past life had been but a preparation for this hour and for this trial.*[8]

One of the keys to the success of the leadership of Winston Churchill was his ultimate trust in the people. Trusting them by never hesitating to give them the truth—no matter how brutal it seemed to be. This created a bond between him and his countrymen which was unshaken throughout the whole of the war. Three days after he ascended to highest office in the land, Prime Minister Winston Churchill stood in the House of Commons and declared to his nation:

> *I have nothing to offer but blood, toil, tears, and sweat . . . We have before us an ordeal of the most grievous kind. We have*

before us many, many long months of struggle and suffering. **You ask what is our policy? I will say: it is to wage war by sea, land, and air, with all our might and with all our strength that God can give us.** *To wage war against a monstrous tyranny, never surpassed in the dark, lamentable catalogue of human crime. That is our policy.* **You ask what is our aim? I can answer in one word. Victory—victory at all costs.** *Victory in spite of all terror, victory, however long and hard the road may be.* **For without victory, there is no survival.**[9]

Hitler had grown accustomed to little opposition is his quest to conquer. It is very likely that Churchill won the battle over Hitler early on in a psychological sense. No leader had dared to confront Adolf Hitler with such audacity and in the face of such overwhelming circumstances. Here was a leader who was not about to accept surrender to tyranny and slavery no matter the cost. Winston Churchill was not just content with directing a *defensive* war. He went full steam ahead with an *offensive* war—to the last man, to the last woman, to the last child. Victory at all costs! Victory or death![11]

During Churchill's first three months as Prime Minister he was called upon to lead his nation through the evacuation at Dunkirk, the fall of France, and the Battle of Britain. If ever there was a man for the hour and the era, it was he. In *Five Days in London, May 1940*, author John Lukacs captures the outcome of the conflict for a grateful posterity:

> *Civilization may survive at least in some small part due to Churchill in 1940. Britain could not have won the war— America and the Soviet Union did that—but Churchill was the one who did not lose it.*[10]

Nine days into his term of office, the Prime Minister delivered the following determined message to his countrymen:

> *Side by side, aided by kith and kin, we must advance to rescue not only Europe, but mankind from the foulest and*

most soul-destroying tyranny which has ever darkened and stained the pages of history. Behind us—behind our [Britain and France] armies and fleets—gather a group of shattered States and bludgeoned races: the Czechs, the Poles, the Norwegians, the Danes, the Dutch, the Belgians. Behind them—behind us—upon all of whom the long night of barbarism will descend unbroken, unless we conquer, as conquer we must—as conquer we shall.[11]

BBC World Broadcast
May 19, 1940

Hitler's invasion of France, heretofore unthinkable, was now inevitable. Churchill still considered the once mighty nation of France his partner in resistance and the French army a strong deterrent to Nazi aggression. But he was under no illusions as to the will of the French government and people. He continually tried to shore up the French nerve, but to no avail. The French had simply given up their will to fight. Holland's fate was not far from their minds. Churchill was summoned to a chateau in the interior of France where the French cabinet had retreated. Attempts were made to persuade him to abandon the flight due to bad weather. The Prime Minister's reply: "I'm going no matter what happens, this is too serious to bother about the weather!" His concerned advisers then went to Mrs. Churchill. Knowing her husband well, she told them, "Lots of young men at this moment are risking their lives for the cause. Winston will do his duty whatever happens." As he was packing for the trip he told his valet, "Give me my heavy pistol and load it. If anything happens and I fall into the hands of the Huns, I want to account for at least *one* before they get me!"[12]

Churchill indeed arrived at the meeting. In a last-ditch effort to plea for France to fight and not surrender, he realized all was lost when the French generals had ordered Paris evacuated. In surrender-mode, the French Prime Minister asked his British ally, "What will you do when they come over to England?" In typical bulldog Churchillian audacity, he replied, "I would drown as many as I could on their way over, and *frapper sur la tete* (hit over the head) anyone who managed to crawl ashore!"[13]

The next day, the German forces entered Paris. Hitler's troops jubilantly strutted down the beautiful tree-lined boulevards. There was no resistance. French citizens stood silently along the parade route. Within an hour, the swastika was flying from the top of the Eiffel Tower. All opposing military forces had been evacuated. Over a quarter of a million British troops and the remains of the First French Army had marched northward as the Germans advanced. The fall of one of the strongest nations in Europe would not take long now.

Only two weeks into the **Blitzkrieg,**[F] Hitler had crushed the French army and trapped 330,000 British soldiers on the northern coast of France in and around the French seaport town of Dunkirk. By the last week of May, the Nazi forces had completely encircled the north of France, cutting off all routes to the east, south, and west. The only route left was the open sea of the English Channel. Sweeping like a sharp scythe, it [the German forces] cut into the British Army, severing it from its allies. Desperately, the Allied forces fought to save their only line of retreat—Dunkirk and its beaches. From the land and from the air, the trapped armies were pounded.[14] With their backs against the Channel and the German forces approaching, the British Expeditionary Force (BEF) was in a most hopeless and helpless situation, struggling to evacuate. For five days the remaining French forces and the British army were under German assault by air, land, and sea. Had he triumphed there, Hitler would have the way cleared to take his most coveted prize—England. Not since William the Conqueror came ashore at Dover in 1066 had Britain faced this serious a threat of invasion. Now, invasion did not only seem probable, but imminent.

What happened at Dunkirk was nothing short of a miracle. The call went out all over England, and hundreds of boats and small seacraft made their way down the rivers to the coast. Escorted by naval vessels commandeered from Dover,[F] they made their way across the treacherous waters of the English Channel. For those few critical days, men from all walks of life ferried over a quarter of a million British soldiers to the safety of their Island home and rescued thousands of their French comrades. Thousands of tons of supplies and ammunition—tanks, trucks, shells, and weapons of all sizes—had to be left behind on the roads and beaches. These were not important now. The order went out: "Save the men! Save the men!" In **Portrait of Churchill**, Guy Eden paints an eloquent word picture of the "disaster-triumph" at Dunkirk:

> *Back and forth, back and forth, went the little ships carrying the men from Dunkirk to their native shores. Back and forth like a restless loom weaving an immortal piece of the tapestry that is Britain's history.*

Then the unimaginable happened. Hitler ordered a temporary halt in the advance of his armies toward the coast, believing his air forces would have no trouble in finishing off the thousands of men stranded on the beaches at Dunkirk. This "blunder" by Hitler delayed disaster and gave the precious time needed for the British army to evacuate. It has been said that this probably cost Hitler the war. He reasoned that since they had no way out, the always cool-headed and rational Brits would have to agree to peace terms. But there was one thing he didn't count on—Winston Churchill. For Churchill, resistance to Hitler was a moral absolute. The key to Britain's survival was in the discernment, the will, and the resolve of the last lion of England.

Dunkirk is considered a military disaster, but also the ultimate of human triumph. Churchill recounted the three factors which contributed to the success at Dunkirk: very few casualties resulted due to the soft sand dunes which muffled Hitler's bombs, the valiant air fights day after day by the British air defense which took out scores of German flyers, and the excellent planning and coordination of the hundreds of civilian, commercial, and military seacraft combined with a disciplined rescue at the French shoreline:

> *A miracle of deliverance, achieved by valour, by perseverance, by perfect discipline, by faultless service, by resource, by skill, by unconquerable fidelity. . . In the midst of our defeat, glory came to the island people—united and unconquerable—*

and the tale of the Dunkirk beaches will shine in whatever records are preserved of our affairs.[15]

The Germans would most probably have finished off the British in June of 1940, but the evacuation at Dunkirk reversed the momentum and the morale, saved the British army, and changed the course of the war. Churchill never forgot for a moment who was responsible for the miracle at Dunkirk. And he was the first to praise those who sacrificed to make it possible—the average British citizen. His steadfast belief in the British spirit would not disappoint him in the days and months to come. A crowded House of Commons fell silent as they listened to the account of the miracle at Dunkirk delivered by a grateful Prime Minister:

> *I have myself full confidence that if we all do our duty, if nothing is neglected, we shall prove ourselves once again able to defend our Island home, to ride the storm of war, and to outlive the menace of tyranny, if necessary for years, if necessary alone . . . We shall not flag or fail; we shall go on to the end . . . We shall defend our Island, whatever the cost may be—we shall fight on the beaches, we shall fight on the landing grounds, we shall fight in the fields and in the streets, we shall fight in the hills—we shall never surrender! We will carry on the struggle until, in God's good time, the New World, with all its power and might, steps forth to the rescue and liberation of the Old.[16]*
>
> Speech following the Deliverance at Dunkirk
> The House of Commons, June 4, 1940

Within a mere 40 days, the Battle of France was over. France had fallen to the overwhelming might of the Third Reich. Although Hitler did not know it the day he entered Paris and danced a little jig under the *Arc de Triumphe*[G] before parading down the famous *Champs Elysees*,[H] he had reached the pinnacle of his power and prestige. His

91

euphoria would not allow him to realize it at the time, but he would not reach those heights again. Yet in those first few weeks, the outcome was by no means determined. In June, Italy officially entered the war on the side of Germany. The noose seemed to be tightening around the British Isles. Britain's last ally on the Continent was gone—she was alone.

> *And now it has come to us to stand alone in the breach and face the worst that the tyrant's might and enmity can do... We are fighting by ourselves alone, but we are not fighting for ourselves alone...But be the ordeal sharp or long or both, we shall seek no terms, we shall tolerate no parley; we may show mercy—we shall ask for none ... This is a war of the unknown warriors. But let all strive without failing in faith or in duty, and the dark curse of Hitler will be lifted from our age.*[17]

> BBC Broadcast
> July 14, 1940

Only six weeks after he became Prime Minister, the German armies were poised to strike across the English Channel. Churchill formed the Home Guard with a million citizens armed with shotguns and pikes ready to take care of enemy parachutists. Although he expected assault and invasion at any time, he went on the offense by organizing an air defense system and forbidding any peace-dealings with the Nazis. Many in the military had to train with broom handles and could only fire two bullets a day per man in practice. Had Hitler known, he would have come immediately. *"The whole fury and might of the enemy must very soon be turned on us ... We cannot tell when they will try to come. But, no one should blind himself to the fact that if the Germans plan to invade, it cannot be long delayed."* [18]

Soon, the grim time gave way to a glorious time as Churchill, refusing Hitler's offers of peace, went on the attack. *Der Fuehrer* had only known from countries in his path, a posture of defense and surrender.

Winston Churchill did not only defend his country, he declared that he, and they, would fight on to the last man. He even had a slogan prepared in case of invasion: *"You can always take one with you!"* [19] The British triumphs between 1940 and 1941 totally exasperated Hitler. He was simply unprepared for the defiance and fortitude of the English bulldog: *"Hitler knows that he will have to break us on this Island or lose the war!"* Commander of the British Army in 1940, Lord Willis later stated:

> *It was as if the man had been waiting for this moment all his life and as if we had been waiting all our lives for this man to come forward. Within six months of Churchill, there was five years of change. Every man rose in spirit—you could almost measure it. We'd have gone down to the coast and beat the Nazis back with broom handles! Such was the magic of Churchill.* [20]

What contributes to the timelessness of Winston Churchill was his ability to impart courage and hope, not only to his own countrymen, but to people everywhere. In October of 1940, the Prime Minister of Great Britain delivered a radio broadcast directed to the occupied country of France. With words such as these, it is little wonder that the French resistance movement (the underground) was one of the most effective in all of occupied Europe. From the War Cabinet Rooms under the streets of London and during an air raid, Winston Churchill spoke the following words:

> *Frenchmen—re-arm your spirits before it is too late! The story is not yet finished, but it will not be so long. We are on his [Hitler's] track, and so are our friends across the Atlantic Ocean, and your friends across the Atlantic Ocean. If he can not destroy us, we will surely destroy him and all his gang and their works. Therefore, have faith, for all will come to right ...Remember, we shall never stop, never waver, and*

*never give in, and that our whole people and Empire have
vowed themselves to the task of cleansing Europe from the
Nazi pestilence and saving the world from the new Dark
Ages. We seek to beat the life and soul out of Hitler and
Hitlerism. That alone, that all the time, that to the end.
Good night then. Sleep to gather strength for the morning,
for morning will come. Brightly will it shine on the
brave and true, kindly upon all who suffer for the cause,
glorious upon the tombs of heroes. Thus will shine the dawn.
Vive la France!*[21]

BBC World Broadcast
October 21, 1940

In the darkest hours of World War II, Winston Churchill rallied his nation. From 1940 to 1941, the Nazi *Blitzkrieg* had conquered the European continent. England without allies, and facing the constant threat of Nazi invasion and air attack, truly stood alone. He described this chapter in his nation's history in the theme of the second volume in his series on the Second World War entitled "Their Finest Hour:"

*How the British people held the Fort alone till those
who hitherto had been half-blind were half-ready.*

In this grim time, the eloquent and emotional speeches given by Churchill united the British nation as she fought for her very survival. But let it be said that words alone—even the most magnificent of words—are not enough without corresponding action. Winston Churchill, of all leaders, understood this. That is why he never failed to give credit where credit was due. He believed in the people, the goodness and courage of his fellow countrymen. On this, he never wavered.

With Dunkirk behind them, a probable invasion ahead of them, and many battles yet to come, the spirit of British determination was captured by *London Times* cartoonist David Low. The drawing depicts a defiant British soldier standing alone at the tip of an island in a storm-tossed sea. His rifle in one hand, his other raised with clenched fist against an angry plane-filled sky. Steely-eyed, he looks above. The caption reads: *"Very well, alone!"*

TUESDAY, JUNE 18, 1940

"VERY WELL , ALONE "   (Copyright in All Countries.)

It has been said that few world leaders in history came to power in the face of such adversity. Britain's Prime Minister would not let the nation consider Dunkirk a victory: *"Wars are not won by evacuations."* He would not let England celebrate just being safe. He knew the difference between peace and freedom. He knew the worst lay ahead. With all of Europe in the grip of the Nazis, the world expected Great Britain to sue for peace—until they heard Winston Churchill speak to Parliament once more. This is Churchill, the immortal, as he delivered the words for which he shall always be remembered:

> *The battle of France is now over…the Battle of Britain is about to begin. Upon this battle depends the survival of Christian civilisation. Upon it depends our own British life, and the*

*long continuity of our institutions and our Empire. The whole fury and might of the enemy must very soon be turned on us. Hitler knows that he will have to break us on this Island or lose the war. If we can stand up to him, all Europe may be free and the life of the world may move forward into broad, sunlit uplands. But, if we fail, then the whole world, including the United States and all that we have known and cared for, will sink into the abyss of a new Dark Age made more sinister, and perhaps more protracted, by the lights of perverted science. Let us therefore brace ourselves to our duties and so bear ourselves that, if the British Empire and its Commonwealth last for a thousand years, men will still say, "**This was their finest hour.**"*

The British *would* fight on alone. Their finest hour—and Churchill's—was about to begin.

^A A Molotov Cocktail is simply a glass bottle filled with gasoline which uses a strip of cloth as a fuse. The fuse is lit and the bottle thrown, spreading the burning fuel on the intended target.

^B Churchill understood this emphatically. The day he assumed the Office of Prime Minister, he chose members from each of the political parties to comprise his War Cabinet and for the prominent positions in his Government.

^C Located in the heart of London, Buckingham Palace is the official residence of the Sovereign of Great Britain. The British monarch at this time was His Majesty, King George VI, who was the father of the current sovereign, Queen Elizabeth II.

^D As he stated in *A History of the English-Speaking Peoples*, Churchill believed that the fighting spirit of the ancient Celtic queen, Boadicea (or Boudicca), leader of the 1st century Britons who fought back the Roman invaders, was part of the fiber of the British race. The valiant Celtic warrior sacrificed herself rather than submit to Roman rule. How fitting it is that a magnificent bronze statue of this great leader atop her chariot led by majestic steeds stands directly across the Houses of Parliament in London.

^E Churchill's description of the *Blitzkrieg*: "an avalanche of fire and steel which rolls across a nation's frontiers, and when resistance breaks out, an overwhelming onslaught is made from the air followed by a close interaction on the battlefield of army and air force with a violent bombardment of all communications and the irresistible forward thrusts of great masses of armour."

^F Dover, England is only 21 miles across the English Channel from Calais, France. Dover Castle, a site established since the Iron Age, was originally constructed by William the Conquerer. During World War II, its miles of subterranean passageways served as a critical command post for British land, naval, and air operations.

^G This famous arch in the heart of Paris was built by Napoleon Bonaparte to commemorate his victories. It is in the style of the Roman arches of victory similar to the Arch of Titus in Rome.

^H This beautiful boulevard was designed by Louis XIV in the 15th century. It is wide, straight, and tree-lined and was quite unusual and magnificent for that time period.

Chapter 8

FIRE OVER ENGLAND

*Never in the field of human conflict was so
much owed by so many to so few.*
Prime Minister Winston Churchill
House of Commons, August 20, 1940

Following the evacuation at Dunkirk, Adolf Hitler was more determined than ever to conquer Britain. His "Operation Sea Lion" was
mobilized to invade. He issued a directive in July of 1940: "Since
England, in spite of her militarily hopeless position, shows no signs of
coming to terms, I have decided to prepare a landing operation
against her, and if necessary, carry it out."[1] The shadow of Nazi
Germany loomed over the English Channel. The situation was not lost
on Britain's "friends across the Atlantic." The United States was not
about to send arms to Britain if there was even a remote possibility of
her surrender to Germany. That was not to be the case. In his memoirs, Cordell Hull,[A] President Franklin Roosevelt's Secretary of State,
recounts the events in the summer of 1940: "France was finished, but
we were convinced that Britain, under Churchill's indomitable leadership, intended to fight on. There would be no negotiations between
London and Berlin. Churchill had made his magnificent [finest hour]
speech in the House of Commons. The President and I believed Mr.
Churchill meant what he said."[2] Germany knew Britain had control of
the seas. The battle had to be won or lost in the air. It would now be a
fight to the finish.

Adolf Hitler stood where Napoleon Bonaparte had stood a century
before and looked out to the chalk cliffs of Dover which seemed to
rise out of the waters from a small, choppy sea. An island only 600
miles long and 300 miles wide—about the size of the state of
Wyoming—was the only obstacle between him and European domination. Crush it and its stubborn people and he would have the combined sea power of Germany and Britain along with a geographic
springboard ready to challenge the "decadent democracy" across the

Atlantic Ocean: *"Where Napoleon failed, I shall succeed. I shall land on the shores of Britain."*[3]

Hitler knew that the English Channel was not like the calm sea around Scandinavia. He knew that for an invasion of this magnitude, thousands of tons of equipment and supplies, as well as his men, had to be transported across the swift waters. Therefore, the first stage of the invasion was to win air supremacy so that his army could cross the Channel unimpeded and unchallenged. His second stage was to break the spirit of the British nation by the destruction of London[B] through the mighty force of the *Blitzkrieg.* In the words of its history-minded Prime Minister, *"Britain was destined to be the 'keep'[C] against the forward march of Hitlerism."* [4]

The first stage of Germany's invasion plan was divided into three phases and seemed like textbook warfare. *Phase One:* Knock out the RAF (Royal Air Force) and its bases, control the air and sea lanes across the Channel, and then follow the successful strategy of communication and transport disruption as in France and the Low Countries. *Phase Two:* Pulverize the coastline with dive-bombers, set up beachheads, blanket the countryside with parachutists, and take over the air bases. *Phase Three:* Launch the invasion using high-speed barges to transport the Panzer Divisions across the Channel under the umbrella of the *Luftwaffe.*[5]

The plan seemed quite probable due to Britain's depleted defenses. Britain had an army, but it had just been dragged from the sea at Dunkirk and was without armaments and weapons. Britain had a navy, but it was sailing all over the globe protecting vital supply lines. Britain had an air force, but it was outnumbered ten to one both in men and machines. In an attempt to drown out England's historical naval anthem, *Rule Britannia,*[D] Nazi troops awaiting their invasion orders sang "We Are Sailing Against England." It was said that the lights of freedom flickered low.

Hitler was convinced by his second-in-command, Hermann Goring, now the Vice-Chancellor of Germany, that air power alone would knock out Britain's defenses quickly. Goring was the personification of a Nazi warlord. He possessed an insatiable desire for power and all its trappings coupled with a visceral hatred of Britain. Goring's vow to destroy England confirmed to Hitler that he had made the right choice for his top lieutenant. A decorated pilot during World War I, Goring had been an airline executive before Hitler tapped him as sole commander of the German air forces. He was the mastermind behind the assault at Dunkirk which seemed all so easy—trap the French and British at the coast and then finish them off by air attack. When he failed to destroy the British army, he now vowed to annihilate Britain itself.[6]

Goring had created the infamous *Luftwaffe* (air weapon), an air force never-before-seen in history. His giant Messerschmitts filled the skies with terror. The British had seen the devastating effects of the *Luftwaffe* over the conquered countries of the continent. Goring perfected the art of strategic bombing, making Germany alone in its capability and supremacy in the air. The Nazis did indeed seem invincible. In almost a millennia, Britain had not seen such a threat to her life as a nation. The treacherous English Channel, which had always protected Britain like the ancient moats which had surrounded her castles, would be of no help now as the threat was from the air, not the sea. The distance across, only 21 miles at its shortest point, would make the air invasion quick and complete. The long-held acknowledgment of Britain's contributions to civilization seemed in peril now: *"A glance at the map of Europe shows the island of Britain anchored off the coast of France. Actually, only 21 miles of water separate Dover and Calais, but these are perhaps the most significant 21 miles in the world. Time after time, they have saved Britain from invasion, and so helped to preserve the liberties of Western man."*[7] Goring vowed to smash the RAF in a month. The Battle of Britain had begun.

Early in July of 1940, England knew she would have to fight for her very survival. Britain's fate lay in the hands of a few hundred pilots. There were no reserves. The motto of the RAF—*there is a time to live and a time to die*—seemed a reality now. But a new detection system became Britain's secret weapon—RADAR.[E] These radio navigation beams would play a key role in Britain's survival.[8] The invisible waves could bounce off large objects like planes, ships, or submarines and then reflect back to reveal their positions. The term RADAR is an acronym, spelled the same front to back, an apt description of its function. Germany was well aware of the new invention and used zeppelins to scout the skies over the coastline. Somehow, they used the wrong frequency, and reported back that "England has no operational RADAR." This report confirmed Goring's bold contention that the new invention would be ineffective against his capabilities.[9]

It only took one year from the development of RADAR, tested in an English meadow,[F] to its installation and activation. One of the most important features of RADAR was that it could be used day or night, in any kind of weather and had a radius of 100 miles. It was a round-the-clock defense system.[10] In less than a year, Britain had installed its "chain home system," a line of towers erected along the southern and eastern coastline which stretched from Portsmouth to Northern Scotland. Relay stations, strategically constructed along the perimeter, were the vital link in the detection system. These RADAR stations were primarily staffed by the WAAF,[G] the first all-female military organization to be used in a war effort. These women became critically important and more than met the challenge. Using long poles, they glided tiny models of British and German aircraft along the surface of a large map of England and the northern coast of France the size of a banquet-sized table top. Equipped with headsets, they used the incoming RADAR reports to monitor the ever-changing locations. They became skilled in detecting the position, the height, and the direction of enemy aircraft. The work area bustled with activity. Often, the Prime Minister sat in the theater-like room overlooking the entire operation observing these efficient women at work. On their recommendation, the commanders dispatched RAF fighters to the target area.[11] Speed and accuracy was vital, for the British pilots could not afford to either waste precious fuel flying over the Channel seeking Nazi warplanes, or to be bombed on the ground waiting for orders. Because of RADAR, the RAF squadrons could intercept the still unseen enemy.

At 11:00 AM on August 15, 1940, RADAR detected massive air squadrons. More than 1,000 German planes were approaching from across the English Channel. Within a half-hour, a life-and-death battle would be fought over the fate of England. As the *Luftwaffe* crossed over the white cliffs of Dover, they made one of the biggest mistakes of the war—they failed to knock out the critical RADAR towers. This major miscalculation, based on Goring's dismissal of the towers as ineffectual, probably cost Hitler his ultimate conquest. Dramatic film footage from this historic battle shows the mighty *Luftwaffe* flying right over the crucial towers, leaving them untouched. Had they been eliminated, the RAF would have lasted a few days at most. On this day, five major actions between German and British fighters along a front of 500 miles were locked in mortal combat, making this the largest air battle of the war. German planes were faster with a better rate of climb; British planes were more maneuverable and better armed. The German flyers had greater numbers and were extremely confident of their abilities and proud of their complete successes over Poland, the Low Countries, and France. But the RAF pilots possessed supreme confidence as individuals and never wavered in their determination to see it all the way to the last man.[12] It was a match for the ages.

For 22 consecutive days, the conflict was unbroken. Germany turned her fury on the English coastline. No civilian target was spared. The naval bases at Portsmouth and Southampton took a pounding, the industrial centers were bombarded, yet the Spitfires continued to go up and out to meet the enemy in the skies. These courageous and tenacious pilots turned back the onslaught. The Dover area was nick-named "Hell's Corner" because of the intensity of the conflict which was continually waged over the English Channel.[13]

Churchill's "gallant squadrons" head toward the Channel. RAF Spitfires fly in "vic" (victory) formation over the English countryside. (Imperial War Museum, CH-740)

Still, Goring was convinced his "air weapon" would prevail. He depended on his seemingly unstoppable Messerschmitts, but they proved to be a liability. They were so heavy that they could only last about 20 minutes in the air before returning to France to refuel. But the lighter RAF fighters could engage the enemy with quickness and maneuverability and stay aloft longer before returning to base.[14] The Germans could not understand where the RAF got their seemingly endless supply of fighters! RADAR had made them seem so much stronger than they really were. Only days actually remained in their arsenal. If Hitler had only known how close they were to depletion, he would have most likely completed the conquest. During the first ten days of the Battle of Britain, Goring launched twenty six major air attacks—the Germans lost 697 aircraft to 153 for the Brits. All the German crews who survived were captured, but over sixty RAF pilots bailed out and were rescued, ready to fight again. In the words of Winston Churchill, these were Britain's "valiant few," her "gallant squadrons."[15]

The spirit of those British pilots was never broken. They shouted the old hunting cry "Tally Ho!" each time they climbed into their cockpits.[16] It was said that the RAF shot down more than the *Luftwaffe*— they shot down the whole Nazi plan of world conquest. Day and night, the 2,000 mile front from France to Norway was protected from invasion. Adolf Hitler put his dastardly invasion plan on hold because the RAF had defiantly defended the skies.

The British success record at the end of the first stage of the Battle of Britain was astonishing. The Brits defeated the Germans by a ratio of almost 2 to 1. This strategic conflict claimed the lives of 503 RAF pilots and 915 British aircraft to Germany's admitted losses of 3,089 crew and 1,733 aircraft.[17] Far from being destroyed, the RAF was triumphant. Each morning Commander-in-Chief of the Royal Air Force Fighter Command, Air-Marshal Sir Hugh Dowding, would walk outside and gaze south over the horizon, waiting for the roar of the Messerschmitts. On September 6, he went out as he always had, not knowing how long he could hold out, waiting for the pre-invasion assault. It would not come again. His few and brave had held their "thin blue line." Hitler was furious with Goring for his failure to knock out Britain's air defenses. Goring later lamented, "I hate the English rogues, but after this is over, I'm going to buy myself a British radio set."[18]

The speech given by the Prime Minister following the initial phase of the Battle of Britain was given as a tribute to the airmen. It was not designed so much to motivate or inspire; instead it was a speech designed to express profound gratitude. Its immortal line sums up the heartfelt feelings of a nation and of a free world:

> *Never in the field of human conflict was so much owed by so many to so few.*
>
> House of Commons
> August 20, 1940

A charming story is told which illustrates the era and the differences between civilization and the barbarism which threatened to destroy it. Vividly it recounts how close to the people's doorsteps the war was brought. With so many downed enemy aircraft, the countryside became littered with "souvenirs" for enterprising British schoolboys. On one occasion, two little ladies were the first to arrive at the wreckage of a downed Messerschmitt "somewhere in England." They found a different kind of souvenir—an injured German pilot wearing the Iron Cross. In excellent English he asked if they were going to shoot him. "No," they replied, "we don't do that in England. Would you like a cup of tea?" Gratefully and eagerly he replied, "Yes!" The ladies made the German flyer a cup of tea before an ambulance arrived to take him to the hospital.[19]

Adolf Hitler certainly held all the cards in the summer of 1940. Yet, against all odds, he would lose. One part of his invasion plan would be put into effect. As his mighty "air weapon" assailed the skies, he unleashed his first large scale attack on London. The Prime Minister had warned his country in June: *"The whole fury and might of the enemy must very soon be turned on us."*[20] Within weeks, peaceful, pacifist Britain had become, in Churchill's words, "a hornet's nest," bristling with activity in preparation of what was to come.

As he prepared his homeland for Hitler's invasion, Churchill speaking to the nation, hearkened back through time, touching the minds of his countrymen with images of the preservation of centuries of their freedom, images created by only his words: *"We shall ready our Island which has not seen the fires of a foreign camp in a thousand years."* [21]

As fire rained down from the sky, all out war ensued over the capital of Britain. What would forever be known to the English as "the Blitz"[H] would test their mettle as nothing ever had before. Author Guy Eden's eyewitness account of those dark days expressed the mood:

> *Then, if as never before or since, words stood between us and possible disaster . . .A wave of patriotism such as no dictator-ridden country could ever know swept over Britain. There can be few who recall those times who would disagree with the statement that the Prime Minister's speeches kept the nation at the fever-heat that was essential. This indeed was their finest hour. Skillfully Churchill brought everyone in the land into the battle, made them feel that on **their** efforts might depend the difference between victory and defeat.*

For 57 consecutive days—almost two months—London was the repository of German bombs and shells. Two hundred German bombers attacked the capital city every night. Bombs fell on Buckingham Palace, Westminster Abbey, the Houses of Parliament, and St. Paul's Cathedral. London became "a smoldering graveyard of 5,000 men, women, and children."[22] As bomb shelters overflowed, thousands found shelter under the streets of London in the underground railways. Thousands of families lost all that they had. On hundreds of bombed-out buildings, anonymous people took chalk and scrawled a message to the world: *"London can take it!"*[23]

The siren—the distinctive sound, like no other—became a part of British national life. When the "all clear"[I] sounded, everyone came out to survey the wreckage and help their friends and neighbors—cheerful, determined, and stronger than ever. Many times Britain's leader walked among his countrymen dressed in his famous "siren suit." A one piece ensemble, it resembled a "jump-suit" and fit the times and circumstances perfectly. If the Prime Minister was asleep when the sirens sounded, he needed only to jump out of bed, step into the suit, and be fully dressed.[24] He was so comfortable he took to wearing it even if there had been no sirens. He wore it all around London and once in the White House Garden! It was uniquely Churchill.

The unassailable quality of determination, melded with unwavering optimism, became the Churchill hallmark. As the bombs fell on London and fire rained from the skies, Winston Churchill counter-barraged with something more powerful—his words:

> *Little does he* [Hitler] *know the spirit of the British nation or the tough fiber of the Londoner. This wicked man, the repository and embodiment of many forms of soul-destroying hatred, this monstrous product of former wrongs and shames has now resolved to break our famous Island by a process of indiscriminate slaughter and destruction...what he has done is kindle a fire in British hearts here and all over the world which will glow long after all traces of the conflagration he has caused in London have been removed. He has lighted a fire which will burn with a steady and consuming flame until the last vestiges of Nazi tyranny have been burnt out of Europe, and until the Old World and the New can join hands to rebuild the temples of man's freedom and man's honour on foundations which will not soon or easily be overthrown.*[25]
>
> BBC Broadcast
> October, 1940

Mr. Churchill's speeches, more bold than ever, touched the heart of every man, woman, and child:

> *The British nation is stirred and moved as it never has been at any time in its long, eventful, and famous history. And it's no hackneyed stroke of speech to say that they mean to conquer or die...they took all they got and could have taken more ... We will mete out to the Germans the measure—and more than the measure—they have meted out to us...to the grisly gang that works its wicked will—you do your worst, we'll do our best!* [26]

107

Churchill spoke of ultimate victory due to the efforts high in the air and in the flaming streets. It was said that it was impossible to be frightened in his presence. He, above all, knew the dangers, yet he continued to go out among the people. Often, he would be met with such throngs that he would hold his derby aloft on his cane, as a king with his banner, so that the crowd would know he was there. As he visited bomb shelters, crowds would shout to him, "Give it 'em back!" Let them have it, too!"[27] So he did. After almost two months of Germany's non-stop bombing of London, Churchill ordered a depleted RAF to go on the offense. He sent what was left of his "gallant squadrons" on bombing raids over Berlin. Hitler—and the world—was stunned at the sheer defiance. It was sheer inspiration.

Coventry, one of the key industrial centers in Britain, sustained the single most devastating raid of the Blitz. The Prime Minister inspects the ruins of Coventry Cathedral, the outline of its magnificent Gothic architecture still standing. (Imperial War Museum, H-14250)

We are doing the finest thing in the world and have the honour to be the sole champion of the liberties of all Europe. . . We shall go on to the end![28]

The British people were inspired time and again to acts of courage because their leader not only elevated them to such ideals, but took no other course than that for himself. During a tour of a munitions factory, he met the workers who tirelessly labored to supply the vital armaments for the struggle. Walking through the crowd, he exclaimed, "You're great people!" They responded with an affection seldom matched, "You're OK yourself!"[29] Once, a bomb fell so close to 10 Downing Street that the windows were shattered and the front door was torn from its hinges. Several soldiers hurried into the street to see if they could be of assistance. A head appeared from an upstairs window, surveying the wreckage. Cupping his hands, one of the soldiers called up to the man at the window, "You all right, mate?" "Fine thanks—are you all right?" came the cheerful reply. A policeman then told the surprised soldiers, "That, you fellows, was the Prime Minister!"[30]

It has been said that Winston Churchill completely created the will of the British people to fight—whatever the cost—to the very end. The people of Britain more than met the challenge. Hitler could kill them, but he could not defeat them. Surrender for Churchill was simply not an option—ever. Churchill and Britain were unbroken and unbowed.

For the first time, Hitler and his forces knew the bitterness of defeat. Gone was their mantle of invincibility. His mighty forces leveled thousands of homes and shops and claimed thousands of lives. Yet not one Nazi soldier set foot on British soil. Adolf Hitler lost the Battle of Britain because his massive and powerful force of arms met a determined and *free* people.[31]

The wolf had met his match in the last lion of England. Author Guy Eden's contemporary account expressed the esteem the British held for their Prime Minister in the summer of 1940: "*We know him as Britain's chief Architect of Victory. And, as we recall that, for a fateful year that seemed a century, Britain stood alone against the almost all-conquering might of the German Third Reich, we may well think that he was the Architect of all Democracy's victory over Dictatorship.*"

At the beginning of the first war of the 21st century, just as in wartime Britain, the American people hearkened to their national leader who exhibited the fortitude and resolve to see them through. In his address to a Joint Session of Congress just ten days after the attack on his country, President George W. Bush rallied the nation in remarks reminiscently Churchillian:

> *Our people are united and resolved as they never have been before . . . We will plant freedom's flag throughout the globe . . . we will not tire, we will not falter, we will not fail.*

After September 11, 2001, Americans witnessed a "smoldering graveyard" of over 3,000 innocent citizens at the site of the World Trade Center, in Pennsylvania and at the Pentagon. Just as in 1940 Britain, the will of the American people galvanized into the determination of one individual with the goal of staying the course, no matter the cost, to rid the civilized world of the terror that threatens its freedom and peace. America has gratefully recognized her "few" to which so much has been owed by so many. The image remains of the unselfish and unflagging firefighters and police officers of New York City who did not run out of the World Trade Center on September 11, but rather ran *in*—into the inferno and certain death. Their sacrifice will forever be etched on the minds and hearts of all Americans. These brave heroes will never be forgotten as long as those who tell the story of September 11 shall make certain. And America proudly continues to recognize those who are prepared to make the ultimate of sacrifices— her fighting men and women who are dispatched throughout the globe. They are, as they were a half-century ago, comrades in arms with America's most faithful and trusted of allies—Great Britain. As in Churchill's day, it is the "Anglo-American Alliance"[J] which is once again called upon to preserve the liberties of Western man.

Very few times in the history of the world has one individual been so vital to the future of his nation. Once in a thousand years does such an individual come on the scene who can inspire his countrymen to indomitable heights of courage and devotion in the face of unimaginable adversity. After the Battle of Britain, Hitler was heard to say to Goring, that something strange had happened in Britain. Yes, something had happened in Britain. Something that Hitler and Goring could have never understood—that in a constitutional democracy, it is not the government that makes war, it is the *people.*

A beautiful film based on Jan Struther's inspirational novel, *Mrs. Miniver,* was made by MGM Studios during the height of the Second World War. Its story centers around an average, middle-class British family who is touched by the war in many life-threatening and life-changing ways. It vividly brings to the screen the example of the indomitable British spirit and its timeless message inspires the spirit of freedom-loving people. Winston Churchill said of this morale-lifting film: "It has done more for the British war effort than a fleet of battle-ships."[32] At the Academy Award Ceremonies of 1942, *Mrs. Miniver* swept the major awards: Best Picture, Best Director,[k] Best Actress, Best Supporting Actress, and Best Screenplay. Its closing scene provides a most moving and memorable climax. It takes place in the village church which has been bomb-damaged by the enemy. The pastor quietly reads from *Psalm 91* then closes his Bible. His final remarks reflect upon the continuing conflict raging about them. His voice builds to a crescendo of confident emotion and leaves no doubt as to the resolve of the free world. President Franklin Roosevelt had these words from the film reprinted and given to the Allied Forces for inspiration on the eve of the D-Day invasion at Normandy. Six decades later, as one reflects upon them, the images of a war that touched a homeland are unmistakable. At the same time, these words of hope and resolve are made relevant in the aftermath of the tragedy of September 11, 2001—a day when families were forever altered and a nation forever changed. These words are a powerful reminder of the true source of the free world's dependency and of its only and ultimate hope:

I will say of the Lord: He is my refuge and my fortress; my God in Him I will trust. Surely He shall deliver thee from the snare of the fowler and from the noise and the pestilence. Thou shalt not be afraid from the terror by night nor from the arrow that flieth by day, nor from the pestilence that walketh in darkness, nor from the destruction that wasteth at noonday. He shall cover thee with His feathers and under His wing shalt thou trust. His truth shall be thy shield and buckler . . .

*We, in this quiet corner of England, have suffered the loss of friends very dear to us. The homes of many of us have been destroyed and the lives of young and old have been taken away. There is scarcely a household that has not been struck to the heart. And why? Surely you must have asked yourselves this question. Why, in all conscience, should these be the ones to suffer? Why these? Are these our soldiers? Are these our fighters? Why should they be sacrificed? I shall tell you why. Because this is not only a war of soldiers in uniform, it is a war of the people—of all the people. And it must be fought not only on the battlefield, but in the cities and in the villages; in the factories and on the farms; in the home and in the heart of every man, woman, and child who loves freedom. **Well, we have buried our dead. But we shall not forget them. Instead, they will inspire us with an unbreakable determination to free ourselves and those who come after us from the tyranny and terror that threatens to strike us down. This is the people's war! We are the fighters! Fight it then! Fight it with all that is in us! And may God defend the right.***[33]

A A native of Tennessee, Mr. Hull received the Nobel Peace Prize in 1945 for his work in laying the plans early in World War II for a post-war international peacekeeping body. FDR called him "the father of the United Nations."

B The ancient city and capital of Britain, Londinium (London), founded by the Romans, was the ultimate prize for Hitler because he considered himself in the line of the Caesars of Rome, patterning all the pomp and pageantry of his reich on the rule of the ultimate of conquerors.

C The "keep" was the stronghold of a castle. Built as a tower and distinguished by its round or square shape, it was the secure place for the family of the owner and was defended to the last.

D The British sailor's anthem which had been sung since before the time of Lord Nelson: "Rule Britannia! Britannia rules the waves! We shall never, never, never live as slaves!"

E RADAR is an acronym for radio detecting and ranging.

F Interestingly, it was in an English meadow, Runnymede, where the invention of English liberties would be crafted, the *Magna Carta*. Now a vital invention that would help preserve those liberties would also be developed in an English meadow.

G Women's Auxiliary Air Force

H Abbreviated form of *Blitzkrieg*; the name the British people "affectionately" gave to Hitler's formidable assault

I A very effective siren system was put into place. "The Alert" signaled everyone to continue daily activity with caution; "The Alarm" ordered "take cover and man your positions"; "The All-Clear" signaled the end of danger.

J The term was used by Churchill to describe the special relationship between the United States and Great Britain.

K Legendary film director William Wyler was unable to receive his "Oscar" the night of the awards. He was flying a bombing mission over Berlin.

Chapter 9

ENGLISH BULLDOG

*I feel greatly honoured that you should have invited me to enter
the United States and address the representatives of both branches
of Congress...I cannot help but reflect that if my father had been
American and my mother British, instead of the other way
'round, I might have got here on my own.*
British Prime Minister Winston Churchill
Address to a Joint Session of the U.S. Congress, December 26, 1941

More than anything else, Adolf Hitler envisioned himself a Caesar.
He patterned his Reich on, and saw it as a legitimate heir to, the power,
pomp, and pageantry of the Roman Empire. One has only to view film
footage of that era to see that, down to the smallest of details—the standards, the banners, the parades, the eagle symbol on every edifice, and
even the salute with outstretched arm that demonstrated ultimate feal-
ty—all were calculated to resurrect the image of ancient Rome. Hitler's
Third Reich was to complete the Roman Empire, which had encompassed the known world from the Atlantic Ocean on the west, to the
Byzantine Empire at the gates of Asia on the east, and from Britannia
on the north to North Africa on the south.

After his rise to power, Adolf Hitler had become accustomed to
conquest and victory. From 1940 to 1942, the British victories were
almost too much for him to handle. He was used to sovereign nations
falling before the might of his forces like stalks of wheat at harvest.
Hitler was totally unprepared for any nation to abandon its posture of
defense and assume the mantle of offense. No country should even
dare. To say that Winston Churchill knocked Hitler off his pedestal is
understating the psychological effect of Britain's defiance. Not only
would Churchill consider a mere defense of his nation as unaccept-
able, but his bulldog determination to fight on to victory was an
important factor in the shift of the momentum of the war.

Winston Churchill has been likened many times to an English bulldog. Tenacious resolve and dogged determination, coupled with a sin-

gleness of purpose—the bringing down of the quarry—characterizes the breed. It applied also to Churchill. A favorite image painted on the sides of many RAF planes was the face of a bulldog wearing a derby on its head and clinching a cigar in its teeth with the "V" for victory sign prominently displayed. It left no doubt as to the message—the Prime Minister was not going to give up, and neither were they.

For the first two years after Churchill took command, the British also suffered a string of defeats. This only made the Prime Minister look for new ways to attack.[1] On close observance of the Prime Minister's utter defiance of the assault of tyranny, one of Churchill's War Cabinet Ministers stated, "We have far too few men, guns, tanks, aeroplanes, shells, and bullets. The only thing we have plenty of is the determination to win through to victory." It was said that at this time, when most were concentrating on plans to resist the invader, Winston Churchill was planning to become the invader and "turn the tables on the swaggering conqueror of all Europe."[2] When Churchill ordered the bombing raids over Germany, Hitler was stunned and infuriated.

> *Nothing impressed or disturbed Hitler so much as his realisation of British wrath and willpower.*[3]

Before Winston Churchill had held the post of Prime Minister scarcely three months, he had in his words "a widening war." Even as he was fighting the Battle of Britain, securing the homeland, and overseeing the evacuation miracle at Dunkirk, he had to prepare for a possible global conflict. At home, the Brits faced German U-boats prowling their waters and harassing their shorelines. They faced the constant threat of invasion and the unrelenting Blitz on their cities and ports. In addition to his duties at home, Churchill had to oversee the effort on several fronts: the Middle East, the Balkans in southeast Europe, and the theatre of war in North Africa. The Prime Minister likened the situation to one not only going over Niagara Falls in a barrel, but also maneuvering the rapids right after the plunge:

We had to keep our heads above water from day to day, do our duty, and prepare for the remorseless development of far larger events.[4]

Winston Churchill saw events in the light of history and destiny. He knew he was just one more leader in the long line of those who had come before him, and would hopefully follow after, who would be called upon to preserve his nation. Lord Ismay[A] once said of his longtime friend, "He thought in terms of history all the time and acted accordingly."[5] Churchill's unflinching call to the duty of defending "the Island home" would just be to him one more scarlet thread which would run through the great tapestry of the fabric of the history of Britain. He believed his destiny now included the preservation of the civilized world. He truly believed what he was once reported to have said, *"The greatest advances come when we recover the things which are lost."*

By the end of the summer of 1940, it was apparent to the world that the mighty *Luftwaffe* of the Nazi regime was no longer invincible. Hitler's bombing of London could not disguise the fact that his plans to invade England had failed. The destruction of the Royal Air Force and the breaking of the spirit of the British nation had been the goals of the Nazis. They failed at both. Bomb-scarred, war-torn London was carrying on. For weeks during the initial phase of the Blitz, Churchill lived on a train specially designed to take him from one position to another along a thousand miles of coastline.[6] Like a watchman perched atop the castle walls, he surveyed any possible places the enemy could land. Adolf Hitler, whose invasions had subjugated country after country, never came to that island off the northern coast of Europe. In October of 1940, he called off the invasion. The Battle of Britain was over.

That same month, General Charles DeGaulle[B] came to Britain. DeGaulle had been the only French leader who chose to continue to fight the Nazis after Dunkirk and before the fall of his country. In the aftermath, he fled France for London to begin organizing the French Resistance Movement that would become legendary. On DeGaulle's flight to London, Churchill stated: "The airplane that brought him here carried the honour of France . . . I always admired his massive strength. He risked it all and kept the flag flying."[7] Asked if he planned to greet the exiled Frenchman in the traditional European fashion, Churchill reportedly replied in typical form: "I'll kiss him on both cheeks or all four if you prefer."

The outcome of the Battle of Britain was, in Hitler's mind, a temporary setback. He was not ready to admit any measure of defeat but prepared to display some audacity of his own. Hitler not only envisioned himself a Caesar, but a Napoleon. However, he was determined to succeed where the Roman Empire and the Empire of France had failed. He would prove it on the Eastern Front where both Rome and France went down to ignominious defeat. The Romans had failed to take the tundra; Napoleon was certain he would succeed where they had failed. It was the beginning of the end for him. Hitler knew he was not going to make Napoleon's mistakes. After all, Nazi Germany had technology never before seen in history. He had the Panzers and the Tigers, the great armored tanks. He had thousands of battle-tested troops and the resources from the countries of a conquered continent. And of course, he had the mighty *Luftwaffe*. In Hitler's mind, just because that island across the Channel did not surrender to his supremacy did not negate his conquest of the European continent and Scandinavia. His early and stunning successes had convinced him and the German people of his infallibility and induced him to push ahead with his plans for total conquest. But, history has a predictable and almost stubborn quality about it. The past is, and always will be, one of the most reliable predictors of the future. Though no one, especially Hitler, could see it at the time, his war on the Russian front would be the beginning of the end of the military might and conquest of the Third Reich.

But in the summer of 1940, Adolf Hitler was riding high. He also had a new ally. In June, Italy declared war on Britain, in Churchill's words, "at the very moment of the fall of France." With help on his southern flank, Hitler could turn his attention eastward toward the Russian frontier. South of Germany lay five countries: Romania, Hungary, Bulgaria, Yugoslavia, and Greece. Romania and Hungary each had a Russian frontier, perfect for Nazi control. Bulgaria had a front on the Black Sea, ideal as a base for German submarines to harass Russian ports. These three countries had leaders who had already "sold out" to the Third Reich. By early 1941 German armies occupied all three. Still left to Hitler's south was unoccupied Yugoslavia and Greece. Nazi strategists knew that these remaining Balkan countries, if not taken, could provide a route for the Allied forces to launch a counter-invasion. Hitler began a massive troop movement eastward. Premier Josef Stalin of the Soviet Union was understandably alarmed. Germany's leader reassured him that their troops were merely practicing for a British invasion. Churchill had warned Stalin about the situation, but Stalin was less suspicious of Hitler than he was of Churchill who had been a very vocal and ardent foe of communism throughout his career.[c] Stalin believed that Churchill's warning was "just a British ploy."[8] Hitler would make full use of the non-aggression pact Stalin had signed with him in 1939. The German invasion of Russia which was to come shortly thereafter certainly did not surprise the Czechs or the Poles.

By the time Germany's new ally Italy declared war, she had a quarter of a million troops in North Africa. By late summer the Italian troops had become active, especially along the Egyptian frontier. Hitler now had an ally with a strong presence just across the Mediterranean Sea that was in place to meet up with his forces.[9] Italy's fascist dictator Benito Mussolini, a cartoonish despot called by many "Hitler's stooge," envisioned himself a conqueror like Germany's Fuehrer. Mussolini rose to dictatorial power by promising the Italian people that he would save them from communism. He did, but with a new form of government—fascism. Churchill, never one to mince words, described him as:

> *That whipped jackal, Mussolini, who to save his own skin, has made all Italy a vassal state of Hitler's empire. He has come yelping not only with appetite, but even of triumph... this absurd impostor!*[10]

During this time, in his typical audacious mode, Churchill sent the cream of his men and supplies to North Africa to oppose Mussolini and engage the formidable German forces. He called this engagement "the hinge of fate upon which our ultimate victory turned."[11] This one decision has been declared by military historians to be one of the boldest strategic moves in history. Britain was at the height of her prestige in the eyes of the free world as, in the words of the Prime Minister, "Hitler's only enemy." Churchill remarked of this move: "Pray God it is the right decision." Churchill knew he was not just sending troops or units of men, but husbands, fathers, sons, and brothers.[12] As he recounted the indispensable contribution to the desert war by the famed 7th British Armoured Division[D], Churchill was later to write that "they arrived in North Africa in the nick of time" and that "they had rendered the highest service and were the best of our fighting men, the like of whom could not be found by us."[13]

The decision was not without cost. During the first two years in North Africa, the British lost battle after battle and stronghold after stronghold to the German army, under the capable leadership of Hitler's legendary general, Erwin Rommel, "the Desert Fox." Churchill later wrote that "the Desert flank was the peg on which all else hung."[14] But, eventually the tide began to turn as the British began to push back and push hard. While the RAF was dropping over 20,000 tons of bombs on Germany, British forces in North Africa were gaining the advantage. Suddenly, the Germans were in retreat. The battles in North Africa were the most hard-fought of all the campaigns and eventually helped to change the course of the war. The world "rubbed its eyes" as it gazed with renewed interest at "the little island to the north-west of Europe and its people who stood alone."[15]

During the initial phase of the North Africa campaign, the Axis powers were poised to strike the Balkans. The invasion of Greece was assigned to Signor Mussolini. It was an unwise decision, because Herr Hitler would have to finish the job. This ancient nation, the birthplace of democracy, is located on a peninsula which has served for millennia as a vital strategic and military point in the Mediterranean. Its exploits have become part of the world's legends.

Hitler could not allow Greece to become a path for the Allies to enter Europe. In October of 1940, Italy invaded the island of

Crete and the western front of Greece. Churchill immediately sent British naval forces to aid in thwarting Mussolini's attack. The valiant Greeks fought in their indomitable and historical fashion and mounted a brilliant campaign which drove the Italians back. It was obvious that Nazi slavery did not appeal to these ancient countries.

Hitler was enraged. The failure of his Italian stooge to protect his southern flank was delaying his invasion of Russia. So he announced his plans to finish the job in the Balkans. At dawn on April 6, 1941, *Luftwaffe* bombs rained down on Yugoslavia. That same day, the Nazi army swarmed down the peninsula of Greece from the north past the famed Mount Olympus.[16] There was little resistance. The Yugoslavian army was cut to pieces. The country surrendered in eleven days. The sudden collapse of Yugoslavia crushed the hope of the Greeks. Churchill later wrote, *"It was another example of one at a time."*[17]

During the height of the conflict in Greece, the British were facing the unrelenting forces of Rommel in North Africa. Against all odds, Churchill sent 60,000 of his desert troops to aid the Greeks even though he thought it was a lost cause. Everything went wrong in Greece and the British had to withdraw at one point. In "another Dunkirk," with British forces in retreat, Churchill's standing at home suffered. He knew he had lost the confidence of many. The back-room whispers included the old charges of warmongering: "Winston can't stand the idea of a war going on without his being in it!" There was mounting opposition to him, but he was determined to face his peers in Parliament, many of whom had declared that "This is the end of him."[18]

The Prime Minister was angry when he spoke to the House of Commons. No wit, no charm, just a strong case for the necessity of the defense of freedom and democracy. He survived this political crisis, but there was still the war in Greece. The Greeks fought hard, but even with British support, they could not prevail. The Germans were overwhelming in men and machines. Greece was overrun. By the end of April, the swastika flew over the ancient city of Athens.

The Greek campaign was one of those unmistakable examples of Winston Churchill's proceeding ahead with what he knew was right, regardless of any personal political consequences. He, of all people, understood that, *"It is impossible in a major war to divide military from political affairs. At the summit they are one."* He also understood valor and recognized it when he saw it. Of the defeat of the heroic Greeks he said, "There were no recriminations. The friendliness and aid which the Greeks so faithfully showed our troops endured nobly to the end. Greek martial honour stands undimmed." Winston Churchill felt that Britain—at all costs—had to uphold the reputation to be faithful to her allies. *"In honour we can do no less."*[19] Greece has never forgotten.

After Germany had taken mainland Greece and the Greek king had been exiled to Crete, Winston Churchill came to that little island and spoke to the citizens of that ancient land whose culture has given so much the world. His words of encouragement and hope bolstered the Greeks in their fight for freedom. His words always seemed to turn defeat into victory.[E] Many proud Greeks to this day remember his impassioned tribute:

> *We used to say that Greeks fight like heroes. From now on, we will say that heroes fight like Greeks.*

This crucial time demonstrated to the world that Britain was in vital need of support from her freedom-loving allies. If Britain was to sustain herself and continue the fight against the tyranny and totalitarianism which she had so valiantly carried on alone, in the days ahead she desperately needed her allies to join her in that fight. In public, Churchill spoke only of victory, but he knew that Britain could not win without help from America. He appealed directly to the American people through their representatives in Congress, *"United we stand, divided we fall."*[F] He later wrote in his memoirs:

> *There is no doubt the Mussolini-Hitler crime of over-running Greece and our effort to stand against tyranny appealed profoundly to the people of the United States.*[20]

It was at this time that Churchill gave a World Broadcast on the BBC:

> *To President Roosevelt: Put your confidence in us. Give us your faith and your blessing, and under Providence, all will be well. We shall not fail or falter; we shall not weaken or tire. Neither the sudden shock of battle nor the long-drawn trials of vigilance and exertion will wear us down. Give us the tools and we will finish the job.[21]*

Help from Britain's closest ally did come. From American ports, tons of arms and supplies began to be shipped from the United States to Great Britain on a "pay later" basis. This was not only a generous gesture by President Roosevelt, but a vital and continuing one as well. This was called the "Lend-Lease Program"[G] and it kept Britain alive with the necessities of life and war.[22] And even though America did not send her sons at this time to aid Britain, Churchill never complained.

"No man should take on himself the awful responsibility of taking a nation into the incalculable dangers and hazards of war unless he is convinced it is the only way." [23] Many times in the months and years to come, Winston Churchill would speak of the Lend-Lease Program and what it had meant to his country during those difficult days. It became another part of the strong bond he called *"the alliance of the English-speaking peoples."*

Britain had been faced with sparse men and weapons against the Nazis who had both to spare. The constant need for supplies, ships, machines, weapons, and ammunition was as necessary as the soldiers and sailors on the frontlines. Churchill called the unabated sacrifice of the thousands of workers at home "the battle of the factories." This "battle" would last the whole of the war. Great courage was needed to ask the men and women who toiled day after day, manufacturing the much-needed supplies and arms, to do more during these years. If anyone else had asked them, they would have walked out. But they took it from Churchill. They forced themselves to make a greater effort. Once in a factory as the rotund figure of the Prime Minister walked among the aisles a weary worker remarked, "If anybody else had asked me to work harder than I am, I'd a' bloody-well knocked his block off! But Winnie—well he's always working himself, and he's a right to ask us to do the same!"[24]

The year 1941 was indeed like a plunge over Niagara Falls. Although the German invasion of Britain seemed no longer a reality, she was not out of danger. In addition to the battles a half a world away, the German navy was harassing the British fleet in her own backyard of the North Atlantic. Thus, the threat to Britain by the Nazis was not only to her forces deployed across the globe, but to her homeland as well. Hitler renewed his **Blitzkrieg** in March of 1941, and through April and May of that year, German air attacks were still a constant and deadly presence over Britain. Said Churchill: "The Blitz continued to assail us." The **Luftwaffe** began to cut off the lifeblood of the British navy—her ports. Portsmouth, the main harbor in Britain, was heavily damaged, its shipyards and dockyards crippled, and thousands killed. In April, London was the target. Portsmouth was attacked again as well as the port cities of Southampton and Plymouth. Immense damage was inflicted, thousands killed and even thousands more made homeless. The indomitable British people "sacrificed their cities to save the navy." They set "decoy fires" across England to save the shipyards and dockyards which were the vital link in supplying both the armed forces and the citizens at home. Their spirits never faltered. The British managed to affectionately call these unrelenting attacks "the Luftwaffe's Tour of the Ports."[25]

May 10, 1941 saw the worst attack on London. When the Nazis returned the last month of spring, they dropped hundreds of incendiary bombs. There were over two thousand major fires across the city which burned continuously. Relief was hampered by damaged water mains and the lowest tide on record in the Thames.[11] That one night, 3,000 Londoners perished. The House of Commons was destroyed. When the Prime Minister visited the ruins, a weeping Churchill vowed to rebuild the chamber exactly as it was.[26] Britain did not know it at the time, but this was, in Churchill's words, "the enemy's parting fling." From June 1940 to June 1941 Britain suffered over 90,000 civilian casualties from Hitler's Blitzkrieg. Over 40,000 of those casualties were deaths.[27] Always with great pride, the Prime Minister said of the courage and determination of his homeland,

> *"It did not matter where the blow struck—the nation was as sound as the sea is salt."* [28]

By the end of the summer of 1941, the entire enemy force had moved to the eastern front to engage the Russians. England had withstood the onslaught. During the worst of the Blitz, Winston Churchill never saw the glass half-empty, but always half-full. In his hallmark posture of optimism and hope, he delivered the following BBC Broadcast on May 3, 1941:

> *While we naturally view with sorrow and anxiety much that is happening in Europe and Africa, and may happen in Asia, we must not lose our sense of proportion and thus become discouraged or alarmed. When we face with a steady eye the difficulties which lie before us, we may derive new confidence from remembering those we have already overcome.*[29]

At the height of the Blitz of 1941, President Roosevelt sent his special envoy, Mr. Harry Hopkins,[1] to meet Britain's Prime Minister. He brought Churchill a special message: "The President is determined that we shall win the war together. Make no mistake about it. He has sent me to tell you that at all costs and by all means he will carry you through no matter what happens to him."[30]

The Prime Minister and the President now planned to meet later that summer. A few months before their first face-to-face meeting, the following exchange of correspondence between Winston Churchill and Franklin Roosevelt took place. It eloquently demonstrates the friendship that was already being forged between these men. Churchill had written to express his determination to stay the course. His closing remarks, recounted here, are laced in typical fashion with his wit and charm:

All my information shows that the Germans are
persevering in their preparations to invade this
country, and we are getting ready to give them
a reception worthy of the occasion.

President Roosevelt responded in a short letter which was written
in his own hand on his personal White House stationery. He quoted a
poem by renowned American poet Henry Wadsworth Longfellow
entitled "Building of the Ship." This poem expressed, like few other
words were able, the resolve to duty and the ultimate consequences
of the outcome of the conflict. The President desired the Prime
Minister to know that he was not alone in the struggle. Churchill had
the note framed as a keepsake.[31]

January 20, 1941

Dear Churchill,

Wendell Wilkie[J] will give you this. He is truly helping to keep politics
out over here. I think this verse applies to your people as it does to us:

Sail on, Oh ship of State!
Sail on, Oh Union, strong and great!
Humanity with all its fears,
With all the hopes of future years,
Is hanging breathless on thy fate!

As ever yours,
Franklin D. Roosevelt

It was during the unrelenting summer of 1941 that the world witnessed one of the most dramatic episodes in the whole of the war—
the sinking of the *Bismarck*. This famous vessel was the German
navy's giant warship and was the most heavily armed ship afloat. The
Bismarck was the most powerful battleship in the world, loose in the
North Atlantic, sinking the freighters supplying England. The
Bismarck weighed over 10,000 tons yet possessed amazing speed
and maneuverability. Its massive hull was virtually invulnerable to
attacking gunfire. When Adolf Hitler launched the great battleship, he
addressed it as if it was a person: "You are the pride of the navy."[32] It
looked as if the Nazis could not be stopped anywhere.

Undaunted, Churchill sent five of his best destroyers to engage the
great German warship. He knew that at all costs, the sinking of the
Bismarck must be done. And sink her they did. But not before the
British battleship, the HMS *Hood* was cut in two by a single blast from
the German behemoth. Fifteen hundred British sailors, including the
captain on board the *Hood*, perished as she sank beneath the waves.
The HMS *Prince of Wales* then engaged the *Bismarck* in an almost
hopeless situation. The *Bismarck* fired upon the bridge of the British
ship killing all the crew except the captain. But, unknown to the

Germans, the HMS *Prince of Wales* had blasted an underwater oil tank on the mighty warship which left a distinctive trail in the Atlantic. The British naval forces set off in pursuit. It took four exhausting days and the unflagging determination of British cruisers, reconnaissance aircraft, destroyers, and battleships to finish off the *Bismarck*. Churchill received the news on a slip of paper handed to him in the House of Commons on May 27, 1941: "I have just received the news that the *Bismarck* is sunk." He sat back down, content.[33]

The Prime Minister of Great Britain had been in communication with the President of the United States for some time during these harrowing months.[K] The two leaders decided to meet face to face in order to draft The Atlantic Charter.[L] At the time, the exact place was kept secret. [M] In Churchill's words, it was held "somewhere in the Atlantic." This historic

At his first meeting with Winston Churchill, the President receives the Prime Minister aboard the USS *Augusta*. Because the extent of FDR's handicap was unknown to the world of 1941, Roosevelt was determined to greet Churchill standing up.
(Churchill Archives Centre; Baroness Spencer-Churchill Papers)

meeting forged not only a military alliance but a true friendship. On the morning of August 9, 1941, Winston Churchill went aboard the USS *Augusta* to meet Franklin Roosevelt. The next morning, the President went aboard the HMS *Prince of Wales* to meet the Prime Minister. On a bright Sunday morning, as the two ships sat stationary on a peaceful and glittering sea, several hundred naval and military personnel from both Great Britain and the United States gathered on the top deck of the British destroyer. Churchill chose the hymns that were "familiar to all and fervently sung." Film footage recounts the very moving event and shows an emotional Churchill taking the lead of all those gathered on the decks in the singing of his selections "Onward Christian Soldiers" and "O, God Our Help in Ages Past." President Roosevelt was "visibly moved" as Churchill later noted:

> *The symbolism was inspiring—the Union Jack and the Stars and Stripes draped side by side on the pulpit. The service was felt by all of us to be a deeply moving expression of the unity of faith our two peoples.*[34]

Perhaps when all those gathered sang the fourth verse of the final hymn, they knew this stalwart anthem would become more than just words:

> *Time, like an ever rolling stream, Bears all its sons away;*
> *They fly, forgotten as a dream, Dies at the op-'ning day.*
> *O, God, our help in ages past, Our hope for years to come,*
> *Be Thou our guard while life shall last, And our eternal home.*[35]

Across a world away was the life and death struggle of a soon-to-be global war. In just sixteen weeks, the United States would be attacked by the Empire of Japan at Pearl Harbor, and America would be forever changed. Winston Churchill wrote poignantly of this unforgettable day:

> *Every word seemed to stir the heart. It was a great hour to live. Nearly half those who sang were soon to die.*[36]

At a pause during the Divine Service aboard the HMS *Prince of Wales*, Churchill and Roosevelt survey the scene. "It was," said Churchill, "a great hour to live."
(Churchill Archives Centre; Baroness Spencer-Churchill Papers)

The Atlantic Charter Conference symbolized for Winston Churchill what was at stake in the great conflict he and his countrymen had long endured. He keenly felt solace in the knowledge that a union of allied support was at a hand. Forces were now forming that would liberate all those under the yoke of totalitarianism. His bulldog determination had not been in vain.

In a BBC World Broadcast given a few days after the meeting at sea, Winston Churchill spoke the following message of hope to the peoples of the conquered countries:

> *There is the signal which we have flashed across the water;*
> *and if it reaches the hearts of those to whom it is sent, they*
> *will endure with fortitude and tenacity their present misfortunes*
> *in the sure faith that they, too, are still serving the common*

*cause, and that their efforts will not be in vain . . . Yield not an
inch! Keep your souls clean from all contact with the Nazis.
Make them feel even in their fleeting hour of brutish triumph
that they are the moral outcasts of mankind. Help is coming.
Mighty forces are arming in your behalf. Have faith.
Have hope. Deliverance is sure.*[37]

Closing his broadcast message, he restated the resolve of all those
present that glorious day at sea: *"Then I felt that—hard and terrible
and long drawn-out as the struggle may be—we shall not be denied
the strength to do our duty to the end."*[38]

With the many notable events of 1941, the year would close with
two of the most pivotal. The invasion of Russia by the forces of the
Third Reich and the attack on Pearl Harbor by the Empire of Japan
would change the course of the war. The Nazi invasion of Russia
would prove disastrous for Adolf Hitler and would reverse the fortunes
of both him and Germany. The Japanese attack on Pearl Harbor would
"awaken a sleeping giant"[N] and, by the concentrated efforts of the
United States, provide the consequential momentum to the Allied
forces—primarily those of Great Britain—across the globe.

For the present, the end was not yet in sight. But Winston Churchill
looked ahead with renewed confidence, bolstered by the fact that he
was not *truly* alone. He and his nation had courageously continued to
exemplify the call to duty. They had held the fort. The world now
paused on the threshold of one of the greatest call to arms in history.

A   Major-General Sir Hastings Ismay was Winston Churchill's Chief of Staff during World War II and his closest military adviser. A career army officer and close friend, he helped plan the D-Day invasion at Normandy.

B   Churchill understood DeGaulle's difficult position and admired him for what he stood for. However, like FDR, Churchill was often infuriated in his dealings with the French leader, especially during the course of the war. A few years after the death of Churchill, then French President Charles DeGaulle surprised few when he ordered all American troops out of France. An exasperated American general remarked, "Does he also want us to remove our boys buried all over France?" In typical form, DeGaulle later blocked Britain from entry into a union of European states.

C   Once, in remarks to the House of Commons, Member of Parliament Winston Churchill had emphatically stated of communism after its takeover of Russia in 1917: "We must strangle Bolshevism in its crib!"

D   This tough and seasoned British army unit is known in history as "the Desert Rats."

E   A naturalized British citizen of Greek ancestry and a businessman in Cambridge, England who owned the lovely inn where the author and her husband stayed during their research trip, told this story at breakfast. This gentleman was barely 40 years old, born after World War II. Yet, he knew the exact date of the Italian invasion of Crete—October 28, 1940—and could remember, to a word, the tribute given by Mr. Churchill to the brave countrymen of his ancestors.

F   Winston Churchill addressed the Congress of the United States in Joint Session three times during the course of the war—an unprecedented number of times by any foreign leader in the history of that body.

G   The Lend-Lease Program could not have been a reality without the measure being passed by the United States Congress. It was no accident that the bill submitted to the Congress was Bill 1776—named for the date of the signing of the Declaration of Independence. It was said that it symbolized "independence from tyranny—1941 style."

H   The Thames River (pronounced *tims*) flows through the heart of London and has served as its most vital artery since the Romans founded the city.

I   A strong friendship between Harry Hopkins and Winston Churchill developed over the course of the war. In a tribute to his friend, Churchill wrote of Mr. Hopkins: "He was a true leader of men. In times of crisis his wisdom has rarely been excelled. His love for the causes of the weak and poor was matched by his passion against tyranny."

J   Republican Wendell Wilkie had been Democrat Franklin Roosevelt's opponent in his most recent election as President of the United States. FDR sent Wilkie as a special envoy to meet with Churchill, demonstrating the unity within the American political system in the crisis at hand.

^K Churchill's code name reflected his lifelong love of the navy. He signed his communiqués "Former Naval Person."

^L The Atlantic Charter was an important document of war aims which later became the cornerstone of the United Nations.

^M The meeting actually took place in Placentia Bay off the coast of Newfoundland, Canada.

^N A well-known phrase attributed to Marshall Tojo following his country's attack on the American fleet harbored in Hawaii on the morning of December 7, 1941. Tojo was an army general and the Prime Minister of Japan when he ordered the attack on Pearl Harbor.

Chapter 10

TO MAKE MEN FREE

Now, this is not the end. It is not even the beginning of the end.
But it is, perhaps, the end of the beginning.
Prime Minister Churchill
At the Lord Mayor's Luncheon, November 11, 1942

Renewed and refreshed by the outpouring of support from his friends across the Atlantic, Churchill began to forge "The Grand Alliance" that would eventually be comprised of the three nations allied to fight Hitler: Great Britain, the United States, and the Soviet Union.^ This alliance would be known to the world as "The Big Three." Mr. Churchill referred to the mission at hand as "the cause" which was, in his words, *"the defeat, ruin, and slaughter of Hitler, to the exclusion of all other purposes, loyalties, or aims."¹*

Winston Churchill was now the man of the hour. After the historic Atlantic Charter Conference, he took up his most extraordinary role of the war. He became a global envoy who traveled anywhere in the world at a moment's notice. On display at Blenheim Palace is a large map of the world with dozens of routes marked which show all the journeys taken by Britain's Prime Minister during those memorable days.² As he traveled the globe, Churchill saw his role of powerbroker as a special one. He believed that the British Commonwealth must always maintain its distinctive relationship with the United States and Europe, thereby achieving a constant "balance of power." During this critical time he considered his role as mediator between the great powers of the United States and the Soviet Union vital to the war effort because he saw the British Empire as the best vehicle for spreading democracy throughout the world.³

This is how Winston Churchill expressed the tenor of those times and the theme of "The Grand Alliance" in his memoirs of the Second World War:

How the British fought on with Hardship their garment until Soviet Russia and the United States were drawn into the Great Conflict[4]

The Grand Alliance was now a reality, secured by the strong partnership between the United States and Great Britain. The friendship forged between Roosevelt and Churchill would last until the death of the President at the war's end. Although the two world leaders sometimes had strong political disagreements, they definitely had a warm and personal relationship.[5] Roosevelt once wrote to Churchill: "It is fun being in the same decade with you." To his Commander-in-Chief, General Dwight Eisenhower, the President remarked of Churchill: "No one could have a better or sturdier ally than that old Tory."[6]

Churchill relaxes at the White House in his famed one-piece "siren suit" he affectionately called "my zip."
(Churchill Archives Centre; Baroness Spencer-Churchill Papers)

A humorous story illustrates the genuine openness between two of democracy's greatest leaders. The first time Winston Churchill visited Franklin Roosevelt as a guest in the White House, the President, unannounced, entered the room just as Churchill had emerged from his bath.[B] Draped in only a towel, he put an embarrassed FDR at ease with his immediate and witty response: "The Prime Minister of Great Britain has nothing to hide from the President of the United States."[7]

By the spring of 1941, Russia had been, in Churchill's words, "drawn into the great conflict." Following his failure to knock out Britain and his conquests of Yugoslavia and Greece, Adolf Hitler made preparations to strike the Soviet Union. He believed the road to Russia was open to his mighty forces. All of his conquests in Eastern Europe had provided the prelude to the main event. The Nazis now had a solid front on Russia's entire western border. Winston Churchill sent a memo to one of his generals:

It looks as if Hitler is massing against Russia…Nobody can stop him in doing this, but we hope to blast the Fatherland behind him pretty thoroughly as the year marches on. I am sure that with God's help we shall beat the life out of the Nazi regime.[8]

On June 22, 1941, an enormous German army approached from five different directions across the western frontier of Russia. This wall of fire and steel encompassed two hundred divisions, comprised two million men, and stretched along a 2,000 mile front.[9] The span of this initial invasion was equivalent to two-thirds the distance across the continental United States. It was one of the most massive assaults in history.

"By December, the banner of the Third Reich will fly over Moscow," Adolf Hitler declared confidently. American newspapers printed the headline: *Russia Has Six Weeks*.[10] The British had believed that Hitler would attack the whole of the Middle East, but instead he turned his army to the east. This fateful decision by Hitler is now considered by military historians as the greatest of his blunders.

Winston Churchill took another one of his gambles and sent aid to Russia at the same time the German army was devouring all in its path. He knew that the Soviet Union was critical to the entire war effort on the eastern front. This was a very unpopular but calculated political risk. At the time of the German assault on the eastern front, the German armies were so strong it was believed that the Nazis could launch an invasion of England and at the same time invade and subdue Russia. Many at home in Britain were trying to convince him that the Russian Army could not last more than a few months. It was said that Churchill had backed the wrong horse this time. Defiantly, the Prime Minister would answer his critics with: "They used to say that about us in 1940, but we're still kicking!"[11]

No military expert or historian at the time gave Russia any chance against the strong, disciplined, and proven forces of the Third Reich. To the Russian people, the historic defense of their land through centuries of unsuccessful invasions was on the line and they were determined to prevail. It was almost a given that Russia would be conquered by the summer's end. Hitler believed it. The world believed it. Everyone but the Russians believed it. Three weeks turned into six weeks. Six weeks turned into six months. Russia could take it—and Russia could dish it out. The Russian army was accustomed to their harsh winters and unyielding terrain. Believing the conquest would not take long, and with incomprehensible arrogance about his invincibility, Hitler did not even send winter clothing or provisions for his troops.

For the first time since Adolf Hitler began his march across the map, his vast war machine met a wall of resistance it had not before experienced. He met a determined people who chose to burn their lands and cities, to fight and die, but not surrender. The unstoppable German army met an adversary which was not deterred by out-dated weapons—or no weapons—or paralyzed by panic. Russia held out. The great *Luftwaffe Blitzkrieg* stalled, sputtered, and died.

The Germans conquered land, but there was just too much land to conquer. Thousands of Nazi stormtroopers lay dead all along Russian roads. At the very gates of Moscow, the German divisions were brought to a standstill by the Soviet troops and the Russian winter. December came, but the swastika did not fly over the capital of Russia. Instead, Russian soldiers in their white snowsuits marched through the streets in defiance. Although his troops fought on for the next eighteen months, Hitler's forces were dealt a blow from which they never recovered. In appraising the situation on the eastern front, Winston Churchill, ever the historian, wryly commented: *"Evidently Hitler hadn't studied Russian history in grade school."*[12]

As events on the eastern front began to unfold, Churchill defended his decision to aid the Soviet Union in their stand against the Nazi invasion. In a BBC broadcast in the autumn of 1941, he encouraged his nation and the world:

> *We are sure that the character of human society will be shaped by the resolves we take and the deeds we do. We need not bewail the fact that we have been called upon to face such solemn responsibilities. We may be proud, and even rejoice amid our tribulations, that we have borne in this cardinal time for so great an age and so splendid an opportunity for service.*[13]

With measured optimism, Winston Churchill looked ahead to successfully winning the war. He knew that the key to ultimate victory over totalitarianism was the entry of the United States into the conflict. That key was made manifest in the early hours of December 7, 1941. On a quiet Sunday morning, the roar of aircraft was heard in the skies over the beautiful islands of Hawaii. The target—the cream of the American fleet moored at the United States military and naval airbase at Pearl Harbor. The attack came suddenly, without warning and without declaration of war. The unthinkable now became reality—death and destruction rained down on Americans.

Trouble had been brewing in East Asia and the Pacific for months. The Empire of Japan had made all-out war on China. They had all but subdued a nation of almost a half a billion people at a time when the total population of the world was just over two billion. The Japanese were now claiming a mantle of invincibility. America had several military bases situated throughout the Pacific Rim, most notably in the Philippines and Hawaii. The American presence in the Pacific was now hindering Japanese expansion throughout the region. The Lend-Lease Program became an economic obstacle to Axis power in the Far East. The United States continued to supply the Allied forces with ships, planes, tanks, and guns across the globe and had managed to aid the Chinese by blocking much of the oil imported to Japan.[14] The Japanese decided it was time to strike.

On Sunday, December 7, 1941 at 1:00 PM East coast time, Japanese envoys were scheduled to meet with American officials at the State Department in Washington, D.C. to talk of peace and friendship. It was seven o'clock in the morning in Hawaii. At 12:30 PM in Washington, D.C. Japanese planes approached Pearl Harbor. At 1:10, Japanese officials telephoned to postpone their meeting.[15] At 1:55 PM-7:55 AM in Hawaii—bombs began to drop over Pearl Harbor.

There were ninety-four American ships anchored at the Hawaiian naval base that morning. Eight battleships were the prime targets. In just half an hour the first wave of the air-launched torpedoes and dive bombers had all but devastated the fleet. The USS *Arizona* was blown apart.[c] The USS *Oklahoma* capsized with hundreds of seamen trapped below the water who never escaped. Both the *West Virginia* and *California* had been sunk. By 10:00 AM the battle was over and the enemy was gone.[16] What remained was a shattered fleet in a maelstrom of fire and smoke—*and* a united America determined to avenge the atrocity.

At Pearl Harbor, hundreds of naval and military personnel—sailors, soldiers, pilots, and nurses—were burned, lacerated, dismembered, and drowned. Over 2,000 Americans perished and over 2,000 were left wounded. The carnage was indescribable. Yet the valor displayed on that fateful morning has gone down in history. A Pearl Harbor survivor wrote the following: "Very ordinary men did very extraordinary things. They lifted objects impossible to lift, moved with broken backs, walked with feet shot off, and serviced guns with broken arms. Some fought on at their battle stations knowing they would drown. Others swam in burning oil to rescue comrades. Mess cooks manned guns, musicians steered boats, machinists tied tourniquets, and nurses hauled lines."[17] Three days later, Germany and Italy declared war on the United States. Churchill later wrote: *"In the immediate aftermath, the Japanese had full battle-fleet command of the Pacific. The strategic balance of the world changed."* [18]

Winston Churchill was at Chequers, the Prime Minister's country home, when he received the news of the attack on America. It was around 9:00 PM British time. Mr. Churchill had just finished a quiet supper with United States Ambassador to Great Britain, Mr. Winant, and President Roosevelt's representative, Averill Harriman. The Prime Minister had been listening to the wireless[D] as was his custom after dinner when he heard the report. He immediately placed a call to President Roosevelt. Within two minutes, the President was on the line. "Mr. President, what's this about Japan?" Roosevelt responded, "It's quite true. They have attacked Pearl Harbor. We're all in the same boat now." Churchill replied, "That certainly simplifies things. God be with you."[19]

Mr. Churchill decided to call Parliament together immediately to discuss Britain's intention to declare war on Japan. He ordered this recall of Parliament to be broadcast over the air waves. It was the first time in history that the British Parliament had been summoned by radio.[20] Churchill was later to record his thoughts on the monumental events that had transpired in December of 1941:

> *No American will think it wrong of me if I proclaim that to have the United States at our side was to me the greatest joy...I now knew the United States was in the war, up to the neck and to the death. So we had won after all! United, we could subdue everybody else in the world. Many disasters, immeasurable cost and tribulation lay ahead, but there was no more doubt about the end."*[21]

On December 8, 1941, President Franklin Roosevelt asked the law-makers of his nation for a declaration of war: "Yesterday, December 7, 1941—*a date which will live in infamy*—the United States of America was suddenly and deliberately attacked by the naval and air forces of the Empire of Japan...I ask that the Congress declare, that since the unprovoked and dastardly attacks by Japan on Sunday, a state of war has existed between the United States and the Japanese Empire." With the attack on Pearl Harbor, and the declarations of war from all sides which followed, the war was launched worldwide.

Winston Churchill, always optimistic, rested in the assurance that the United States would make the difference in the final victory. America's declaration of war justified his optimism. War factories across the United States poured out machines and arms and exported them to their friends across the Atlantic. The island of Britain became "an unsinkable aircraft carrier launching the air power to sink the Nazi-occupied fortress."[22] Just three weeks after Pearl Harbor, Britain's Prime Minister addressed the United States Congress. In tongue-in-cheek understatement, Churchill referred to Japan's decision to bring America into the conflict: *"They have certainly embarked upon a very considerable undertaking."* [23] His remarks were met by resounding applause.

America's entry into the fight was in Churchill's words, "the high point of the war." In his memoirs, Winston Churchill wrote poignantly of his first night in the aftermath of Pearl Harbor:

> *I went to bed and slept the sleep of the saved and thankful.*
> *After seventeen months of lonely fighting, we had won the*
> *war. England would live.* [24]

Within a week of Pearl Harbor, Churchill sailed for the United States to meet with President Roosevelt. He agreed with the President that the defeat of Germany must come before the defeat of Japan. During the course of the war, he traveled six times across the Atlantic to meet with the American President. Churchill's friend, Lord Ismay, recalled the "procedure" on these sea crossings: "On the first day out on every voyage he would insist on a lifeboat drill and that his boat be heavily armed. I think he secretly hoped to battle a German U-Boat."[25]

In December of 1941, British Prime Minister Winston Churchill addresses a Joint Session of Congress in the Chamber of the United States House of Representatives.
(Churchill Archives Centre; Baroness Spencer-Churchill Papers)

During this time Winston Churchill delivered his first speech to a Joint Session of the United States Congress. With rolling cadences, lilting prose, and a substantive message, he eloquently framed the resolve of the Allies to take up the weapons of warfare until the job was done:

> *If you will forgive me for saying it—the best tidings of all— the United States, united as never before, has drawn the sword of freedom and cast away the scabbard.*[26]

The friendship forged between Winston Churchill and Franklin Roosevelt has served as a model for the Anglo-American bond of unity that has lasted to the present day. In the immediate aftermath of the September 11th terrorist attacks on America, the world witnessed again the unbreakable bond of friendship between the United States and Great Britain. Churchill's "Anglo-American unity"[E] was as strong as ever.

Six decades after World War II, British Prime Minister Tony Blair continued to carry on this important tradition. What a comfort to the American people and to President George W. Bush that immediately after the attacks on the United States, and over the course of the events in later months, Britain's Prime Minister stood shoulder-to-shoulder with the American cause. Mr. Blair's government continued to support the United States throughout every phase of the war on terror, even though at times Mr. Blair, like Winston Churchill, took much personal political risk. America has not, and will not, forget.

Just two weeks after September 11, 2001, the only world leader President George W. Bush invited to attend his speech to a Joint Session of the Congress was British Prime Minister Tony Blair. *Newsweek* diplomatic correspondent Richard Wolffe recounts the event in a historical context: "For Bush and Blair, their alliance harkened back to the glory days of World War II."[27] Mr. Blair sat in the House gallery next to First Lady Laura Bush. That night a grateful President looked up to an emotional and smiling Tony Blair as Mr. Bush declared his "war on terrorism" to the United States Congress, to the American people, and to the visiting Prime Minister:

> *America has no truer friend than Great Britain . . .*
> *Once again we are joined together in a great cause.*[28]

Prime Minister Blair gave several interviews on American television which reaffirmed his nation's solidarity with the United States. In an interview on CNN, Prime Minister Blair said the following: *"Well, we've made it very clear that we stand side by side with the United States...we will see it through; it will be done."* Mr. Blair stated on America's Public Broadcasting System: *"From this nation goes our deepest sympathy and prayers for the victims and our profound soli-*

darity with the American people. We were with you at the first. We will stay with you to the last."[29]

Over the weeks which followed, echoes of the Churchill style and substance was heard from Prime Minister Blair as the leaders of the world's two greatest democracies purposed to stand against the newest form of global aggression. Just one month after the attacks on America, Tony Blair was quoted by the British newspaper, *The Guardian:*

> *This is a moment of utmost gravity for the world. None of the leaders involved in this action want war. None of our nations want it. We are peaceful people. But we know that sometimes to safeguard peace, we have to fight. Britain has learnt that lesson many times in our history. We only do it if the cause is just. The cause is just. We will not let up or rest until our objectives are met in full.*[30]

In his first address to the Congress of the United States in December of 1941, Prime Minister Winston Churchill closed with the following statement so characteristic of his boundless optimism and his belief in the ultimate triumph of good over evil. Although his words were aimed at a world at war a half-century ago, his expressions are remarkably relevant and powerfully suited for all those nations who still have the will to make men free:

> *It is not given to us to peer into the mysteries of the future. Still, I avow my hope and faith, sure and inviolate, that in the days to come, the British and American peoples will for their own safety and for the good of all, walk together side by side in majesty, in justice, and in peace.*[31]

A   Winston Churchill would return to his anti-communist stance before the war's end.

B   The other version of the story recounts a surprised and totally nude Churchill greeting President Roosevelt with the subsequent famous remark. When this version circulated among the press, Churchill became a bit miffed and declared that "I would have never received the President without at least a bath towel around my middle."

C   Only the USS *Arizona* was totally and permanently lost. All the other vessels were salvaged and many were returned to active duty. The *Arizona* may still be seen today under the shallow waters of Pearl Harbor.

D   This is the term used by the British to describe the radio.

E   This phrase was used by Winston Churchill many times to describe the special relationship between the United States and Great Britain.

[The chapter title is taken from a phrase from the second stanza of the hymn Churchill chose to be sung at his funeral, the powerful American anthem "Battle Hymn of the Republic." This hymn became a stalwart of the American Civil War and was a personal favorite of President Abraham Lincoln.]

Chapter 11

INTO THE BREACH

In war, you don't have to be nice, you only have to be right.
Rt. Hon. Winston Churchill

So much of what the world knows of the interdependent events of the Second World War comes from the vast and detailed first-hand account of Sir Winston Churchill. For history and posterity, he, in a sense, recorded an entire era—all the battles, all the conferences so vital in the planning of events, the intricate relationships of those in leadership, the personalities with their conflicts and comradeship, the communication between the principals from all sides—an era carefully preserved in the volume of pages written down immediately following the war. Within the now yellowed and fragile pages he penned a half-century ago, his monumental times come to life. Six decades have not diminished the impact of his written words. His life and times provide a model of how the world fights for all that is good and right. His record has become a priceless account of how people and events shaped an era and molded a generation.

As the year 1942 dawned, the Allied forces began their forceful presence on the world stage. During this year and into the next, the military might, political will, and the psychological terror of the Third Reich and the Axis of Germany, Italy, and Japan would be breached.^ By standing alone against such power, Britain and her Prime Minister bought the precious time needed for the ascendancy of the Great Alliance—the Allied powers—to halt the forces of tyranny. As he looked back on the years between 1940 and 1942, his words recall a time of loneliness and struggle, laced with a quiet confidence in the eventual outcome:

I cannot recall any period when its stresses and the outset of so many problems all at once or in rapid succession bore more directly on me and my colleagues than in 1941. Greater military disasters fell upon us in 1942 but by then we were no longer alone—our fortunes were mingled with those of the Grand Alliance.[1]

On all fronts across the globe—from the theatres of war across Europe to the deserts of North Africa and the Middle East, to the vast frontiers of Russia and the boundless oceans of the Atlantic and the Pacific—freedom was on the march. Although many battles lay ahead and much blood and treasure would be required, the tide had turned and no force on earth was going to stop it. It was, in Churchill's memorable words, the end of the beginning:

By steadfastness of purpose, by steadfastness of conduct, by tenacity and endurance such as we have so far displayed— by these, and only by these—can we discharge our duty to the future of the world and to the destiny of man.[2]

The world was about to witness the impossible made possible. The British presence in North Africa resulted in their stunningly successful Desert Campaigns. In North Africa, the British fought doggedly in the desert, eventually defeating Hitler's greatest general and winning the crucial victory that, along with the American landings in Morocco and Algeria, led to the liberation of the northern coast of that continent. American naval victories throughout the Pacific secured a hemisphere and, in Churchill's words, made the conflict "truly a world war." The Russians provided a turning point in the whole of the war in the East when they valiantly defended their homeland against the German onslaught and brought to a standstill a previously unstoppable army. Winston Churchill captured the mood of the times with his punctuated descriptive of the massive Allied deployments across the globe: "Aloft, Ashore, and Afloat!"[3]

Adolf Hitler also used powerful words—words that made good sound like evil and evil sound like good. During his meteoric rise to power, he had declared years before that only one view of the world would prevail:

Two worlds are in conflict...two philosophies of life...
one of these two worlds must break asunder![4]

Hitler's words now took on a meaning he had not intended. One view *would* prevail—but that view would not be his. It was Hitler who had broken the boundaries of Europe and aligned his ambitions with the powerhouse of the East—Japan. It was Hitler who had introduced a virulent strain of genocide unparalleled in human history. His power was unchecked. His will was unchallenged. He had begun to expect that the world might break under his domination. Within just three years, it would be Adolf Hitler and his maniacal tyranny and oppressive totalitarianism, coupled with the Empire of Japan and its cruelty and religious fanaticism, that would be broken asunder by the forces of liberty, peace, and restoration. The proofs of history teach an irrefutable fact—earthly empires rise and fall; none are eternal. In the long run, gaining power by force is not as difficult as the maintaining of that power after the conquest. History is the ongoing story of the prevailing human spirit seeking the fresh winds of freedom and the shining light of liberty.

There were many decisive battles in every theatre of war during the crucial years of 1941-45. Every inch of ground and every sector of sea had to be won at a heavy cost. Most historians cite the huge victory of the Russians over the forces of the Third Reich at the Battle of Stalingrad as the turning point of the Second World War. Winston Churchill believed that the turning point was the entry of the United States into the struggle after the Japanese assault on Pearl Harbor: *"It was clear that the cause of Freedom would not be cast away."* [5] He called each turning point a "hinge of fate." Always an optimist, Britain's Prime Minister was still a realist. He knew that the road to victory would be long and hard. He later remembered the many pressures in the early years of the Second World War:

One war at a time was next to impossible. . . So it went on, with disaster and triumph, triumph and disaster as the companions of our journey. [6]

In the Desert Campaigns, disasters and triumphs were keenly felt by the British. The conflicts in North Africa and the Middle East were aided or hindered by the side controlling the central area to the battle fronts—the Mediterranean Sea. The British held a piece of land vital to control of the Mediterranean and, therefore, important to the desert wars—the colony of Gibraltar. Famous for its massive rock which seems to rise from the depths of the sea, it is located on the southern-most tip of the Iberian Peninsula, the area comprised by Spain and Portugal. This vital seaport guards the isthmus and passageway from the Atlantic Ocean to the Mediterranean Sea known as the Strait of Gibraltar. The doorway to the Mediterranean, it stands at the edge of two continents. This narrow sea lane is the waterway between Spain and Morocco—or between Europe and North Africa. It has been one of the most strategic points on the globe throughout history. Gibraltar's battery of eight huge cannons, hidden under a shelf of solid rock early in the war, protected it from attack from Axis forces.[B] Churchill considered its airfields with one-mile runways constructed just for the war to be Gibraltar's greatest contribution. "Britain's Gibraltar made possible the invasion of North Africa," recalled General Eisenhower.[7]

The British also held a small island in the center of the Mediterranean Sea—Malta. With both Gibraltar and Malta in British hands, the Allies had a good foothold in the Mediterranean. The Axis desperately wanted control of at least one of these strategic pieces of real estate. With Malta located not far from Mussolini's Italy, it was the most likely possibility. The arrogant Italian dictator boasted that he would have no trouble securing the Mediterranean, or "that Italian lake" as he referred to the famous sea to the south of his country.

In February of 1942 the Allies began, according to Churchill, "the supreme struggle for the life of Malta." This small island fortress was critical to both sides in the campaigns of North Africa and the Middle East. To Churchill, Malta was "a faithful British sentinel which guarded a vital sea corridor." President Roosevelt saw the island of Malta as "the key to all our hopes in the Mediterranean." The Germans consid-ered its capture imperative because it would destroy British military power in the Middle East. Hitler called in the *Luftwaffe:* "At all costs, Malta must be captured!"[8]

Churchill understood fully the strategic advantage of Malta. For the entire spring and summer of 1942, a life and death battle for the little island ensued. If the Axis forces had taken Malta, only two to three days would have been needed for the Germans and Italians to cross the Mediterranean with the arms and supplies for their troops all along the front. The loss of Malta would have forced the British to make a voyage of two to three months around the whole of the African coast in order to supply their troops in the Middle East. A voyage around the Cape[C] would be made perilous by the constant threat of German U-boat[D] attacks along the west coast of Africa. The British knew full well the constant danger from the formidable German U-boats.

Churchill believed that Hitler made a major blunder by not realizing that he had such a strong weapon: *"The U-boat attacks were our worst evil in the seas. It would have been wise for the Germans to stake all upon it."*[9]

In May, Mussolini decided to help capture Malta. He offered Italian parachute divisions to aid German air and naval forces in their attempt to take the island. Mussolini held Sicily,[E] where airfields had been constructed to hold a large concentration of Axis aircraft, ready at a moment's notice for a call from Rommel and his Afrika Corps. [F] Relentless air attacks crippled the island. "Malta cried aloud for help," wrote Churchill. The Prime Minister appealed for aid. He got it. FDR sent one of his largest aircraft carriers to England, the USS *Wasp.*[G] Loaded with British Spitfires, it headed to the Mediterranean. In the great conflict that ensued, the tiny Mediterranean outpost survived. Churchill signaled to the Captain and crew of the USS *Wasp: "Who said a wasp couldn't sting twice?"*[10]

During the struggle for Malta, the battles in the deserts of North Africa continued. One of the most important campaigns of the desert wars was over one of Italy's permanent holdings in North Africa, the fortress at Tobruk.[11] Before the siege of Malta, General Rommel prepared to launch a surprise attack on the fortress. For the better part of a year Tobruk was one of the most famous battlefields of World War II and expressed, like few others, the conflict between German and British determination and will. The garrison had been captured by the Australians in January of 1941, bolstering British morale considerably. Churchill summed up their success at that time: *"Good news arrived from Tobruk where the audacious and persistent enemy met their first definite rebuff."* Of the stand by the tenacious Australians, Churchill later wrote: *"We can never forget the noble impulse which had led Australia to send her only three complete divisions, the flower of her manhood, to fight in the Middle East, or the valiant part they played in all its battles."*[11]

On a moonlit night in May of 1942, Rommel besieged Tobruk. Forces comprised of British, South Africans, Australians, and Canadians held firm. An eight-month battle for the fortress ensued. During many of the weeks of conflict, the RAF and the *Luftwaffe* engaged in fierce fighting over the skies of the desert seaport. By July, the famed British 8th Army was hit hard and in full retreat. But, they were not alone. Churchill later wrote proudly of the sacrifice by his forces on the ground and in the air:

> *The valiant, remarkable, and devoted aid of the RAF was seen again as it protected the escape of the 8th Army against the advancing enemy…the days of the Battle of Britain are being repeated far from home.*[12]

The Prime Minister was visiting the President at the White House in June when he received the news that Tobruk had fallen to the Germans. Winston Churchill wrote of this difficult time: *"The surrender of Tobruk reverberated around the world. It was a bitter moment…one of the heaviest blows I sustained during the war."* Over 30,000 Allied prisoners were taken by Rommel's forces. President Roosevelt's immediate response to his friend was, "What can I do to help?" Churchill requested as many Sherman tanks as the United States could spare. The President sent 300 tanks on six of his fastest ships. One ship sank on the voyage over. Without a word, FDR sent another carrier with seventy tanks right off the assembly line. *"A friend in need is a friend indeed,"* Churchill gratefully recalled.[13]

The fall of Tobruk was one of the biggest defeats for the British. General Eisenhower was later to reflect on the unshakable optimism of Winston Churchill: "In the face of such defeat, Churchill spoke only of victory."[14] At home, Winston Churchill experienced an all too familiar ritual—another political crisis. Headlines in American papers read: *"Anger in England" "Tobruk Fall May Bring Change in Government" "Churchill to be Censured."*[15]

Churchill recalled that the tension in Parliament toward him was very similar to that which was directed to Neville Chamberlain after Hitler invaded Poland. His ministers stood firm in their support: *"They were a strong, unbreakable circle...preserving the common cause through every disappointment."* America awaited Churchill's fate. In Parliament, a "no confidence" vote on the Prime Minister was taken. The measure was defeated by 475 to 25. Franklin Roosevelt cabled his friend: "Good for you!" Winston Churchill did not relish the moment or relax in personal jubilance. He recognized where the power to rule originates in a democracy and was grateful for the governmental structures of a free people:

> *It is important that not only those who speak, but those who watch and listen and judge, should also count as a factor in world affairs. After all, we are still fighting for our lives, and for causes dearer than life itself. We have no right to assume that victory is certain. It will be certain only if we do not fail in our duty.*[16]

The situation in North Africa was at a turning point. The Prime Minister and commander of his nation's armed forces made a decision that would change the fortunes of the British in the Desert Wars. Once more in the midst of disaster, he was preparing for victory.[17] Winston Churchill promoted General Bernard Law Montgomery[1] to commander of the British 8th Army in North Africa. A decorated soldier from the

First World War, General Montgomery was known as a superb military strategist who focused on precise details. He required his troops be in top physical condition and insisted that the equipment they used be carefully checked and prepared. Understandably, he inspired trust and loyalty from those he commanded. "Monty" as he came to be known to his countrymen, was the first British general to lead a decisive victory over German forces.[18] He told the Prime Minister: "It can be done— it will be done!"[19]

Montgomery led the valiant 8th Army, affectionately known to the world as "The Desert Rats,"[J] to their highest level of fame. These troops, battle-hardened and desert-worthy, had provided the margin of victory in numerous decisive conflicts. But now the noted battalion had been demoralized by the German onslaught at Tobruk. Throughout July, the battle swayed back and forth. When General Montgomery assumed command in August, he formed a strong defensive line and oversaw the buildup of massive armaments and weapons to be used on the frontlines across Egypt.[20] Rommel himself led charge after charge in attempts to break through the British line. It was a draw. Then, on the last day of August in 1942, British troops under the command of General Montgomery advanced on the German-Italian positions in Egypt at El Alamein, a coastal town located on the Mediterranean only 150 miles west of Cairo. The Italians began to founder as the New Zealander forces proved invaluable with their valiant attacks. Throughout autumn, the conflict raged. Churchill likened this conflict to the fierce World War I battles on the Western front. The first four days of November saw the most intense fighting—all hung in the balance. He recalled the overall mood of those days: *"Monty was determined to fight the battle out to the very end."* [21]

The battle in Egypt began on October 23, 1942. Within two weeks, at 1:00 AM on November 2, the Australians led a spectacular forward drive that tipped the whole battle in favor of the British. The steadfast German line was breached at last. The next day, a great tank battle began. Fighters of the RAF roared over the Mediterranean and swarmed over the battlefield. For the first time, the enemy was held back. Churchill remembered the importance of this decisive battle to

Germany's hopes in North Africa: *"Germany felt the pinch. Hitler gave the 'no retreat' but the issue was no longer in his hands."[22]*

During the war-altering Desert Campaign, a visit by the Prime Minister inspired British troops at Carthage who gathered to catch a glimpse of him. (Imperial War Museum, NA-3252)

On November 4, 1942, the Battle of El Alamein was won. Rommel and his Afrika Corps were in full retreat. General Montgomery's forces pursued the German army across the open desert. Italian soldiers by the thousands were left stranded by the Germans on the battlefield and waited only to surrender. The mighty *Luftwaffe* abandoned the skies. Great news followed. A long-awaited victory at Tobruk was won. The fortress was recaptured by the British on their drive from El Alamein. Of these victories, Churchill recalled: "To Rommel fell all the disasters, to the Allies the triumphs."[23] In his second speech to a Joint Session of the United States Congress in May of 1943 the Prime Minister jubilantly declared: *"A continent has been redeemed!"* [24]

The decisive and determined drive to victory by all the British divisions was crucial to the outcome, especially the contribution by the RAF. Their Prime Minister was generous with his praise: *"Our fighters made the difference again, becoming a dominant force in the Desert campaign. They inflicted severe injury to Rommel's army."* Later, Rommel himself praised the role of the Royal Air Force in the Allied victory in the deserts of Egypt.[25]

Perhaps Rommel was merely returning a compliment, for during the height of the Desert wars the Prime Minister of Great Britain delivered a few words of praise in the House of Commons for Hitler's best general. Churchill later summarized his remarks about "the Desert Fox" in his memoirs of the war: *"A new figure sprang upon the world stage—a German warrior who will hold his place in their military annals. His ardour and daring inflicted grievous disasters on us, but he deserves the salute I gave him in the House of Commons in January, 1942. He also deserves our respect because, although a loyal German soldier, he came to hate Hitler and all his works and took part in the conspiracy in 1944 to rescue Germany by displacing the maniac and tyrant. For this he paid the forfeit of his life."[26]* The Prime Minister was later criticized for his positive remarks about Hitler's best general, but Churchill respected honor and courage, and Rommel[K] was a man who possessed both.

El Alamein was the turning point in Africa and the Middle East and gave the Allies control of the Mediterranean. Hitler's army was on the defense from then on. Now, Germany felt the brunt of assault from an enemy above, behind, over, and around them. On the day of the victory, British and American troops landed in Algiers. From the northwestern coast of North Africa at Morocco to the northeastern coast of North Africa in Egypt, the Allies had blanketed the deserts along a 2,000 mile front. *"The magnitude of the war effort involved in the desert struggles must not be underrated,"* wrote Winston Churchill years later as he reflected on the war years. It was twelve days that turned the tables on the Axis in North Africa: *The Battle of Alamein will ever make a glorious page in British military annals...It differed from all previous fighting in the Desert...It marked in fact the turning of "the hinge of fate" . . . It may be said that before Alamein we never had a victory—after Alamein we never had a defeat.*[27]

Through all the trials and tribulations which beset the British during the Desert campaigns, the undeterred optimism and redoubtable presence of Winston Churchill cannot be forgotten. A story is told of the consistent encouragement given to the British troops in North Africa by the indefatigable Prime Minister. It seems there was an often-seen "Mr. Bullfinch," who furiously rode around the desert in a jeep, flashing the "V" sign with uplifted fingers. A vital lift to morale, "Mr. Bullfinch" was always grinning and making short speeches, then was quickly gone in a puff of cigar-smoke.[28]

Just days after the victory at El Alamein, the Prime Minister requested the ringing of church bells all over London, church bells that had been silent for three years. Churchill called these "the Bells of Thanksgiving" and told his advisers: *"Tonight there is sugar on the cake."*[29] A few days later, at the Lord Mayor's Luncheon at the Mansion House, he uttered the memorable phrase that put into words a sense of hope and comfort, coupled with an understanding of how the past and present can shape the future:

> *The Germans have received back again that measure of fire and steel which they have so often meted out to others...*
> *Now this is not the end. It is not even the beginning of the end. But it is perhaps the end of the beginning.*[30]

The forces of totalitarianism had indeed been breached by the forces of liberty. Those forces now faced a true world war, encompassing over three-quarters of the area of the world, three of the four oceans, four major seas, and the continents of Europe, Asia, North Africa, and the Middle East. Yet to come was the long-awaited culmination of the enormous struggle—the invasion of Europe. Plans for this mammoth undertaking were begun in 1943, but the designated day, or "D-Day," would not be a reality until 1944. Thus continued the great work of defending freedom to the ultimate victory—the task Winston Churchill called "the noblest work":

As long as we have faith in our cause and an unconquerable will-power, salvation will not be denied us. In the words of the Psalmist: 'He shall not be afraid of evil tidings; his heart is fixed, trusting in the Lord.' [31]

Likewise, in the weeks and months following the attacks on America in September of 2001, President George W. Bush laid out for the American people a scenario not unlike the one that Great Britain faced in the 1940s. Mr. Bush effectively made the case that the free nations of the world faced a widening war—a global war on terrorism. The United States and Great Britain once again took the lead as they formed a coalition to eradicate the shadowy networks of terror beginning with al-Qaeda, the group led by the mastermind of September 11, Osama bin Laden.[L] Within six months of the attacks on New York and Washington, Allied troops were deployed to Afghanistan. In six weeks, Allied forces liberated that nation from the grip of the repressive Taliban[M] government. As the initial phase of the war on terrorism was launched, President Bush delivered a speech at Elgin Air Force Base in Florida. On February 5, 2002, the Commander-in-Chief dispatched the troops with words of inspiration reminiscent of the elements of the great wartime leader of a half-century before:

We shall rally the nations of freedom . . . History has called us, and we will not rest until the threat of global terrorism has been destroyed . . . Our cause is right—our cause is just.

One year later, in February of 2003, President George W. Bush delivered the annual State of the Union Address to both houses of Congress, his Cabinet, and the American people. The Leader of the Free World framed the issues at hand and the challenges ahead with regard to the expanding war on terrorism. Within a context of history and reliance on a higher authority, he closed his address:

Americans are a resolute people who have arisen to every test of our time. Adversity has revealed the character of our country to the world and to ourselves . . . Americans are a free people who know that freedom is the right of every person and the future of every nation. The liberty we prize is not America's gift to the world, it is God's gift to humanity.

During this time, America's closest friend and ally prepared to send her sons and daughters to the frontlines. In the great tradition of his nation, Prime Minister Tony Blair captured the tenor of the times with the following:

I cannot recall a time when Britain was confronted simultaneously by such a range of difficult and dangerous problems . . . Though the concerns are real and justified, we are well placed to face up to them . . . If the world makes the right choices now—at this time of destiny—we will get there. And Britain will be at America's side in doing it.[32]

On February 27, 2003, the President invited several world leaders to the White House to discuss the coming days. He made privy the result of months of gathered intelligence information to those he respected—several from the opposite side of the political spectrum—and whose support he desired most. One of these was Jewish Holocaust survivor and Nobel Peace Prize winner, Elie Wiesel. When Mr. Wiesel emerged from the meeting, he spoke to reporters. Of all people, he knew what the costs of freedom entailed. He gave his public support that day to America's continuing war on global terrorism. In an historical context and with stunning succinctness he expressed a critical call to the free world with a reminder of the consequences should the forces of evil be left unbreached:

Evil must be stopped before it becomes too powerful. Had the great powers of the world recognized this in 1938, perhaps there would not have been a world war.

Each era possesses unique and specific challenges. Each civilization is, from time to time, required to collectively preserve that which is vital to its continuance. In the illustrious military history of Great

Britain, few battles capture the essence of heroism and glory more than the early 15th century Battle of Agincourt. At the close of the Hundred Years War, during the reign of King Henry V, both thrones of England and France were at stake. Henry led his army, outnumbered by three to one, to stunning victory. Trapped on the northern coast of France with their backs against the Channel, ravaged by hunger and disease, Henry's situation was desperate. England's rag-tag forces were pitted against resplendent mounted French noblemen. Against all odds, the English advanced. The French warriors and their horses stood motionless. Then, the English let go a volley of ten thousand arrows.[N] The French attempted a cavalry charge, but the field was sodden and their horses sank ankle deep in mud. With muddy ground below and a hail of arrows above, disaster followed. Only one in ten French knights reached the English. Shrieking men and horses fell back on their own forces. The French line was broken. The impenetrable wall was breached.[33]

These ageless and immortal lines from Shakespeare's *Henry V* capture the essence of this point in the renowned battle. They speak to any time or any era when the valiant are called upon to muster the courage, fortitude, and determination to see the contest through:

> *Once more into the breach, dear friends, once more!*
> *On, on, on, on, and on! To the breach, to the breach!*[34]

A   breach: to make a gap in a wall of fortification

B   Prime Minister Churchill was given a personal tour of the defensive preparations by the Governor of Gibraltar in 1942.

C   The Cape of Good Hope is the southernmost point on the continent of Africa.

D   U-boats were simply German submarines or "undersea boats" armed with torpedoes and deck guns. Germany was the first country to use submarines in war. Constant all-out attacks were made on the scores of U-boat nests throughout the Atlantic. Many enemy nests were situated all along the eastern seaboard of the United States.

E   Sicily is the large triangular-shaped island off the coast of Italy, located at the tip of "the boot."

F   The Afrika Corps were formidable desert troops comprised of German and Italian units under the command of Hitler's most capable military leader, Field Marshal General Erwin Rommel, "the Desert Fox."

G   After this gallant mission, the *Wasp* headed for duty in the Pacific. Sadly, the ship was sunk by Japanese torpedoes. Happily, all the crew was saved.

H   Tobruk, a town in Libya on the Mediterranean Sea, is situated on the coastal highway approximately 350 miles from Alexandria, Egypt. It was one of the finest seaports on the coast and was occupied by the Italians in 1911 as part of their African colonial empire.

I   After his stunning success in the Desert Campaigns, General Montgomery had a major role in the Allied invasion of Italy in 1943 and was appointed commander of all ground forces. He led British troops into France prior to the invasion of Europe by Allied forces in June of 1944. After the war and during his retirement, the Queen bestowed upon him one of the highest honors of the realm, the Order of the Garter, the highest order of British knighthood.

J   This famed unit was an active presence in the War in Iraq in 2003.

K   Believing that Hitler was leading Germany down a path of total destruction, General Rommel took an active part in the plot to assassinate Hitler which was planned by several members of the German High Command. Hitler survived and was only wounded by a bomb planted under the conference table in his bunker. Following this incident, Hitler believed that "Providence has preserved me" and he set out to punish all those involved. Erwin Rommel was the most notable of the several officers executed for this "crime."

L   The terrorist network known as al-Qaeda was founded by Osama bin Laden, a native of Saudi Arabia from a wealthy family. Its stated goals: "dedicated to opposing non-Islamic governments with force and violence" and "to drive the United States out of Saudi Arabia and Somalia by violence." The network has a command and control structure for conducting major terrorist operations and has ties to major terrorist fronts throughout the Islamic world: "For the purpose of working together against common enemies in the West, particularly the United States."

[M]   The Taliban was possibly the most repressive governmental structure in the Islamic world. Located in Afghanistan after the capture of Kabul, that nation's capital, it was comprised of young men called "God's Students" who were trained in Islamic schools in Pakistan. Its original aim was "to set up the world's most pure Islamic state." There are no basic rights or freedoms granted to women and children—including education or health care—under Taliban rule. Its strict codes are taken from a narrow interpretation of the Koran, the holy book of the Islamic faith, and were harshly enforced throughout the regime.

[N]   Unknown to any country on the continent, Henry V of England had the largest contingent of archers in Europe.

Chapter 12

THE NOBLEST WORK

Those who expect to reap the blessings of freedom, must,
like men, undergo the fatigues of supporting it.
Thomas Paine
The American Crisis, September, 1777

Many lessons were learned in the years between 1940 and 1945. Foremost was the lesson that tyrants must be stopped—no matter the cost. Adolf Hitler labored under the misconception that the free world—the democracies and constitutional monarchies—were too weak to fight and die.[A] Often, many believe that liberty makes men and women soft and unable to mount serious challenges to their ways of life. It is precisely the preservation of freedom within democracies that compels people to fight to the last full measure. History clearly shows that Italy underestimated the Greeks, Germany underestimated the British, and Japan underestimated the Americans. During those difficult days in the life of his nation, Prime Minister Winston Churchill delivered a speech to the Canadian Parliament colorfully capturing the events of the past few years:

> *When I warned them* [the French] *that Britain would fight on alone, their generals told their Prime Minister and his divided Cabinet: "In three weeks England will have her neck wrung like a chicken." Some chicken! Some neck!*[1]

At the height of the Desert Wars, three simultaneous events transpired: the war in the Pacific led by United States naval forces, the continuing war on the Russian front as it approached its climax at Stalingrad, and the first meeting between Winston Churchill and Josef Stalin. The redoubtable Prime Minister of Great Britain had presided both politically and militarily over two of his nation's most eventful and perilous years. He, of all people, knew the challenges before them:

The fact that we were no longer alone, but instead had the two most mighty nations in the world in alliance, fighting desperately at our side, gave indeed assurances of ultimate victory.[2]

While war was raging in the deserts of North Africa and all along the Russian front, many decisive battles were waged over thousands of square miles of ocean. This area was known as "The Pacific Theatre of War." This immense territory stretched from the Aleutian Islands off the coast of Alaska, to Samoa and the Fiji Islands off the northeast coast of Australia. It encompassed the islands in the center of the Pacific Ocean known as Midway,[B] the tropical nations of New Guinea, Borneo, and Burma just west of Siam (now Thailand), as well as the Philippines, Guam, and the Coral Sea. An entire hemisphere was at stake. Many famous battles that would decide the final outcome of the war against the formidable forces of Japan were fought here between 1942 and 1944: Wake Island, Midway, Guadalcanal, the Philippines, and the Coral Sea. In February of 1945, there was an immortal battle on a dot in the Pacific—Iwo Jima.

In June of 1942, the turning point of the war in the Pacific came at the Battle of Midway. It was here, for the first time in history, that an aircraft battle at sea took place. Churchill wrote: *"Nothing like it had ever been seen before."* Planes were launched from both the Japanese and American aircraft carriers. The opposing aircraft engaged over the tiny Midway Islands and the vast ocean surrounding them. It was also the first time in history that two surface ships at sea did not exchange a shot. Midway was the turning point in the Pacific theatre because the flagship of Admiral Nagumo, the commander-in-chief of the Japanese navy, was destroyed along with three-quarters of his irreplaceable fleet. Churchill later wrote of those days:

The memorable American naval victories were of cardinal importance, not only to the United States, but to the whole Allied cause. . . The moral effect was tremendous and instantaneous. At one stroke the dominant position of Japan in the Pacific was reversed. The glaring ascendancy of the enemy which had frustrated our combined endeavors throughout the Far East for six months was gone forever. No longer did we think in terms of where the enemy might strike the next blow, but where could we best strike at him to win.[3]

Two and a half years later, one of the most famous battles—and the bloodiest—in the whole of the Second World War was fought on a tiny volcanic island in the Pacific.[c] This small piece of ground, only five miles long and two miles wide, became a crucible of liberty. On Iwo Jima, over 4,000 Americans died to plant the flag of freedom.[D] Of the United States Marines who prevailed at Iwo Jima, Fleet Admiral Chester Nimitz[E] uttered the now famous phrase: "At Iwo Jima, uncommon valor was a common virtue." More decorations for meritorious service were given to the men of Iwo Jima than all the other military awards combined in over 225 years since the founding of America.[4]

In a moving tribute to his friends, the Americans, Winston Churchill expressed his view of the War in the Pacific:

"The annals of war at sea present no more intense, heart-shaking shock than these battles in which the qualities of the American race shone forth in splendor. The bravery and self-devotion of the American airmen, sailors, and marines and the nerve and skill of their leaders was the foundation of all."[5]

In the midst of the great conflicts in the waters of the Pacific and on the deserts of North Africa, Winston Churchill traveled to Moscow to meet Josef Stalin for the first time. The Soviet Premier now fully grasped the threat to his country from his former ally, Adolf Hitler. Churchill assumed the role he seemed to relish most of all, that of powerbroker. The Prime Minister cabled President Roosevelt: *"I have somewhat a raw job."* This would prove an understatement.

Churchill and Roosevelt enjoyed a warm, personal relationship, even though they sometimes had political disagreements, especially over Stalin's role at the end of the war.[6] No such relationship was possible with Stalin who, in Churchill's words, *"could not be courted, only withstood."*[7] Roosevelt had been Governor of New York before he was elected President and was not accustomed to the confrontation and one-on-one debate within a deliberative body. Churchill's lifelong political career provided experience in that arena. He believed the often raucous give-and-take of political debate in Parliament better prepared him to face the harsh disposition of Stalin.

> *I pondered on my mission to this sullen, sinister Bolshevik State I had once tried so hard to strangle at its birth, and which, until Hitler appeared, I had regarded as the mortal foe of civilised freedom.*[8]

Although Winston Churchill was an ardent anti-communist, he recognized that the greater threat to the stability of a free world in the years during the Second World War was not from communism, but from fascism. He surveyed the geopolitical landscape when Hitler came to power and realized that although communism was a menace, it was contained, for the most part, within the boundaries of the Soviet Union.[F] After the rise of National Socialism (Nazism) in Germany, he saw the deadly consequences of fascism and its immediate threat as it left the borders of Germany and was exported throughout Europe and beyond.[9]

Even as Churchill prepared to meet his Russian ally, he was no less astute in his political understanding. He regarded the Soviet Union as he always had: *"a riddle wrapped in a mystery inside an enigma."* He knew his difficult task was to convince Stalin to remain in the Grand Alliance and to stay in the war. Stalin was unhappy with the British and the Americans for, in his view, failing to protect the Allied convoys which traveled through the North Sea bringing the vital arms and supplies to Russian ports, and for not relieving pressure on the Russian army by creating a Second Front in Europe. The Arctic convoys had been relentlessly attacked by German U-boats and the lifeline to the Soviet Union was in jeopardy.[G]

In their first face-to-face meeting, Churchill was both scolded and charmed by Stalin. Churchill gave as good as he got. Stalin knew in the realm of confrontation he had more than met his match. During this encounter, the Premier entertained the Prime Minister at a lavish state dinner. Amid glittering toasts and lively conversation, Stalin rose to his feet to relate to his distinguished guest a story that was of personal interest. Many years before this memorable evening, Stalin had been visited by Lady Nancy Astor and noted author and playwright George Bernard Shaw, both political adversaries of Winston Churchill. At this time, Mr. Churchill and the government of which he was a part were out of power, and he was busily making speeches with few listening about "the Soviet menace." Lady Astor was pleased to report to Josef Stalin, "Churchill's finally finished!" "I'm not so sure," Stalin told her, "If a great crisis comes, the English people might turn to the old war horse." When she suggested to the Soviet leader that the Prime Minister of the current Labour Government, Lloyd George, be invited to Moscow, Josef Stalin gave her a lesson in how one respects those with unwavering convictions and principles—even when those convictions and principles are held by an opponent. Stalin did not need to mention the name of Winston Churchill in his reply to her request to invite Lloyd George: "Why should I invite him? We like a downright enemy better than a pretending friend." Churchill was delighted.[10]

After dinner, Stalin invited Churchill to his private quarters. Through translators, the two men discussed strategy in dealing with the Germans. Stalin demanded more action by the British in protecting the convoys. He demanded the opening of "a second front" or another major offensive in the theatre of war. The Soviet leader made a rude remark about the British navy's failures. Churchill replied, "I know we did what was right. I do know about the navy and sea war." Stalin erupted. "And I know nothing?" In diplomat mode, Churchill calmly replied, "You Russians are land animals, we British are sea animals." Stalin sat silently for a moment. He then smiled and regained his good mood.

At the close of the meeting, around 2:00 AM, Churchill asked Stalin about the war on the Russian front, "Can you hold out?" Stalin took out a large map and the two men surveyed the options. Quietly, Stalin told his guest, "We shall stop them."[11] And stop them they did.

While the British and Americans were engaged in "two great operations at both ends of the Mediterranean," the Russians were victoriously defending their frontier and their homeland. The great Russian victories broke the back of Hitler's European forces and turned the tide in favor of the Allies in the European theater of war. Churchill described these victories—most notably the victory at Stalingrad—as "the Soviet thank-you."[12]

Against advice from his top leaders including General Rommel, Adolf Hitler proceeded with his war on the eastern front. By the fall of 1942 the combined armies of the Third Reich were aimed at the whole of the Soviet Union and held a solid front along the entire western border of Russia. One Russian city after another had been overrun by the Nazi invaders, and the German armies were deep into Soviet territory. The Russian people burned their own homes, crops, and lands rather than hand them to the enemy. The Russian strategy was a costly one at the beginning, but ultimately provided victory. The Russians employed their historically validated tactic. By falling back on the scorched land, they drew the invader further and further into the immense wasteland. The enemy was worn down and cut off from all aid.

The German High Command was declaring victory as its armies captured hundreds of square miles of terrain, making the same mistake Napoleon had made a century before.[H] Within a mere thirty days, Hitler's forces were within 125 miles of Leningrad.[I] It all seemed so easy—too easy. But for seven and a half months Leningrad held out. Hunger, numbing cold, no water, no fuel, no relief from Nazi shelling—but no surrender.[13] By the following summer, help from the United States and Britain arrived.

By late summer of 1942, Hitler turned his focus on the city of Stalingrad. This important city, strategically located on the Volga River and centered between the Black and Caspian Seas [J], is called "the gateway to Asia."[14] As the German armies quickly advanced toward Stalingrad, their pattern repeated. In just thirty days, the Nazis reached the outskirts of the city. But this time, Russia had at her disposal her most dependable ally—the Russian winter. By October, snow covered the city and the lakes and ground were frozen. Thousands of stalled German tanks littered the landscape, but the Russians remained a potent mobile force. The Red Army deployed hundreds of their "ice drivers" or armed tanks mounted on giant ice skate-like blades.[15] The previously unstoppable German army was overwhelmed. The tide had turned.

The Battle of Stalingrad lasted well into 1943 and delivered the knockout punch to the armies of the Third Reich. The Red Army successfully used the German tactic which had worked so well for Hitler in conquering the countries of Europe—the pincer. This classic military maneuver calls for an army to divide itself and close in around the enemy from opposite sides. The mighty German 6th Army was trapped.[16] By December, the Germans tried desperately but futilely to break through the Russian lines. Unprepared for the bitter winter weather, Hitler's ensnared army was decimated. The cream of his forces in the east was "swallowed up."[17] Over 300,000 Nazi troops[k] had been promised by Hitler that they "would winter in Stalingrad."[18] They did, but as cold, hungry, wounded, and crushed prisoners of war. A hundred thousand Nazi soldiers lay dead on the battlefields and along the roads. Four major Nazi generals were either captured or surrendered along with entire German units. "A catastrophe," proclaimed der Fuehrer. *"A crushing disaster for the Germans,"* wrote Churchill.[19]

The Battle of Stalingrad is considered by most historians as the turning point of the Second World War. Perhaps all would have been lost without the stalwart Russians who prevailed there. The truth of this, however, must be overshadowed somewhat by the persistent efforts and dogged determination of the British and American forces on all fronts and in all theaters of war throughout those three previous critical years. It must be noted that it is not really the last straw which breaks the back of the proverbial camel, *it is all the straws*. Of the invaluable contribution by Russia to the defeat of Nazism, Winston Churchill recalled its place in history:

History will affirm that the Russian resistance—its magnificent struggle and decisive victory—broke the power of the German armies and inflicted mortal injury upon the life-energies of the German nation.[20]

Just weeks after Stalingrad, Axis allies Romania and Hungary were destroyed by the Red Army. Eighteen months later, Italy, Germany's strongest European ally, surrendered. Those Axis allies not destroyed began to defect from the Third Reich's great crusade. Gone now was any real prospect for a German victory. Many of Hitler's remaining military and political leaders began to plan his assassination and determine how best to sue for peace. It is not known exactly what Adolf Hitler believed about the outcome of the war post-Stalingrad and El Alamein, but he certainly became more and more reclusive. He ordered that "only good news" be brought to him. But there was not much good news now. Gone was the great orator. He gave only two major speeches during the remainder of the war.[21]

Winston Churchill likened the victories at Alamein and Stalingrad to the Battle of Gettysburg during the American Civil War. After each of these hard-fought conflicts, there was no doubt about the outcome of the respective larger wars. There was also no doubt that after each of these costly conflicts, more blood would be shed before the end would come. Churchill knew that the invasion of Europe known forever as D-DAY[L] was inevitable. With succinct eloquence he expressed the situation: *"Heavier work lies ahead."*[22] It did.

At the height of the war in Russia, with the Battle of Stalingrad not yet decided, the Prime Minister of Great Britain met with the President of the United States to plan the most important event in the whole of the war—the invasion of Europe by the Allied forces. The secret meeting was held in January of 1943 in one of the most famous cities in the world—Casablanca, Morocco. The Casablanca Conference, as it would come to be known, was held, in Churchill's words, *"on liberated territory."* Located on the western coast of North Africa and on French soil, Casablanca[M] has long been considered one of the most exotic locales on the globe—a place evoking romance and intrigue.

Also present for this historic conference was General Dwight D. Eisenhower, later named Supreme Allied Commander in Europe, who was ultimately responsible for the largest invasion in history. In addition to "Ike," as General Eisenhower was affectionately known to friends and colleagues, Lord Louis Mountbatten, great military hero, member of the British royal family and Chief of Combined Operations, was present, along with the hero of Alamein, General "Monty " Montgomery.

General Charles DeGaulle was invited but refused to attend because his chief rival for French leadership was to be there, the former Vichy^N commander who had come over to the Allies, Admiral Darlan. After many haughty refusals, Churchill issued DeGaulle an ultimatum: "If you reject this historic opportunity, we will endeavor to get along well without you, but you may well be replaced and your movement [the French Resistance] may suffer." DeGaulle reluctantly arrived two weeks later.[23]

Described as "a picturesque scene of Churchill and FDR in action," this conference laid out preparations for the final victory over the totalitarianism that had engulfed the continent.[24] With eloquent brevity, Winston Churchill remembered it this way: *Thus we approached the great military climax upon which all was to be staked."*[25]

It was at the Casablanca Conference when the term "unconditional surrender"[o] was first used—a phrase that would profoundly affect both sides of the conflict. Initially, it gave hope to the Allied nations and despair to the Axis nations. The question has always remained of its psychological impact: Did it prolong the war or help end it more quickly? Churchill was criticized in some quarters for the use of the phrase, for it was believed that many Germans, Italians, and Japanese would fight harder, entrench themselves, and refuse to surrender to the point of death, since they had believed that they had nothing to lose. His critics also feared that the Allies would become overconfident, thus armed with a false sense of security. Proponents of the phrase contended that it gave a much needed boost to the Allied forces as they considered the sacrifice required for ultimate victory and was a necessary component in sustaining the momentum of the

171

remaining battles. Politically, the use of the term may have been important for relations with Stalin, as it proved Anglo-American commitment to the war on all fronts and showed that a separate peace with Germany was not an option.[26] In June of 1943, just weeks after the conference in Casablanca, the Prime Minister delivered a speech at the Guildhall in London boldly using the term:

> *We, the united nations, demand from the Nazi, Fascist, and Japanese tyrannies unconditional surrender. By this we mean that their will and power to resist must be completely broken, and that they must yield themselves absolutely to our justice and mercy . . . We plan a world in which all branches of the human family may look forward to what the American Declaration of Independence finely calls "life, liberty, and the pursuit of happiness.*[27]

After this historic meeting, Churchill and Roosevelt drove together 150 miles across the desert to the famed oasis city of Marrakech.[P] In his memoirs, Churchill's description of their journey provides an exciting picture for the reader: *"On our five hour journey, we drove between thousands of American troops assigned to protect us. All along the route, dozens of airplanes circled ceaselessly overhead."* During their stay, Churchill invited his friend to witness the breathtaking spectacle of the sun setting over the snows of the Atlas Mountains. FDR was brought in a chair to the roof of their villa where they observed the scene together.[28] An avid and accomplished amateur artist, Winston Churchill painted the spectacular landscape.[Q] Later, he presented his work to the President. It was a very special gift, for it was the only picture he painted during the entire war.[29]

Early in 1943, Churchill declared, *"things are definitely looking better!"* Victory was in sight. Germany felt the full force of the United States Army Air Force as American bombs rained down "night after night and day after day."[30] Winston Churchill traveled to North Africa once again. At Algiers, he met with his top advisers and American officers, including General Eisenhower. The agenda included devising a strategy for the invasion of Italy and setting a date for the Channel crossing and subsequent invasion of Europe. He and Eisenhower got along famously. Recalled Churchill, "He fully shared the British view."[31] Upon returning from these meetings, the Prime Minister learned that a commercial airplane had been shot down over the Atlantic. Desperate to eliminate Churchill from the world stage, a German agent reported that "a thickset man smoking a cigar" had boarded at Lisbon, Portugal for England.[R] Churchill later wrote that this incident only confirmed that the enemy was not as cunning as most at the time believed: *It is difficult to understand how anyone could imagine that with all the resources of Great Britain at my disposal I should have booked a passage in a neutral plane from Lisbon and flown home in broad daylight."[32]

In May, the Prime Minister traveled to the States for his third visit to Washington. There he delivered his second address to a Joint Session of Congress. His speech was carried live on American radio and broadcast around the world on the BBC. While a guest in the White House, he received word of the great Allied victory at Tunis, Algiers. During the final phase of the war in North Africa, Free French divisions had captured thousands of Germans. Over all, the Allies took over a quarter of a million prisoners of war. Wrote Churchill: *The magnitude of victory at Tunis held its own with Stalingrad...Africa was clear of our foes."[33]

During this visit, Mr. Churchill was invited by the President to spend a weekend at the Roosevelt family home in Maryland. Along on the trip were Mrs. Roosevelt and Harry Hopkins. As the entourage approached the town of Frederick, Churchill asked to see the home of Civil War patriot, Barbara Frietchie, the 90-year old lady who defied the Confederate army by hanging the American flag out the window of her house as General Stonewall Jackson rode by. Touched by the old woman's courage in the face of death, General Jackson ordered his troops to not harm her. The encounter is immortalized in a ballad by American poet John Greenleaf Whittier. Mr. Hopkins began quoting its most famous lines: *Shoot if you must this old gray head, but spare your country's flag, she said."* To the delight of his

American hosts, Churchill then began to recite from memory, the entire poem. As he reached the most famous stanza, all those in the automobile joined in the reciting. He remembered this day with fondness.[34]

September of 1943 was just as eventful. The Prime Minister of Great Britain traveled to Harvard University whereupon he received an Honorary Doctorate. His stirring address to the faculty and students possessed the Churchill timeless quality:

> *Tyranny is our foe, whatever trappings or disguise it wears, whatever language it speaks, be it external or internal, we must for ever be on our guard, ever mobilized, ever vigilant, always ready to spring at its throat. In all this, we march together . . .Let all of us who are here remember that we are on the stage of history, and that whatever our station may be, and whatever part we have to play, great or small, our country is liable to be scrutinized not only by history, but by our own descendants. Let us rise to the full level of our duty and of our opportunity, and let us thank God for the spiritual rewards He has granted for all forms of valiant and faithful service.*[35]

Three days later Winston Churchill received word of the surrender of Italy. British and American forces had invaded Sicily just weeks before. The Italian provisional government made plans to surrender to the Allies after Hitler decided not to send troops and supplies to aid them. The consequences: the loss of his only European ally and one-third of the Axis. Mussolini prepared to flee. British and Canadian forces under the command of General Montgomery swept into Italy and captured the deposed dictator. But before Mussolini could be handed over to Allied command, German parachutists descended on the area and rescued him. This only delayed his fate. In a little over eighteen months he was captured again, not by enemies, but by his own countrymen. He was shot by a cadre of Italian communists as he attempted to escape to Switzerland disguised as a German soldier. In April of 1945, his body was mutilated and strung upside down in Milan Square along with his mistress and one of his top leaders.

Toward the close of 1943, the full realization of a victorious end was not far off:

> *Nearly two years of intense and bloody fighting lay before us* [but] *soon the German nation would be alone in Europe—surrounded by an infuriated world at arms. The leaders of Japan were already conscious that their onslaught had passed its zenith. Together, soon Great Britain and the United States would have the mastery of the Oceans and the Air. The hinge had turned.*[36]

In late November of 1943, the Grand Alliance, or "the Big Three," met a final time before the most historic event of the war—the cross-Channel invasion of Europe by the combined forces of America and Britain, code-named OPERATION OVERLORD. The first day of this mammoth military operation would be forever remembered as D-DAY or "designated day."

Together in Teheran, President Franklin Roosevelt and Prime Minister Winston Churchill, along with their highest military advisers, planned the event in detail. The target date: June or July of 1944. It was at this meeting that Soviet Premier Josef Stalin insisted upon the opening of a second front.[5] Stalin's Red Army was fighting the Nazis alone in his homeland, and he demanded that the Allies relieve the pressure by invading German-occupied territory. Stalin would not be disappointed. Before he departed for Russia, the Soviet leader would know the outline of the invasion plans. Toward the close of the conference, in the spirit of celebration, the Prime Minister hosted a lovely dinner at the British Embassy. It was his 69th birthday and an evening of reflection:

This was a memorable occasion in my life. On my right sat the President of the United States, on my left, the master of Russia. Together, we controlled practically all the naval and three-quarters of all the air forces in the world... I could not help rejoicing at the long way we had come on the road to victory since the summer of 1940 when we had been alone and, apart from our Navy and Air, practically unarmed against the triumphant and unbroken might of Germany and Italy with almost all Europe and its resources in their grasp.[37]

At the Teheran Conference in November of 1943, the three Allied leaders enjoy a few moments of relaxation from the work of planning the invasion of Europe. Churchill celebrated his 69th birthday at this meeting. (Imperial War Museum, E-26615)

From the time he was a boy playing "French and English" in the Great Hall of Blenheim Palace through his years at Sandhurst, Winston Churchill was captivated by military strategy. From his time as a young Member of Parliament to his service as First Lord of the

Admiralty, Winston Churchill sought new technologies and innovative discoveries by which to advance his nation's position in the world. When he answered destiny's call and was elevated to the leader of his country during World War II, he led in every aspect the military activity of his nation. Because he was personally daring, he expected the officers under his command to be the same. Because he was an innovator, he expected his ideas and plans be carried out. But, often the Prime Minister's "ten ideas a day" frustrated his advisers: "One is good, but which one?" It has been said that Churchill was both a trial and inspiration to his generals, whom he "bullied, charmed, exhausted, and led." Many professional military leaders often criticized him as "an amateur strategist who interfered with everything." Churchill never overruled his chiefs-of-staff when they were united against him, but his close association with all operations made him, in effect, a member of his own staff.

Of his relations with his often frustrated advisers he was said to remark in typical Churchillian fashion: *"All I wanted was compliance with my wishes after reasonable discussion."* Sir Alan Brooke, Chief of the Imperial General Staff, once remarked, "Winston never had the slightest doubt that he had inherited all the military genius of his great ancestor, Marlborough. His military plans and ideas varied from the most brilliant conceptions at the one end to the wildest and most dangerous ideas at the other."[38]

Always with an ability to put things into proper perspective, Winston Churchill expressed the exasperation he and those he so closely worked with experienced with each other throughout the war: *"There is only one thing worse than fighting with Allies, and that is fighting without them."*[39] Through all his bubbly plans and ambitions, Winston Churchill learned from his mistakes. His errors at Gallipoli in the First World War aided him in planning the naval strategies used at D-DAY and helped him in developing the art of seaborne assault. This knowledge brought victories at Normandy and later at Okinawa and helped ultimately to crush the Axis Powers.[40] Winston Churchill's life experiences provide encouragement, for they demonstrate that failure is not final.

One of the most fascinating aspects of studying the events that have shaped the world is the understanding of what went on behind the scenes. Throughout the Second World War, especially during the many difficult months of the Blitz as bombs rained down on London, the business of defending the homeland carried on. Prime Minister Winston Churchill could meet with his Cabinet, his War Cabinet, his staff, and British intelligence organizations whenever necessary in a fortified basement complete with several rooms. This secure area is located in Whitehall,[T] the famous area in the heart of London which is "the home of the British government." These subterranean chambers provided shelter from air raids and provided a place for the Prime Minister to work, to sleep, and to live in safety as long as necessary. They are known as "The War Cabinet Rooms."[41] Visitors today are treated to four of the main areas. **Churchill's Room** is preserved just as it was when the Prime Minister used it. He spent many a night there when it was not safe for him to return to 10 Downing Street. **The Cabinet Room** was the "inner sanctum" of the British government and was used for meetings of the Prime Minister and his closest advisers throughout the whole of the war. **The Map Room** was used from the very first day the rooms were established and until the very end of the war. This room was considered "the hub of the whole site." **The Transatlantic Telephone Room** contains the computer-sized scrambler which was state-of-the-art in 1940. It created the original "hot line" and allowed Churchill and Roosevelt to conduct vital strategy discussions in complete security. This scrupulous commitment to security would never be so vital as to the guarding of the plans for OPERATION OVERLORD. During this time of secret strategy, Winston Churchill expressed the critical role played by the need for discernment and discretion—discernment of what was true and what was false and discretion for the protection of that which was true: *"In war, truth is so precious, it must have an escort of lies."*[42]

It has been eloquently and succinctly said that D-DAY was the day when freedom met tyranny. American historian and author Stephen Ambrose[U] put it this way: "D-DAY was the most important day of the 20th century—everything led up to that day and everything was affected after it."[43] Plans for the largest invasion force in history had to be shrouded in total secrecy, complete with an elaborate deception designed to confuse the Germans as to where the Allies would land in northern France. A second smaller seaborne assault, code-named ANVIL, was aimed at Southern France. This operation was to be carried out at the same time as OVERLORD with the hopes of drawing German troops away from the northern coast.[44]

The obvious and most practical choice for a Channel crossing was from Dover, England to Pas de Calais, France. At that point, the distance between England and France is only 21 miles across the Channel as the port of Calais provides the most direct access route through the heart of France. But the initiation point of the invasion would not be chosen for its ease or convenience, but to confound the German High Command. The fine art of subterfuge was most definitely part of the equation in the planning of D-DAY. Because the enemy believed the invasion would be launched from Dover with the landings at Calais, the elaborate scheme to convince Hitler he was right included the very colorful General George S. Patton.[v] General Patton was given the task of commanding decoy forces at Dover. His "forces" were complete with dummy tanks, artillery, planes, and obsolete ships moored off port. The point chosen to initiate the greatest liberation force in history would not conform to conventional wisdom or configure to the plans of the German High Command. The great armada sent to liberate Europe from the grip of tyranny would launch from Portsmouth, England and land on the sandy beaches of Normandy, France.

While the Allies were planning to invade Europe, the armies of the Third Reich were not idle. They had been building the most elaborate land defense system in history—The Atlantic Wall. Hitler had to defend his conquered territory. He could not fight a war on two major fronts, so he ordered an "impenetrable wall" be built so he would not have to choose. This "wall" consisted of coastal batteries and beach obstacles which stretched unbroken the entire length of the northern coastline of Europe—from the fjords of Scandinavia to the Pyrenees Mountains.[w] Over the three thousand miles from Norway to Spain stood this formidable rampart that made the entire

European continent a virtual fortress. The Atlantic Wall consisted of thousands of miles of barbed wire, thousands of miles of trenches manned by thousands of batteries of guns, millions of tons of steel and concrete, and millions of land mines. The Atlantic Wall required tens of thousands of German defenders who waited patiently for the fateful day in dugouts all along the front. Coastal waters were littered with mines attached to long wooden spikes that stood above the water. These were called "Rommel's asparagus." Each was powerful enough to blast a landing craft out of the water.[45] The beaches were lined with three-dimensional steel barriers made from large wooden spikes and entwined with barbed wire and land mines. These "hedgehogs"[x] were difficult to cross and dangerous to engage. Concrete bunkers lined the coast. These "pillboxes" housed protected machine gun nests able to sustain continual barrages along the beach front. Each bunker had walls over three feet thick and could withstand heavy bombardment with minimal damage. Every inch of coastline was defended from a land assault. It would take the largest invasion in history to defeat Hitler's Atlantic Wall. And it did.

During the height of Germany's war on the Russian front, Hitler called in his most able commander, General Erwin Rommel, "the Desert Fox," to oversee the ongoing construction of his massive defense system. Rommel understood the weakness of the Atlantic Wall—it could not be defended against aerial bombardment, and the general was well-acquainted with Allied air power. Astute as he was brilliant, Rommel knew the war was lost: "Surrender now while we have something to deal with!" He believed if the Wall could be made impenetrable, it could be used as a bargaining chip for the Germans to force a peace with the Allies.[46] The Atlantic Wall delayed the invasion, but could not stop it. Rommel knew that when the inevitable invasion came, if the battle was not won on the beaches, it would not be won at all. He was proven right. In six days, three and one-half million men landed on the beaches of Normandy—5,000 ships along a 60-mile stretch of coastline protected by 10,000 Allied aircraft which took out much of Hitler's Atlantic Wall. General Rommel knew the first 24 hours of the invasion would decide the outcome for either side. He rightly dubbed it "the longest day."

The edge Winston Churchill possessed over Adolf Hitler—his innovative spirit and his knowledge of history with its resultant far-sightedness—was used to its fullest now. A veteran of the First World War, Adolf Hitler was stuck in time. He had experienced such light-ning success with his land war throughout Europe, naturally he believed he would prevail on the ground. In fact, Hitler's Atlantic Wall would have worked beautifully in World War I, primarily a land war. For all its seemingly unstoppable presence, the Atlantic Wall could not halt the indomitable forces of freedom when the actual invasion came. Thousands of Allied planes simply flew over it, dropped their bombs, and helped clear the way for ground forces. As almost a quarter of a million men stormed the sandy beaches of Normandy, even with the heavy casualties inflicted upon them from the entrenched German forces on the cliffs above, the numbers of invading soldiers were simply too great for the Wall to hold. After the first 48 hours, the "impenetrable wall" was virtually irrelevant and was nothing more than an impediment as millions of soldiers crossed its boundaries. Hitler's Atlantic Wall has been called one of the great-est military blunders in history.[47]

In the months leading up to D-DAY, the Allies would prove to the world the superiority of the ingenuity of free peoples. Two of the most bold and dramatic innovations in the whole of the war had been specifically designed for the Allied invasion of Europe. One had been planned three years prior to D-DAY. The other, planned just a few months before the designated day. Each was absolutely critical to the successful outcome of the crossing, the landings, and the sustaining of the invasion. And each was credited to the innovative bravura of Winston Churchill. These respective operations were code-named PLUTO and MULBERRY.

Both sides of the global conflict knew the outcome would be decided on the availability and acquisition of oil. Trucks, tanks, planes, and ships cannot move without fuel. Because Hitler con-trolled oil production and distribution in Europe, the vital commodity had to come via England. So in 1941, not long after Britain declared war, work on PLUTO (Pipe Lines Under the Ocean) was begun.

PLUTO was an elaborate system of underground pipes deeply placed in grid-fashion under the meadows, towns, and villages of Britain. This ambitious project was the brainchild of young Royal Engineer Geoffrey Lloyd and Lord Louis Mountbatten. Workers and citizens were told it was a much-needed water system. This cover story was made plausible by the fires set during the Blitz. The major line was laid on the seabed across the floor of the Channel. Off the coast of Britain, American ships could unload the precious cargo in safety. When completed, the pipeline ran from Liverpool, England to the battlefields of southern France—right up to the Rhine Valley. Declared a smashing success, it became "oil on tap." A soldier or airman just had to turn on a faucet to get his vital supply of oil all the way from northwest England. A million gallons a day ran through this pipeline, freeing up trucks and tankers for other important duties. Never once did a lack of fuel hinder the Allied air or land forces. It was truly an astonishing achievement. PLUTO was in full operation one month prior to D-DAY.[48] It was another excellent example of the determination, farsightedness, and optimism of Britain's wartime Prime Minister. Three years before the invasion, Winston Churchill was preparing to have the resources available to defeat Adolf Hitler.

But it was to the project, code-named MULBERRY, the Prime Minister devoted his full attention. Because of the Atlantic Wall, deep harbor ports were necessary if the Allied invasion of Europe was to succeed. There were, of course, no ports along the northern coast of France, only German fortifications. Invasion planners knew the initial offensive in the liberation of Europe had to be sustained. For mobility and speed, the men who would land on the beaches could only carry 48 hours worth of supplies and ammunition—back up supplies were critical. Tanks and armored equipment needed for the first weeks of the invasion had to be able to come ashore quickly.[49] Failure in this meant failure of the entire operation. Ever the innovator, Winston Churchill's idea of constructing floating harbors to be set down off the French coast during the first wave of the landings became absolutely indispensable to the Normandy invasion.[50] Knowing well the hazards posed by the treacherous English Channel to an invasion of the magnitude required to liberate Europe, Mr. Churchill pressed his advisers to use any and all resources to solve the problem.

Two artificial floating harbors with pontoon docks from ship to shore had to be invented, designed, and constructed. These self-propelled docks would be set in place during the initial assault. One dock would be built for the British forces, a second for the American forces. They would be constructed on the south coast of England, ferried across the German-infested sea, and assembled on two beaches designated for the landings. Churchill demanded these harbors be both strong and flexible, have the ability to float up and down with the rising and falling tides, and remain viable in unpredictable waves and currents. Each harbor had to be linked to the shore by a steel roadway a mile long. This roadway had to be strong enough to carry heavy vehicles and secure enough to survive in heavy seas and storms. Each harbor would be the size of New York City's Central Park and both had to be completed in less than one year.[51] Nothing like this had ever been proposed, much less attempted. When his advisers endeavored to explain the near impossibility of it all, he replied in typical fashion: *"Don't argue for the difficulties. The difficulties will argue for themselves."*[52]

It was vital that the harbors be protected. A plan to devise the means to shelter them from the winds and waves of the Channel was proposed. A man-made breakwater[v] consisting of obsolete ships and barges would be placed in a perpendicular line from the French coast, extending over two miles out into the water. Massive concrete blocks or caissons weighing over 6,000 tons would provide anchors for the harbor wall. These caissons would be towed on barges across the Channel and then sunk in a line, supporting the discarded vessels.

Royal Navy Engineers sailed into the project. Several designs for the Mulberry Harbors were submitted, but the design by a young Royal Engineer named Allan Beckett was chosen. He designed a flexible bridge span apparatus attached to floats that ably rose and fell in the strong waves. The steel pontoons were secured at the bottom of the sea bed by his revolutionary style anchors. The harder the anchors were pulled, the deeper they held. All associated with the project—

especially Mr. Churchill—pronounced the plan "fantastic."[53]

Through sheer determination and will, muscle and might, and unsurpassed intelligence and creativity on the part of the British, a wall was made in the sea and harbors constructed in the ocean. United States Naval historian, Dr. Edward Marolda summed up the triumph of the man-made floating harbors: "Operation Mulberry was brilliant—a phenomenal feat in British engineering history. The harbors and the breakwater sustained the offensive that ultimately defeated Germany."[54] Members of the Royal Navy who recalled those days remembered the driving force of OPERATION MULBERRY: *"No doubt about it, it was Winston Churchill who kept us going. He was the man of the hour. He inspired us—this had to be done—it was demanded of us, and we felt his presence. Churchill was truly the dynamic force behind the whole thing."*[55]

Sir Winston's impressive study at Chartwell displays an aerial map of the Mulberry Harbors of D-Day, set down during the early morning hours of the Normandy landings off the coast of Arromanches, France, June 6, 1944. (Jeremy Whitaker, MCSD)

Without the Mulberry Harbors, the Allies would most certainly have been pushed back into the sea. The harbors and their protective breakwater kept the forces supplied so they could keep fighting—and keep liberating. Over three million men, a half million tanks and vehicles, and four million tons of supplies passed over the floating roadways which extended out into the English Channel. For the first time in history, a harbor had been constructed in one country, towed across the sea, and set down *during battle* on an enemy's shore. In commemoration of this extraordinary accomplishment, Arromanches, France[z], the little coastal town overlooking the British beaches at Normandy, was for a short time renamed "Port Winston."[56] Visitors there today cannot miss the monuments to the vision of Winston Churchill. Parts of the breakwater constructed many years ago to sustain the most important event in the 20th century can still be seen today in the waters off the beaches of Normandy.

It was decided that June 5, 1944 be the initial target date for the Allied invasion of Europe. Now, the largest armada in history would be dependent upon the surging tides that affected the treacherous waters of the English Channel and the beaches of France and Britain. These tides, affected by the phases of the moon, determine when conditions in the Channel are most favorable to crossings and landings. D-DAY planners knew the window of opportunity was just three days, with June 7th the last day the launching could take place. If not, the entire operation would be have to be postponed for two weeks until the next lunar phase.[57] All was in readiness. A quarter of a million men, five thousand seacraft, ten thousand aircraft, the floating harbors and their breakwater, thousands of supply vehicles—all were on hold on the southern coast of England waiting to cross the Channel to the northern coast of France.

Unbelievably, the worst Channel weather in twenty-five years occurred on June fifth. The storm was so hazardous, the invasion had to be postponed. But for how long? Confident that German agents had infiltrated the ranks, the Allied commanders knew a postponement would surely allow time for word to reach the German High Command and place the entire operation in jeopardy. The Allies had little choice. The invasion had to proceed. The decision rested solely on General Eisenhower. Because of the weather, an 11-day delay was discussed. But with the small window of time allowed during the current lunar phase, the next morning appeared to be the best option. As Supreme Commander of the Allied Forces, Ike had the responsibility of the sole decision to go or stay. Winston Churchill was well acquainted with difficult decisions. He admired Dwight Eisenhower greatly because of his strength and courage, but never more than at this time.[58] The lives of millions of men and the fate of nations rested on the resolution of the Supreme Allied Commander. Given all the facts and all options, Ike carefully weighed his decision. In one confident command, he told his generals, "Let's go!" At that moment his order was irrevocable. It was as if a button had been pushed setting great events in motion. The outcome was no longer in his control. OPERATION OVERLORD had begun. Historian Stephen Ambrose eloquently described the scene: "At once he [Eisenhower] moved from being the most powerful man on earth to the most powerless."[59] The commanders on all fronts, the President of the United States, and the Prime Minister of Great Britain could only observe the outcome. On D-DAY, Winston Churchill remarked to his Service Chiefs: *"The invasion has been launched. The result is with God."*[60]

General Dwight Eisenhower referred to D-DAY as "the great crusade to liberate Europe." In his speech to the troops before the final order to embark, the Supreme Allied Commander in Europe gave a stirring address to the forces of freedom:

> *Soldiers, sailors, and airmen of the Allied Expeditionary Force: you are about to embark on a great crusade over which we have striven these many months. The eyes of the world are upon you. The hopes and prayers of liberty-loving people everywhere march with you.*[61]

At 4:00 AM the sixth of June, 1944, the first bomber squadrons left England. These seasoned fighter pilots were the first wave of the invasion. Their target: take out the section of the Wall directly over the beaches. By 6:00 AM, the RAF dropped the first bombs on Normandy. By dawn, the United States Air Force was on the scene. Churchill later wrote: *"No doubt we achieved a tactical surprise... The troops on the ground were protected not only by 10,000 bombers in the skies, but by 70,000 guns and rockets which rained down upon the enemy. There was no sign of the Luftwaffe. How different things were four years before!"*[62]

In the early morning hours of June 6, 1944, German soldiers on France's most northern coast were stunned as they woke up to see the greatest land and sea operation in history. An angry gray sky over the tempest-tossed and icy waters of the English Channel beckoned the liberators toward the cold, windswept beaches along the crescent-shaped coast of Normandy. Allied warships set out in a great convoy. Allied planes blanketed the skies "as far as the eye could see." Behind the great armada, under protective air cover, the most precious cargo of the invasion was carried across in troopships—a quarter of a million of the finest fighting men in the world. Tugboats pulled the massive concrete blocks and the sections of the artificial harbors. As each part of the harbor and breakwater floated across the English Channel, observers from the air declared, "It looked like a gigantic jigsaw puzzle."[63] That puzzle would soon reveal one of the most incredible successes in military history.

A three-division assault was originally planned with landings on three beaches. Strategists concluded this would not be enough force. The final plan called for five simultaneous landings on five beaches divided by the following forces: the Americans would land on two beaches code-named *Utah* and *Omaha*, the British would take two beaches code-named *Gold* and *Sword*, and the Canadians, joined by the Free French who were anxious to help liberate their homeland, would land on a beach code-named *Juno*.[a] All five beaches, when secured by the Allied forces, would make a single bridgehead, or front, from which to successfully engage the entrenched enemy. All five beaches would become stained with the blood of self-sacrifice.

The first to hit the beaches were the men of the 2nd and 5th Ranger Battalions of the United States Army. Their target: Point du Hoc. Their mission: take out the massive, 12-mile range German guns atop the 100 foot cliffs overlooking Omaha Beach. Before the landings could proceed, these behemoth armaments had to be stopped. The ramps on their

British landing craft went down and the Rangers poured out into the shallow waters. Under heavy gunfire and a shower of grenades, these elite units headed straight for the sheer cliffs of Point du Hoc.[b] Nothing protected these courageous warriors who dared to charge up the sandy battleground. With small ladders made of rope, they began the climb. As one was cut down, the next took hold and continued upward. Within ten minutes, the Rangers were atop the windswept objective. On D-DAY, 225 Rangers set out to scale the desolate cliffs overlooking the beaches of Normandy. At the end of the day to end all days, only 90 were left standing.

The great convoy of battleships, cruisers, minesweepers, and destroyers drew close to the coast of France, fell in line, and aimed their huge guns at the enemy. British, Canadian, and American soldiers huddled on the decks of their troopships as the warships barraged the German fortifications.[64] All of a sudden, the shelling stopped. It was time to hit the beaches—this was "H-Hour,"[c] or the moment the landing craft made contact with the beaches. Waiting soldiers tumbled forth from the transports. Immortal battalions stepped onto land—and into history.

Each landing craft was equipped with a trap door at one end that opened and fell with a hard slap as the transport hit the beach. The soldiers had to climb down a net of heavy rope attached to the side of each troopship and drop down into the landing craft that would transport them to shore. They had trained for this, but not in these perilous conditions. Many men slipped, plunged under the turbulent waters, and with their heavy packs, sank beneath the surface, never to come up again.[65] Hundreds of men drowned before they could reach the shallow water of the beaches. Those who made it faced the unimaginable—the crushing barrage of enemy fire as they maneuvered around and between the hundreds of deadly beach obstacles. Amid the shouts from their commanders: *"Keep moving forward! Don't stop! You must keep moving!"* the liberators charged ahead. Thousands were cut down in the first wave of the assault. For so many brave men, the longest day was already over.

In two hours, and accompanied by the thrilling sound of bagpipes, the British and Canadians secured the beaches of Juno, Gold, and Sword. In less than an hour, the Americans at Utah Beach had prevailed. But it was at Omaha Beach that the battle was the most costly. The Americans who landed on Omaha Beach were met with the most ferocious fire and aggressive assault of the day. It became "a shooting gallery."[66] Omaha Beach sustained the heaviest casualties on D-DAY. Unconscionable carnage was the price paid by the valiant there. By nightfall, 4,000 Americans lay dead. The five beaches along the sixty miles of rugged and rocky coastline of Normandy became hallowed ground.

On D-DAY the Prime Minister of Great Britain entered the House of Commons. He was greeted by a low reverberation of cheers. At the end of the traditional question time posed to the leader of His Majesty's Government, Winston Churchill rose to his feet once more:

> *I have also to announce to the House that during the night and the early hours of this morning the first of a series of landings in force upon the European Continent has taken place.[67]*

The House of Commons broke wildly into cheers. Then all fell silent. For one of the few times during his long career of speech-making, Winston Churchill used no flowery oratory, no grand historical themes, no references to the sacrifices being made as he spoke. His colleagues needed no reminder. As the good journalist he once was, he recognized that a great story is quite capable of telling itself. Mr. Churchill quietly continued:

> *So far, the commanders report that everything is going to plan. And what a plan! This vast operation is undoubtedly the most difficult and complicated that has ever occurred. It involves tides, wind, waves, and visibility, both from the air and sea, and the combined employment of land, air, and sea-forces in the highest degree of intimacy and in contact with conditions which could not and cannot be fully foreseen. There are already hopes that actual tactical*

*surprise has been attained, and we hope to furnish the
enemy with a succession of surprises during the course
of the fighting...Nothing that equipment, science or
forethought can do has been neglected, and the whole
process of opening this great new front will be pursued
with the utmost resolution, both by the Commanders
and by the United States and British Governments
whom they serve.*[68]

The House fell silent. The Prime Minister sat down, then stood
abruptly and walked out to a waiting car that took him directly to
General Eisenhower's quarters located on a field in southern England.
Winston Churchill was eager to advance to France. He crossed the
Channel four days after the invasion "to see for myself and to encour-
age and thank our forces at Normandy."

Britain's Prime Minister later recalled the day that changed
the world:

*Our long months of preparation and planning for the
greatest amphibious operation in history ended on D-Day,
June 6, 1944. The immense cross-Channel enterprise for the
liberation of France had begun. All the ships were at sea.
We had the mastery of the oceans and of the air. The Hitler
tyranny was doomed. Here we might pause in thankfulness
and take hope, not only for victory on all fronts, but also
for a safe and happy future for tormented mankind.*[69]

Winston Churchill's grasp of history gave him a perspective and
an understanding so critical during those years. His remarks reflect
the term he used to describe the entire enterprise of securing freedom
at all cost:

*... And after all, we are doing the noblest work in the world,
not only defending our hearths and homes, but the cause of
freedom in other lands.*[70]

A British veteran of Normandy recalled the valiant, the courageous—the young men of D-DAY:

> *Remember their supreme sacrifice—honor the real*
> *meaning of that sacrifice. . . They gave away all*
> *their tomorrows for your today.*[71]

Once again, immortal lines penned by William Shakespeare a
half-millennium ago speak to a time just a half-century ago. The following words resound at the climax of Shakespeare's masterpiece,
Henry V. From an impassioned speech by a warrior-king who always
placed himself on the front lines of battle, the words by King Henry
V are delivered to his troops on the eve of the final battle of
Agincourt—troops that crossed the Channel to face an implacable
foe with a seemingly unstoppable army. Agincourt, the deathless battlefield at Pas de Calais, decided the fate of two continents. These
timeless words speak of those things that bind men together as
brothers: duty, honor, courage, loyalty, sacrifice, and selflessness.
The lasting things—the things which shall never pass away:

> *From this day to the ending of the world,*
> *But we in it shall be remembered.*
> *We few, we happy few, we band of brothers;*
> *For he to-day that sheds his blood with me*
> *Shall be my brother...*[72]

^A A true believer in the principle of "the divine right of kings," Winston Churchill once poignantly observed:"Monarchies are the surest protection against dictatorships."

^B These strategic islands are located due west of Pearl Harbor and due east of Tokyo.

^C The Battle of Iwo Jima left 20,000 American casualties with over 4,000 killed. The Japanese lost 21,000 men during the conflict. The highest point on the island is Mount Suribachi where six Marines raised the American flag on February 23, 1945. They were immortalized in a photograph wired to every news service around the world and captured for history the essence of the world at war.

^D The same number of American soldiers would sacrifice their lives for freedom in just one day on Omaha Beach, Normandy, France—D-DAY.

^E Admiral Chester A. Nimitz, born in the small town of Fredericksburg, Texas, became the Supreme Allied Commander in the Pacific. Churchill described him as "most vigilant and active." Admiral Nimitz, remembered mostly for his leadership at the battles of Midway and the Coral Sea, was present at the surrender of the Japanese which took place in 1945 aboard his flagship, the USS *Missouri*. The largest aircraft carrier in the United States Navy is proudly named for him.

^F Churchill would revert to his staunch anti-communist stance within months after the end of the war.

^G The British government understood that the liberation of Norway was the key to protecting the convoys. A free Norway would provide a base in securing the safety of the cargo ships critical to Russian aid as they passed through the North Sea. An active, willing, and courageous Norwegian underground network was a component in this strategy.

^H At the beginning of the 19th century, King Charles of Sweden learned this lesson the hard way when he took on the forces of Peter the Great, the most famous of the Russian Czars, who by defeating one of Europe's mightiest armies, brought his nation into the modern world, and whose victory relegated Sweden to a minor European power. Napoleon Bonaparte, Emperor of France, attempted to take Russia in the same manner a century later. Commanding the largest European army in history, Napoleon led his troops deep into Russia. His forces were all but obliterated by the forces of Czar Alexander I who used his country's geography and weather to defeat the great Continental army of France and effectively end the career of one of the world's greatest military leaders.

^I Leningrad was called "the Venice of the North" because of its system of beautifully constructed canals. Since the fall of the Soviet Union, the city has been renamed to the original—St. Petersburg.

^J The capture of the area around the Caspian Sea was a desired goal for the Germans as it was a site of abundant Russian oil reserves and production.

^K Ironically, this was the exact number of British and French soldiers trapped by

Hitler's army at Dunkirk.

L The "D" in D-DAY stands for "designated." Hence, the term meant "designated day."

M During the Second World War Casablanca was a vital port-of-call for those fortunate enough to have permission from the Nazi controlled Vichy government of France to leave the occupied territory of French North Africa and travel to freedom. This was one of the themes of the celebrated classic film *Casablanca* released in 1942 and given the Academy Award for Best Picture in 1943. *Casablanca* is considered one of the finest films ever made, capturing the spirit of patriotism and self-sacrifice as have few others. Amazingly, its release coincided with the Casablanca Conference.

N Vichy was the name of the Nazi-controlled government which held power in the northern half of occupied France. After the fall of France, surrender terms stipulated France be divided into two zones: one under full German military control, the other in control by the French in name only. This puppet regime collaborated with the Germans and eventually became nothing more than a tool for Nazi policy, even to the point of betraying French Jews and anti-Nazi French. The valiant Free French Resistance Movement not only had to fight the invaders, but also many of their own countrymen.

O Franklin Roosevelt believed in the positive effects of declaring "unconditional surrender" and used it in many speeches. Both he and Churchill knew of its supposed origins, in the personage of General Ulysses S. Grant whose first two initials earned him the nickname "Old Unconditional Surrender."

P This ancient locale was renowned as a city of wealth and pleasure. Its beauty and French influence earned Marrakech the nickname of "the Paris of the Sahara."

Q Winston Churchill tackled painting like he did everything else in his life—with gusto. Of all his pastimes, painting was by far his favorite. He once described it as "a lifelong joyride in a paint-box" citing the first quality of an amateur painter—audacity. Above all his other hobbies, painting was a lifelong passion. Wherever he traveled and whenever he could, he found time to paint.

R Fourteen civilian passengers perished along with noted British stage and screen actor, Leslie Howard. An outspoken British patriot, Mr. Howard had done several wartime documentaries and short films on the Allied war effort. He is best known to American audiences for his film role as Ashley Wilkes in *Gone With the Wind*.

S The term "second front" refers to more than one major operation in a theatre of war established to divide the resources of an enemy.

T This area of London includes the Houses of Parliament, Buckingham Palace, and 10 Downing Street.

U The late Stephen Ambrose was one of the most prolific chroniclers of American military history. An author of many books on history and war, he was founder and president of the D-Day Museum in New Orleans, Louisiana.

[v] George Smith Patton was one of America's most colorful and memorable generals. A graduate of West Point, he served in the tank corps in World War I. In the Second World War, he led operations throughout North Africa and in Sicily. His bold methods and unquenchable love of warfare coupled with his highly disciplined leadership earned him the nickname "old blood-and-guts." He is best remembered for his ivory-handled side arm and for slapping a soldier he believed was cowardly. He had a seemingly ignoble death. After the war, he died from complications of a car crash in Germany. The George S. Patton Museum is located on the military base at Fort Knox, Kentucky.

[w] This range of mountains runs the width of the Iberian Peninsula and separates Spain from France.

[x] These obstacles resembled giant jacks—3-D star-like metal objects from a common childhood game, Ball and Jacks.

[y] The breakwater was code-named Gooseberry. Gooseberry was a man-made breakwater of seventy old merchant ships and four obsolete war ships. This mile-long structure subdued the choppy Channel waters.

[z] The British sector was located at Arromanches; the American sector, 10 miles west down the French coast.

[a] The original names for the British and Canadian beaches were: Goldfish, Swordfish, and Jellyfish. Someone in the London War office decided that the use of the word "fish" might imply the landings would be amphibious and, therefore, posed a severe breach in security. The word fish was dropped leaving Gold, Sword, and Jelly. RAF Wing Commander Michael Dawnay, one of the planners of Operation Overlord, suggested that British families might not find it dignified should a husband, sweetheart, or son die on Jelly. Noting the letter "J" already in use for the beach designation, Wing Commander Dawnay suggested it be named after his wife, Juno. Everyone agreed, including Churchill. (Jeremy Whitaker, MCSD, Hampshire, England; lifelong friend of Juno Dawnay.)

[b] As the Rangers secured the summit of Point du Hoc, they discovered the guns had been moved due to the Allied aerial bombardments. The elite force headed across the nearby farmland and found the menacing munitions hidden in an apple orchard. Using light thermite bombs, the remaining Rangers rendered the weapons inoperative. The gravest danger to the invasion force was eliminated and the way was cleared for the Allied forces to move inland.

[c] Because of the varying tides, each beach had to have a different "H-Hour."

Chapter 13

ON THE RAMPARTS

The price of greatness is responsibility.

Prime Minister Winston Churchill
Honorary Doctorate Acceptance Speech, Harvard University, 1943

Stirring words from Mr. Churchill's address at Harvard University in 1943 seem to have been tailored for the monumental events that took place between the summers of 1944 and 1945:

> *By singleness of purpose, by steadfastness of conduct, by tenacity and endurance such as we have so far displayed— by these, and only by these, can we discharge our duty to the future of the world and the destiny of man . . . As long as we have faith in our cause and an unconquerable willpower, salvation will not be denied us.*[1]

The long, hard road to grand and glorious freedom was nearing its end. Four years of struggle and sacrifice, of triumph and tragedy would soon reap the bountiful rewards of victory. It would take only fourteen months from D-DAY to the surrender of both Germany and Japan. After the first wave of the landings at Normandy on June 6, 1944, the combined Allied forces fought through France, the Low Countries, and into Germany. The strategy was brilliant. Massive air power, combined with heavy ground power in the form of armored tanks, led the way. Potent field artillery aided the disciplined and determined infantry in their desire to rid the world of the stench of totalitarianism. Nazi troops were never dispatched to meet the invasion forces. The would-be conquerors of the world were in retreat and fighting merely to hold ground that, by the hour, was giving way to the forward and unyielding thrust of the forces of liberty. Town by town, village by village, vanquished Europe would be free again.

The Allied invasion of Europe was certainly the most significant event in 1944. To Britain's Prime Minister it was "the supreme climax of the war." But it would take several strikes on Nazi Germany before Europe would be liberated. In July, the Americans landed in southern France, the Russians flooded from the east into Poland and the Balkans, and British-led forces drove northward from the Mediterranean across the entire length of Italy.[2] By August, the world-famous city of Paris was liberated, and by the end of September, the Anglo-American forces had reached Germany's western frontier and the Russians had arrived at her eastern border. The Allies closed in on Germany.

The determined march toward total liberation began only five days after D-DAY. On June 11, 1944, the Allies formed a continuous and moving front inland. The Americans moved swiftly from the west toward the heart of France. On June 19, Hitler received some help—the worst weather in a quarter century. For four long days an incredibly intense storm in the English Channel battered the coast of France. One of the artificial harbors was destroyed and the other severely damaged. After the storm, parts of the decimated harbor were salvaged to repair the remaining one.[3] The valuable shipping lifelines were preserved, and the vital supply operations carried on. Britain's Prime Minister visited the coast to survey the damage. Upon his arrival his officers, undaunted by the circumstances, greeted him by singing **Rule Britannia!** The mood was uplifting and the morale high.

Many times during Winston Churchill's political career, adversaries called him an old warhorse. There is an element of truth in this— never more so than at D-DAY. Britain's bold Prime Minister planned to accompany the Allied Forces in order to "watch the dawn attack in this historic battle." Deaf to protests by his advisers, staff, and commanders, Britain's leader was determined to personally cross the Channel and take part in the invasion. Nothing or no one could persuade him otherwise. All those around him feared for his security and safety. The danger was too great. This Prime Minister was irreplaceable. Everyone knew it—except Winston Churchill. Finally the King himself was prevailed upon to step in. At this point, only a request by

His Majesty could dissuade his headstrong Minister of State. King George effectively told him, "Winston, if you go, I go."[4] Knowing he could not place the life of his nation's Sovereign in peril, and ever the obedient and faithful servant, Winston Churchill relented. He stayed behind in London—even if it was only for six days. In his voluminous account of the Second World War, Churchill recalled the incident. With his classic persistence in holding to what he believed was right, he was unrepentant about his desire to cross with the troops on D-DAY. He believed that a man who had to order millions of other men into battle should share, in even a small way, in their risks. He could not resist an "I told you so" for posterity when he recalled with satisfaction that the squadron with which he would have made the historic crossing was untouched during the momentous day: *"I should have gone. I would have been all right after all."*[5]

Allied ground troops began their rapid advance across France within six weeks of the victory at Normandy. Churchill described the strategy: *"Once ashore, the first need of the Allies was to consolidate immediate defence of their beaches and form a continuous front by expanding from them."*[6] But all was not easy and much blood would still be shed. As the ground forces moved inland, they encountered an obstacle few had considered—the centuries old hedgerows that crisscrossed the French countryside. These natural fences had long been part of the charming features of English and French terrain. Now, they would prove deadly to the approaching Allied advance. The hedgerows became more of an impediment than Hitler's Atlantic Wall. Most of these ancient boundary lines were one storey high, one storey deep and miles long. Their dense composition made it impossible for an infantryman to merely push through, cross over, or walk around. Hundreds of men who lived through the initial landings on the beaches of Normandy were cut down by enemy fire coming from behind the hedgerows. The enemy effectively hid behind them, formed a protective shield, and unleashed a barrage of death. It took the might of Sherman tanks to break through these natural barriers. When the way was finally cleared and the enemy driven back, the Allied forces moved swiftly inland.

The entrenched enemy fought hard and was not easily over-come. The German army was not about to relinquish conquered territory to their hated foe. Allied infantry fought all the way, taking the ground in front, holding it, and pushing forward hour by hour, mile by mile. Historian Stephen Ambrose beautifully captures the tenor of those times:

> *Only two words can truly express those days in the summer of 1944—pain and sacrifice. The courageous men of those battles endured both on the beaches and in the hedgerows of France...We can never honor the men of D-DAY enough. It is to them we owe our freedom today.*[7]

The Allies were further aided by a major military miscalculation by the Germans in the immediate aftermath of Normandy. As it hap-pened, Adolf Hitler's most able general, the formidable desert com-mander and defender of the Atlantic Wall, Field Marshal Erwin Rommel, was absent from the coast on D-DAY. Unlike Hitler and his top advisers who believed the invasion would be at Calais, Rommel was convinced the invasion would be at Normandy. He lost the argu-ment, and as a result, the German High Command left their forces seriously depleted, trusting in the Atlantic Wall to stop any landing threat. The Germans also believed that any Allied invasions plans would have to be postponed due to the bad weather menacing the Channel. Subsequently, Rommel departed to Germany for his wife's 50th birthday. Because he was not personally in command when the Allies landed in France, the Nazi counter-offensive was poorly coordi-nated and in disarray.[8] And because of the structure of the Hitler's chain of command, no next-in-line commander dared to take respon-sibility. Officers in the field had to wait for orders all the way from der Fuehrer. Not so with officers in free and independent countries—they just saw what needed to be done and did it.[A] Also conspicuously absent on D-DAY was the mighty force that had so menaced Britain just four years before—the *Luftwaffe.* The skies over the Channel were now literally covered with Allied planes. Veterans remember this aspect as providing the most hope to them as they hit the beaches. The Allies had thirty times the planes held by the enemy. Many years later, a *Luftwaffe* pilot recalled: "We'd go up with thirty to meet three hundred. In fifteen days, all our planes were gone."[9] Just four summers before, the mighty *Luftwaffe* commanded the skies over Europe. The founder and chief of Hitler's air armada, Hermann Goring, had vowed "to smash Britain in a month." The Third Reich's invincible air weapon was now only a memory. So it should go with all who seek to tyrannize free peoples.

On September 1, 1944, General Dwight David Eisenhower took direct command of all Allied land forces in Europe—four years to the day since the Nazi armies invaded Poland, launching the Second World War. The enormous combined Allied forces in Europe were comprised of the British 21st Army, commanded by General Montgomery; the United States 12th Army led by Ike's second-in-command, General Omar Bradley; the United States 3rd Army under General George S. Patton; and the Allied Tactical Air Force, commanded by British Air Chief Marshal Leigh-Mallory.[10] The sheer numbers in the Allied armies, combined with non-stop night and day Allied bombing, dominated the entire scene, in Churchill's words, *"driving the remnants of Hitler's European forces to their end."* By the end of the summer of 1944, the Russians had launched their great offensive from the east, preparing to meet the Allies from the west as these great armies closed in around Germany. Together, the advancing Allies formed a wide loop. The result: the German army was entirely encircled. This was what Churchill termed "closing the ring." By the end of September, the Allied armies had reached the borders of Germany.

The breakout force in Western Europe was on the march, led by the United States 3rd Army under the command of General Eisenhower's most controversial and most capable commander, General Patton. No longer in charge of a decoy force, Patton was called into action—and action he provided. Patton's forces were aided by over 30,000 eager fighters of the French Resistance. His formidable troops swooped down from the Brittany Peninsula, and in no time western France was clear. The victorious army headed toward Paris[B] and joined the forces moving inland from Normandy. General Patton ordered his weary warriors, "The Germans are just as exhausted as you are—keep moving!"[11] General Rommel's Chief of Staff, Hans Speidel later wrote, "An orderly retreat became impossible. The Allied armies surrounded the slow and exhausted German foot divisions and smashed them. There were no German ground forces left and next to nothing in the air."[12]

Patton's 3rd Army continued to move at almost breakneck speed eastward toward Paris. There was little German resistance left. One by one, Nazi-occupied French towns fell to the Allies. Jubilant crowds greeted the troops with waving flags and showers of fresh flowers. Ecstatic men, women, and children filled the streets of their ancient towns and villages—free at last! Flower-strewn tanks rolled through the center of each rescued village and on to the next as the French people cheered and waved to their victorious liberators.

In mid-July, just six weeks from D-DAY, the Allies engaged the enemy in two major battles for the control of two key towns in northern France—Caen and Falaise. Fierce fighting ensued and heavy casualties were sustained in these crucial conflicts. General Eisenhower ordered Patton to proceed south to Caen and famed British commander Montgomery[C] southeast to Falaise. Located on the northern coast of France, not many miles south of the landings, Caen was a German stronghold and firmly in Nazi hands. Caen lay in the direct path of the Allied forces on the route into Paris. Its capture was key. It had to be taken. Allied heavy bombers prepared the way for the British infantry. A violent battle ensued over many days with the Germans roundly defeated. From released records of the German army obtained after the war, Churchill recounts the mood of the German command at Caen. As his battalions were barraged from the air and from the ground, the German commander in charge of the Nazi-controlled town telephoned his superior officer: "What shall we do?" The reply came from someone in Hitler's headquarters: "Make peace, you idiots! What else can you do?"[13]

After the critical victory at Caen, the Allies pushed down the road to the famous French town of Falaise. This ancient town whose name means "the cliff" is nestled amid the mountainous beauty of northern France. A thousand years before, Falaise had been the birthplace of William, Duke of Normandy, immortalized in history as William the Conqueror. The castle in which he was born still stands majestically on the cliff overlooking the historic town. The Allies met strong resistance there. Five days of relentless fighting ensued before the Allies could claim victory. The German army broke into two divisions in a last attempt to stop the Allies. The American line held—the German line was broken. The Nazis were devastated. Unrelenting rocket attacks delivered cascades of intense heat and volleys of blazing fire. Allied air advantage was again on display. General Von Kluge, the German commander at Falaise reported to Hitler: "The enemy air superiority is terrific and smothers almost all our movements…losses of men and material are extraordinary. The morale of the troops has suffered heavily under constant, murderous enemy fire."[14]

The battle for Falaise was a tremendous Allied victory. The German army in France was destroyed. All escape lines were cut. The bodies of 10,000 German soldiers were piled in heaps. Over 50,000 men were taken as prisoners of war. Hitler's once proud army was totally demoralized.[15] Desperately, the Nazi forces tried to evacuate. British, Canadians, Poles, and Americans tightened the noose. No hope for the Germans remained—their occupation of France was virtually over.

Seven weeks from the breakout at Normandy, Patton and his forces were at the gates of Paris. Fearing its decimation, General Eisenhower had ruled out a battle over the famed and magnificent city. He was determined to encircle the French capital and force surrender. Churchill concurred. In this, as in many decisions, the two men were on common ground. Winston Churchill was always grateful for the friendship he forged with Dwight Eisenhower during the war years. Their friendship was to last his lifetime. He appreciated Ike's diplomatic skills in his sometimes delicate dealings with strong Allied commanders, be they British, Canadian, Australian, or American. Churchill remembered that "Ike fully shared the British view and comprehended the work of his British comrades." In his memoirs, Britain's Prime Minister recounted the significance of the two vital victories in northern France when he cited General Eisenhower's assessment from a memo sent him by the Supreme Allied Commander in Europe:

> *Without the great sacrifices made by the Anglo-Canadian armies in the brutal, slugging battle for Caen and Falaise the spectacular advances made elsewhere by the Allied forces could never have come about.*[16]

By summer's end, Patton crossed the Seine River[D] and opened Paris to the Allies. Known as "the city of lights," this glittering gem was on the threshold of liberation. Because one of the main goals of the Normandy invasion was to rescue France, Churchill insisted that a Free French division be landed early in the operation so that the French people *"would know their troops were fighting once more on the soil of France."* Britain's Prime Minister desired the citizens of Paris to remember their own countrymen set them free. The German garrison in Paris prepared to surrender. At the moment of liberation, the Allied troops paused on the outskirts of the famed city to allow the Free French troops and members of the heroic French Underground to proceed first through the streets of the beautiful—and now free—capital of France. Now, it was east to Belgium, east to Holland, and south to Germany!

During the summer of 1944, over four million Allied troops were on the march and anxious to place the noose around Germany's neck. Of all the advancing units the Germans feared most, it was not the British or Americans, but the Poles. Although their numbers were small, no fighting force fought with more valor or courage than did the Polish brigades and fighter pilots. The Germans knew what they had done to the Poles, and were more afraid of them than any other segment of the Allied armies. According to Churchill no nation suffered more. The Poles never forgot Germany's atrocities, and the Germans knew it. As long as the story is told, the courage and pride of the Polish fighters will be remembered. Even though the Germans had crushed their country, the spirit of the Polish people was never diminished.

Winston Churchill was as effusive in his praise and admiration of the Poles as he had been of the Greeks, whose nation was liberated by Allied forces in the fall of 1944. During the liberation of Greece, an unforeseen situation developed. In October, the British intervened in Greece to oust a communist insurgence that attempted to fill the vacuum left by retreating German forces. Bands of communist guerilla fighters began to take control, spreading disorder and anarchy. Order had to be restored, so the Greek government requested immediate aid. British parachutists were dispatched, followed by ground troops, and the crisis was soon quelled. Although the situation in Greece was an unexpected diversion, Britain could hardly turn its back on the nation responsible for the birth of democracy. Churchill later recorded the importance of this episode to the peace and stability of the post-war world. The incident in Greece became a foreshadowing event. In his account of the war, Mr. Churchill succinctly captured the essence of the struggle against communism within an embattled nation the Allies sought to liberate:

> *Thus ended the six weeks' struggle for Athens and for the freedom of Greece from Communist subjugation...The spasms of Greece may seem petty, but nevertheless they stood at the nerve-centre of power, law, and freedom in the Western World.*[17]

Neither Poland nor Greece could ever accept defeat, clinging rather to the notion that one may be beaten, but not vanquished. Perhaps it is no coincidence that during the 1980s it was from Poland that a movement was born, crucial in bringing down decades of communist oppression in Eastern Europe.[E] The example of Poland—a nation which would not surrender tamely—has remained on the side of history and of freedom.

As the advance upward through southern Europe had begun to form that section of the "ring" by which Germany would be encircled, Allied forces from the breakout at Normandy knew stiff challenges lay ahead. Critical to the control of northern Europe was the key port city over which the Germans held firm control—Antwerp, Belgium. Until the Allies gained control of Antwerp, no sustained drive into Holland, the Rhineland, or Germany itself was possible. Patton's 3rd Army had all but secured the Lower Rhine following its drive south from Paris. In Churchill's words, Antwerp was "a valuable prize" that had to be won as the Allies pressed on to the ultimate goal—invading Germany via crossing the Rhine River. The 1st British Airborne Division was ordered to parachute over the Belgium city followed by a Polish brigade protected by American and British bombers. The objective: take the northern sector of the Rhine Valley. It was at a heavy cost and took over a month of severe fighting around Ardennes,[F] but the Allies prevailed. Antwerp and the Upper Rhine were won. The formidable German line on its western flank was pierced during the pitched battles at Ardennes. The Nazis were pushed back into Germany. By late November, Belgium, Holland, and the Rhine Valley were secured. But there was more to come. Unknown to the Allies, they were soon to be in direct confrontation with Hitler's final, last-ditch, and long-planned counteroffensive known as "The Battle of the Bulge."

Preparations now began in earnest for the all-important Allied offensive toward the plains of Germany. But the battles at Ardennes left a weakness in the Allied line. The Germans now had their chance. They prepared to divide the Allied forces and prevent the Allies' inevitable invasion of "the Fatherland." It was here that Adolf Hitler decided to take one last stand. In December of 1944, the Allies engaged the remaining forces of the Third Reich in one of the deadliest battles in the war.

The Allies were caught unaware and unprepared for the German counteroffensive. Through the element of surprise, the Germans initially had stunning success. Hitler ordered Panzer Divisions of his super-tanks, manned by the elite of the elite, his brutal SS officers, to push through the line at Ardennes. A bulge in the Allied line was quickly formed. Hitler called his ultimate armored tank the "King Tiger" and considered it his masterpiece. The Allies had nothing like it. Of these gigantic tanks, American officers later recalled, "Ninety Tigers did the work of two hundred Shermans [tanks]. The Tiger could destroy an Allied tank at 1,000 yards, but a Sherman could not take out a Tiger at 200 yards."[18] But, the Allies had something the Nazis did not—the valiant RAF above, sheer numbers of Sherman tanks on the ground, the arrival of the United States 3rd Army, and George S. Patton.

The forces of freedom reacted quickly to the Nazis' aggression. The Allied soldiers reinforced the weak section of the line and dug in for fierce and heroic fighting. Throughout mid-December to the last day of January, 1945, the last major battle of the Second World War took place. The most brutal and brave fighting of the conflict came on Christmas Day. Snow-covered ground and freezing conditions made the Battle of the Bulge one of the most difficult in the whole of the war. Both sides sustained severe casualties. But by January, the Allies began to gain the advantage. The Germans withdrew across their western border. Their depleted forces could not sustain their counteroffensive or hoped-for drive to the North Sea at Antwerp. The Nazis knew their time was running out. Massive and continuous aerial bombardment by the Allies finished off Hitler's Ardennes adventure. The honor of victory at the Battle of the Bulge was not lost on Britain's great general and hero of Alamein. "Monty" Montgomery had nothing but admiration for his American comrades: "The Battle of the Ardennes was won primarily by the staunch fighting qualities of the American soldier."[19] All that remained was the final push into Germany. A quick end to the war in Europe was in sight.

Always effusive in praise of the brains and brawn of the stalwart American fighting forces, Prime Minister Churchill delivered the following remarks in a speech to the House of Commons in January of 1945 at the close of the major conflict in the Ardennes and its climax, the Battle of the Bulge:

> *In the terrific battle on the American front, the United States troops have done almost all the fighting and have suffered almost all the losses... We must not forget that it is to*

*American homes that the telegrams of personal loss have
been going during the past months...In the recent battle the
highly skilled commanders handled their very large forces
in a manner which I think I may say without exaggeration,
may become the model for military students in the future.*[20]

With these hard-fought victories, the year 1945 had dawned.
Although the war was far from over in either the East or the West,
Europe not yet liberated and Japan not yet defeated, portends of trouble
in a post-war world lay ahead. As the long-sought and complete
victory approached, remarks made by Winston Churchill at the
Tehran Conference just eighteen months before took on a concrete
quality now. Never totally living in the present but always looking to
the future, the words spoken by the British Prime Minister to his
Allied partners at their first meeting in 1943 were now more relevant
than ever:

*We are the trustees for the peace of the world. If we fail,
there will be perhaps a hundred years of chaos. If we
are strong, we can carry out our trusteeship. . . I ask
for the freedom and for the right of all nations to
develop as they like.*[21]

It was the desire of an ailing President Roosevelt to have one more
meeting with "the three." FDR cabled his friend his wish to hold a
summit meeting, this time in Russia, "...in hopes Stalin will meet us
halfway." Little did the President know this meeting of the Grand
Alliance would be his last. He would live but three months more. The
summit was held in February of 1945, at the beautiful resort city along
the Black Sea in the Crimea—Yalta. At first Churchill was displeased at
the choice of location. Meeting in Russia in the dead of winter held little
appeal: *"No worse place could've been found if we'd spent ten
years looking for it."*[22] But the ultimate powerbroker knew the necessity
and importance of such a meeting—and at this time:

The advance of the Soviet armies into Central and Eastern Europe in the summer of 1944 made it urgent to come to a political arrangement with the Russians about those regions. Post-war Europe seemed to be taking shape.[23]

When Mr. Churchill received the details of the summit meeting, he requested President Roosevelt meet him at Malta and then travel on together to the Russian rendezvous with Premier Stalin. Ever desirous to put a positive face on possible difficulties, Winston Churchill could not resist the impulse to inject a bit of humor in the message to his friend. In the memo the Prime Minister sent the President on the first day of January, 1945, the obvious rhyming qualities in the destination points served his purpose well:

No more let us falter! From Malta to Yalta! Let nobody alter![24]

On the morning of February 2, 1945, President Roosevelt arrived in the harbor at Malta aboard his American steamer, the USS *Quincy*. Prime Minister Churchill came alongside in the British warship, the HMS *Orion*. Churchill recounts the moment when he came into view of Mr. Roosevelt seated on the bridge of the *Quincy* as RAF Spitfires circled above and both American and British military bands played "The Star-Spangled Banner:" *"It was a splendid scene."* Later, the two met privately in the President's cabin. Churchill confided his concerns over possible Soviet advance and control, especially in Italy, Poland, and Greece. He ended his lengthy conversation with: *"...it is undesirable that more of Western Europe than necessary should be occupied by the Russians."*[25]

The next day a long, cold flight lay ahead. Churchill arrived first and waited for Roosevelt. After reviewing the Soviet troops with the Russian delegation, the contingency set out for the Crimea. An austere eight-hour drive through countless villages and roads lined with Russian soldiers ensued. The entourage traveled over snow-covered mountain passes and descended towards the Black Sea. Churchill remembered, *"We suddenly passed into warm and brilliant sunshine and a most genial climate."*[26] Welcomed with accommodations in a beautiful villa situated in a valley between snow-covered mountains and adjacent to the glittering waters of the Black Sea, the Anglo-American leaders were greeted by warm and pleasant weather *and* Premier Stalin.

It has been rightly said that at Yalta the feelings of pride and friendship among the three world leaders—especially between Roosevelt and Churchill—were never stronger. With war still raging on the battlefields of Europe and the high seas of the South Pacific, the lofty goal of world peace was paramount. The victors-to-be prepared to decide the boundaries and destinies of the nations of post-war Europe as, in Churchill's words, *"four million Allied troops poised for a final smash into enemy territory."*[27] At Yalta, the final assault on the Axis powers was planned. At Yalta, the future of the Western world was proposed. At Yalta, agreements were made which affected two hemispheres for the next half-century.

President Roosevelt suggested only five or six days for the summit meeting in the heart of Russia. Winston Churchill feared that so few days would not be nearly enough to resolve the monumental problems certain to arise in a mass undertaking such as mapping out the post-war world. Quick-witted as always, the Prime Minister astutely appraised the enormous task in remarks to his staff:

> *I don't see any way of realising our hopes of World Organisation in six days. Even the Almighty took seven.*[28]

Humor and wit aside, Winston Churchill rightly realized the somber winds of Red domination were about to storm across Eastern Europe. He understood the untold sacrifices made for the liberty of Western man might well be exchanged for a quasi-peace in the shattered nations of a continent Premier Stalin sought to carve up for himself. Churchill desired *"a stern and honourable peace...where a united Europe might be formed in which all the victors and vanquished might find a sure foundation for the life and freedom of all their tor-*

mented millions."[29] He stood fast to this goal even as he faced the harsh reality of being "squeezed out" from the emerging power and influence over the post-war world that America and the Soviet Union would wield.[30]

At Yalta, Britain's Prime Minister prepared to muster his formidable negotiation skills. As much as he admired and appreciated the Russians for their invaluable role in preserving the freedom of the West, Winston Churchill felt the West was paying—and would pay— a heavy price. Although his friendship with Mr. Roosevelt was at its strongest, the most severe rift in their relationship would occur over Stalin's plans to dominate Eastern Europe—beginning with the question of Poland. In his historic account of those days, Mr. Churchill reflected on the vital importance of the decisions that loomed before the three most powerful leaders in the world:

> *The political situation in Eastern Europe was by no means satisfactory...Greece, it seemed,* [post British intervention] *would establish a free and democratic government...But Rumania and Bulgaria had passed into the grip of Soviet military occupation. Hungary and Yugoslavia lay in the shadow of the battlefield. And Poland, though liberated from the Germans, had merely exchanged one conqueror for another.*[31]

An avid student and articulate communicator of history, Winston Churchill realized a maxim of war and peace was now in play. Over a century before, French philosopher Pierre Manent used the term *pouvoir revelatuer* (power to reveal) to explain an often overlooked effect of war: "The ordeal of war exposes essential truths of a situation that the distractions of peacetime would otherwise have left hidden indefinitely."[32] Churchill's lifelong concerns about the aims and goals of communism seemed to fit this political theorem as the conference at Yalta began to reveal a troubling direction a world at war was taking even before the guns were silent.

At the historic summit meetings at Yalta, the focus was on the plans for world peace. Winston Churchill believed the two most important questions facing his allies centered on world security and the future of the nation whose egregious violation by Hitler was the catalyst for the Second World War: *"Poland was the most urgent reason for Yalta. Its fate would prove the first of two great causes which led to the breakdown of the Grand Alliance."* He was not about to give on the question of Poland's freedom and independence—its future was discussed at seven of the eight Yalta meetings. Sandwiched between Germany and Russia, its unique geography positions it as the gateway to either country from its east or west frontiers. Britain's Prime Minister put forth an impassioned declaration of the Polish question: the security of its boundaries, its critical need for a single government, the guarantee of free elections, and its safeguard from advancing Soviet armies. For Winston Churchill, it was a question of honor. His passionate pleas for Poland were expressed in imagery and eloquence: *"It is why Britain went to war! It is why we had drawn the sword."*[33]

During the often tense negotiations, the President attempted to moderate the emotional give-and-take between Churchill and Stalin. Astonishingly, at one point during the talks Roosevelt told Churchill: "Don't gang up on Uncle Joe!"[G] Regardless, Churchill felt he had no choice but to oppose the Soviet dictator who appeared to have plans for the eastern half of the continent of Europe. For Churchill, there was no question—he had to fight courageously for the rights of the smaller nations that lay in the path of the Red Army.[34] In the decades which followed the Second World War, Franklin Roosevelt's moderation on the encroachment of communism proved disastrous, and the concerns expressed by Winston Churchill proved sound. The series of agreements between the American and Soviet leaders not only led to the division of Germany with its subsequent Berlin Wall,[II] but further led to the loss of Poland, Hungary, and Romania to the communists— an outcome most distressing to Churchill.

As the inevitability of the ascendancy of American and Russian leadership at this stage of the war became apparent, Winston Churchill now knew his time of leadership in the capacity of power-broker was in its twilight. His independence had to give way to pragmatism. At the final Summit dinner at Yalta, the Prime Minister, always the prophet, remarked to an aide:

> *If a permanent peace between the Allies and all of Europe is not achieved, it will be a tragedy history will never forgive.*[35]

The subsequent forty years of Communist domination in Eastern Europe and the escalation of tensions during the Cold War[1] that accompanied it bore the truth of his prescient statement.

Although Winston Churchill was the consummate politician, at his core he was principle-driven. Principles—first, last, and always. His stand during the 1930s in regards to the preservation of freedom and democracy for all nations under the heel of fascism was a remarkable display of principle over politics. His valiant efforts at Yalta, employed to prevent the totalitarianism of communism over those same embattled nations, were no less vital to who he was as a leader and statesman.

The principled positions advocated by Winston Churchill at Yalta are a key component of his legacy. His defense of liberty in the hearts of people in every nation has paid tremendous dividends to this day. From the Polish fighter pilots who engaged the *Luftwaffe* at the Battle of Britain and the Polish brigades which participated with the Allies in D-DAY and beyond, to the Poland of the 21st century as one of the first nations to join "the coalition of the willing" at the onset of the war on terror, Poland has been at the side of America and Britain as a steadfast and faithful ally.

It has been well said that a politician is one who cares about the next election, but a statesman is one who cares about the next *generation*. Often difficult for people present in any age to distinguish between the two, it is rarely difficult for those who live in the generations that come after. A great statesman is ever on guard from his position on the ramparts. Like a watchman who stations himself on protective barriers raised as fortification, the statesman guards all that is precious. He may slumber, but he never sleeps. He is always prepared to issue the critical warning that danger approaches. As the end of the Second World War loomed, Winston Churchill positioned himself on the highest point of the castle walls and prepared to warn the West to be ever on guard against *all* forms of tyranny.

In this tradition, leaders of the great democracies of America and Britain and their allies took their places atop the ramparts as the widening war on global terrorism was launched six decades later. The forces of liberation prepared to sacrifice their blood and treasure to free a people and bring peace and stability to one of the world's most important countries and a true nation of antiquity. Once called Mesopotamia, or "the land between the rivers," the nation of Iraq, known as the cradle of civilization, is one of the most historically important nations of the world.[J]

In the Churchillian tradition of proclaiming the steadfastness of the Anglo-American Alliance, British Prime Minister Tony Blair, in 2003, addressed a Joint Session of the Congress of the United States as the widening war on global terror reached the borders of Iraq. With courage and conviction, Mr. Blair laid out broad themes of history as he affirmed universal and lasting truths:

> *The spread of freedom is the best security for the free. It is our last line of defense and our first line of attack. And just as the terrorist seeks to divide humanity in hate, so we have to unify around an idea. And that idea is liberty. We must find strength to fight for this idea and the compassion to make it universal. Abraham Lincoln said, 'Those that deny freedom to others deserve it not for themselves.' And it is this sense of justice that makes moral the love of liberty. . .America, don't ever apologize for your values . . . My nation takes enormous pride in our alliance and great affection in our common bond—our job is to be there with you. You are not going to be alone. We will be there with you in this fight for liberty. And if our spirit is right and our courage firm, the world will be with us.[36]*

In March of 2003, one of America's premier weekly publications reprinted a report from a leading newspaper in Great Britain, *The*

Daily Mail, regarding the beginning of the War in Iraq. British reporter Sarah Oliver hailed Lieutenant Colonel Tim Collins of the Royal Irish Regiment as "Britain's first hero of the Iraq War." The press took notice of his stirring address delivered to the troops of the 1st Battalion on the eve of a decisive battle in the Iraq War.[K] The report declared the remarks made by Lt. Col. Collins as being in the finest of the British tradition of eloquence on the battlefield and were said to be reminiscent of Winston Churchill:

> *We go to liberate, not to conquer. We will not fly our flags in their country. We are entering Iraq to free a people, and the only flag that will be flown in that ancient land is their own. Show respect for them . . . But if you are ferocious in battle, remember to be magnanimous in victory. . .We will bring shame on neither our uniform nor our nation. . . Iraq is steeped in history. It is the site of the Garden of Eden, of the Great Flood, and the birthplace of Abraham. Tread lightly there. You will see things that no man could pay to see, and you will have to go a long way to find a more generous and upright people than the Iraqis. . .Don't treat them as refugees, for they are in their own country. Their children in years to come will know that the light of liberation in their lives was brought by you. . . As for ourselves, let's bring every one home and leave Iraq a better place for us having been there.[37]*

The positions advocated by Mr. Churchill before, during, and after his war years illustrate a doctrine he believed was consistent in the continuum of history—the "great man theory." This theory holds that as individuals rise to lead in any age, events occur and are driven and shaped according to the course taken by individuals who comprehend the mantle of destiny, decide according to conviction, and act upon principle. The "great man theory" describes those leaders as willing and able to withstand the buffeting winds of enormous challenge and contention, for they possess an innate understanding that great achievement often accompanies great controversy. Such leaders never lose sight of objectives and goals, even though at times their view can be obscured by dark or cloudy horizons. The "great man" operates from a posture of principle and possesses an unshakable faith and optimism that light and sunshine will burst forth again. Such a leader never refers to himself as what he really is—a statesman.

Three years before the horrific events of September 11, 2001, historian and author Mark Helprin wrote about war and those who comprehend its terrible price and enormous stakes. Ominously prophetic, these words describe the hard truths of history and the enduring qualities of the statesman:

> *It is difficult for individuals or nations to recognize that war and peace alternate. But they do. No matter how long peace may last, it will end in war. Though most people cannot believe at this moment that the United States of America will ever again fight for its survival, history guarantees that it will. And when it does, most people will not know what to do. They will believe of war what they did of peace—that it is ever lasting. The statesman, who is different from everyone else, will, in the midst of common despair, see the end of war—just as during the peace he was alive to the inevitability of war, and saw it coming in the far distance as if it were a gray wave moving quietly across a dark sea. . . .As others move in the light, a statesman moves in darkness so that when others move in darkness, he may move in the light. This tenacity is given to those of long and insistent vision. This tenacity is what saves nations.[38]*

It has been said Winston Churchill saw the battlefield not with a general's eye, but with the eye of a statesman. His statesman's spirit now steadied him to stand on the ramparts. Liberty had yet to be won. Peace had yet to be secured. As the forces of freedom prepared to finish the job, the foundation of all worth fighting for was waiting to be proclaimed once more.

A   Mr. Ambrose recounts that the situation was quite the reverse on the Allied side—especially from the Americans. The independent, take-charge junior American officers never waited or wavered in assuming command if the situation called for action.

B   Paris was originally settled on an island by a tribe of prehistoric Celts called the Parisii. These ancient people named their city Lutece. Julius Caesar renamed the city Paris in honor of its founders after he conquered Gaul (now France). Since that time, the island is known as *Ile de la cite* which means "island of the city." The world-famous cathedral, Notre Dame, sits on the original *Ile de la cite* and all distances on French maps are marked from its entrance making this fabulous gothic edifice, by design, the heart of France. Paris possesses a distinctive culture, world-renowned cuisine, fabulous art works and is home to one of the most recognizable landmarks in existence— the Eiffel Tower.

C   A healthy rivalry between Patton and Montgomery only aided the Allied advance through Europe—each was determined to reach the gates of Germany before the other.

D   The Seine River runs through the heart of Paris.

E   The Solidarity Movement was born of a trade union strike led by a Polish factory worker, Lech Walesa, whose courageous leadership ignited a spark which lit the fires of democracy throughout nations previously in the grip of the Soviet Union. Although the communist-controlled government of Poland outlawed the trade union movement he helped organize and mobilize in 1980, Mr. Walesa received the Nobel Peace Prize in 1983. Just five years later, Lech Walesa was elected President of Poland in that country's first direct election in its long history.

F   The Forest of Ardennes is located in northwest Europe and includes territory from three countries: Belgium, Luxembourg, and France. Its dense forests have provided cover for severe and important battles in both the First and Second World Wars.

G   In several private cable communications between Roosevelt and Churchill during the course of the war, this term was used to describe Josef Stalin. At Yalta, Stalin discovered this and became extremely angry at what he believed was a derisive term. Ruffled feathers were soon smoothed by the quick thinking of Churchill. He explained to the Soviet leader that the term was one of regard, as is the term "Uncle Sam" which is often used to affectionately describe the United States.

H   The infamous Berlin Wall was a concrete barricade topped by barbed wire and guarded by fortified watchtowers. Erected in 1961, it was built after two and a half-million East Germans fled their communist-controlled government in the years after World War II. The wall divided Germany's capital city in half—the east was communist, the west was free. Hated and feared, it effectively closed off access by any East German who sought to flee to the freedom of the West.

It became a visible symbol of a divided Europe and a constant reminder that the world was engaged in a continuing struggle between freedom and tyranny—the Cold War.

[I] The term "Cold War" was first used in a 1947 congressional debate by financier and FDR adviser, Bernard Baruch. The opposite of a "hot war," or a war openly engaged with violent force of arms, the Cold War, which spanned the last half of the 20th century, was open, yet militarily restrained, and was waged ideologically, covertly, politically, and economically. In the immediate post-war years beginning in 1946, the rivalry and hostility between the pro-democracy West and the communist East escalated. At its peak during the 1950's and 1960's with the formation of NATO, the communist victory in the Chinese Civil War, the Korean and Vietnam wars, and the Cuban Missile Crisis, a build-up of weapons on both sides commenced. It was only a matter of time before the economic, social, and political failures of communism, driven by the unrealistic utopianism of the ideology of Marxism, brought the Soviet Union to the brink of collapse. The system could no longer be maintained or compete with the rapidly increasing domestic and military technologies advancing on the world stage. The unwavering stance of President Ronald Reagan, supported by British Prime Minister Margaret Thatcher, for the development of a strategic defense initiative (SDI) helped bring the Cold War to an end. Soviet President Gorbechev could not overcome the economic hurdles that designing such a system represented.

[J] The meaning of Mesopotamia refers to the Tigris and Euphrates Rivers recorded in the book of Genesis as two of the four rivers which flowed through the Garden of Eden. Thus, the reference to this area as "the cradle of civilization" is established and accepted in all cultures. The first settlements in the region are documented from 10,000 BC. In the 4th millennium BC, the advanced civilization of Sumeria was established. The 3rd Dynasty of the Sumerians was the city of UR. The 4th Dynasty, established in the south, was Babylon. In the 7th century AD, the region was conquered by Arab Muslims who dominated until the Mongols conquered them in AD 1258. The Ottomans re-conquered for Islam in the 15th century and ruled until the 17th century. Following the First World War, the region was established as a British mandate and the lines were drawn by Gertrude Bell, aide to Winston Churchill, and a new nation was born in 1922 and named Iraq—which should be more accurately referred to as URAQ for its designation of origin of the land of the Biblical patriarch Abraham, Ur of the Chaldeans.

[K] At the time of the commencement of the Iraqi war in March of 2003, Iraq's brutal dictator, Saddam Hussein, had over the course of many years repeatedly violated several United Nations resolutions regarding weapons of mass destruction (WMD). Definite links to the financial and collaborative organs of global terrorism by Hussein were documented by both British and American intelligence agencies.

Chapter 14

FOR LIBERTY

May God prosper our arms in the noble adventure
after our long struggle for King and Country,
for dear life, and for the freedom of mankind.
Mr. Churchill's message to the troops
Last Battle of the Rhine, March 23, 1945

As the furies of war played out on the battlefields of Europe, half a world away in the vast waters of the Pacific Ocean there raged no lesser a life-and-death struggle by the forces of liberty for the freedom of mankind. As the climax of the war in the West approached in the winter months of 1944 to 1945, the Allies were still fighting a formidable enemy in the East—the Empire of Japan. To those who live in the 21st century, it can be quite difficult to fully understand the sacrifices made during World War II for the freedom, peace, and prosperity experienced in the Western world. During the first five years of the 1940s, the breadth of the conflicts on three continents and across the world's two largest oceans made the Second World War truly that—a world war. And because three-fourths of the globe is covered by water, the conflict in the Pacific was particularly an immense undertaking.

The year 1942 witnessed tremendous American victories at Midway under the command of Admiral Nimitz and the Battle of Guadalcanal which launched the Allied advance to the Philippines led by General Douglas MacArthur.^ The year closed with the unimaginable suffering inflicted by the Japanese to the Allied forces following the fall of Bataan and Corregidor. The year 1943 brought the hard-fought battles on the Solomon Islands and New Guinea in a two-year struggle for command of the regions of the Coral Sea. By 1944, both the Allied and Axis Powers knew Japan's only hope for survival lay in victory at sea. Winston Churchill later noted of the battles across the southern Pacific and their meaning for Japan: *"With every passing day their doom was nearer."*[1] After eighteen months of fighting through the jungle-covered mountains of Burma and on the southern

217

tip of the Indonesian Peninsula, the challenge to the determined Allied forces was met. In 1945, the Allied victories on the islands of Okinawa and Iwo Jima became the precursors to the proposed Allied invasion of Japan herself.

In naval coat and cap, Britain's Prime Minister is surrounded by admiring U.S. sailors. (Churchill Archives Centre; Baroness Spencer-Churchill Papers)

Winston Churchill marveled at American willpower and know-how in the development and production of the countless armaments of war during the first years after the attack on Pearl Harbor. In his account of the war he noted how swiftly and determinedly a free people act when challenged. When the war in the Pacific began, the United States Navy possessed only three aircraft carriers. One year later the Americans had fifty. And by the end of war, the United States had manufactured and put out to sea over one hundred of these massive ships of war, carrying the powerful aircraft required to span the skies over the chain of island groups from Japan to the Philippines and from the northern coast of Australia to Indochina.

The Japanese controlled the myriad of connected islands that formed an arc across an area over 2,000 miles in length, or two-thirds the distance across North America. The Japanese built airfields on most of these fortified and defended islands and were ready and waiting for any threat to their territory. This chain of islands is called "the southwest Pacific rim." The nation of Japan could not be taken until this chain was broken. Allied strategists knew it would take too long to secure every island, so United States naval forces took them in "leap-frog" fashion. The Americans had to win one island at a time in a three-pronged approach: aerial bombardment, amphibious landing, and battling inward. After an island was secured, it was used as a base to assault the next. With determination, persistence, and thoroughness, the pattern was repeated again and again. This strategy broke the enemy's hold as the enemy defenders lost their mobility, communication, and power all along the 2,000 mile front. Britain's Prime Minister never admired the will, strength, and capability of the United States Navy more than at this time as the forces of Britain's closest ally simply pressed on with the job ahead: *The Americans took it all in their stride.*[2]

After Pearl Harbor, the Japanese had immediate advantage: the immobilization of the U.S. fleet and the control of the waters between North America and Asia which prevented aid from reaching the Allied outposts throughout the Pacific. Just hours after Pearl Harbor, Japanese air squadrons assaulted the lone American outpost in the Pacific—Wake Island. The tiny coral island, manned by only 400 Marines to protect a thousand civilians, held out for fifteen days until a thousand Japanese troops landed to take it. Wake Island earned the title "Alamo of the Pacific." Japan's early advantage made repercussions of the fall of the Philippines, Bataan, and Corregidor acutely severe. At Bataan, no offensive was possible. Few supplies and munitions were available. Starvation and disease set in. Yet the heroic Allied defenders held on for four months of stubborn fighting. Cut off from all outside help, and left to themselves to fight it out, American forces were overwhelmed by the Japanese—beaten by their circumstances but not defeated. At Corregidor, the small island off Bataan

Peninsula at the entrance to Manila Bay, the situation was repeated. Upon the last Allied stronghold in the Philippines, Japan mounted intense and relentless bombing which shattered the inland forces. Capture was quick and sure. Then, in acts of inhuman cruelty, the half-starved, disease-ridden, yet courageous captives were marched to prison camps in Manila. This is known in history as "the Bataan Death March." Those who died along the way were left to litter the landscape. With poignant understatement, Winston Churchill described how the world would remember the barbarities of a savage enemy: *"…the pitiless Japanese."*

The climax of the War in the Pacific came at the Battle of Leyte Gulf in the central waters of the Philippine Islands. Admiral William "Bull" Halsey[B] was in command of naval forces as MacArthur's forces advanced toward the islands. But the decisive conflict was almost lost. The formidable Japanese Fleet converged on the gulf. In a brilliant stroke, the Japanese put forth a decoy force. Their gamble paid off. Admiral Halsey pursued with abandon and was led into a trap. His forces fought valiantly but were hit hard by Japanese bombers on suicide missions. These fanatical, religious-driven pilots—known as *Kamikazes* or "divine wind"—menaced American aircraft carriers and killed hundreds of men with exploding fuel and fire on the decks of the battleships.

MacArthur's fleet, positioned in the Gulf, was at stake now. Victory looked sure for Japan's formidable naval commander, Admiral Kurita.[c] Suddenly, the Japanese commander withdrew and turned back. His reasons are unclear to this day. Did he believe he was alone and unsupported? Were signals between his warships misread or misunderstood? Was this an ironic twist of fate or did Providence take a hand during those critical days in the Pacific when victory was held in the balance? In his account of the war, Winston Churchill noted that the Japanese at sea were hindered by, of all things, their language. Because war increases the development of new and ever-changing technologies, the art of electronic signaling between warships at sea became a vital tool during the Pacific War. Because the English alphabet consists of only 26 letters, it is relatively easy to transcribe the language into abbreviated messages used in ship-to-ship communication. The Japanese had much greater difficulty converting their character-based alphabet and language into concise signals. Therefore, the chances of confused or misread transmissions became an impediment for the Japanese during those critical moments when communication was necessary for victory or survival. The decision to retreat, for whatever reasons, by the Japanese admiral probably saved the American forces from disaster.

The Battle of Leyte Gulf fulfilled General MacArthur's famous promise to return and liberate the Philippines. The resolution of the Allied cause was captured in a famous photograph of the general and two of his commanders wading ashore to prepare to direct the land forces. From October of 1944 through January of 1945, the glorious victory there gave the United States naval forces command of the South China Seas. In just five days the Japanese Fleet was destroyed. No doubt remained as to the eventual outcome of the war in the Pacific. By the end of 1944, a quarter of a million Americans had landed in the Philippines. Japanese resistance there was broken. Sixteen thousand Japanese soldiers perished amid the ruins. In his war memoirs, Winston Churchill recounted the all-important victory in the Philippines:

Long should the victory be treasured in American history. Apart from valour, skill, and daring, it shed light on the future more vivid and far reaching than any we had seen.[3]

Even though Japan's hope of victory was gone, the proud and defiant nation refused to surrender and continued fighting with the same fanatical zeal as in the first days of the war. Both sides knew that an Allied invasion of the island country was inevitable. The Allies had to make a decision-how many men would be sacrificed to take Japan herself? Tens of thousands? A million? Said Churchill, *"The western coast alone of Japan was defended by a million men well-trained, well-equipped, and fanatically determined to fight to the last."[4]* To launch such an invasion, two strategic islands off the southern coast of Korea would have to be taken—Iwo Jima and Okinawa.

If an Allied victory was to be assured, the Japanese knew the Americans would have to battle them on a strategic point in the Pacific. So in October of 1944, over 21,000 troops were sent by the Empire to defend the pork chop-shaped island of Iwo Jima. The small volcanic island was honeycombed throughout by an elaborate system of interconnected underground tunnels dug over thirty-five feet deep for protection against aerial bombardment. It was a virtual fortress. In February of 1945, the bloody work of destroying the Japanese defenders of Iwo Jima began. The loss of human life, the carnage, was staggering. After several unimaginable days and nights, over 40,000 casualties from both sides lay across the tiny island, but at the end of the battle, the flag of the United States of America waved proudly atop the island's highest point. Only 200 Japanese surrendered at Iwo Jima, the rest fought to the death—over 20,000 in all. Almost 7,000 Americans died and 18,000 were wounded. The world must never forget the sacrifices made for freedom there. The image of the six Marines proudly hoisting the colors is forever etched in the American psyche.

The drama played out in the Pacific Theatre of War was most costly. Great and unimaginable sacrifices were made by the Allies— particularly the Americans, the Australians, and the New Zealanders—to bring Japan to her knees. Few knew this more keenly than Winston Churchill:

> *The struggles in the Pacific, where the stubborn resistance of the enemy, the physical difficulties of the islands, the ravages of disease, and the absence of communications made the campaigns as arduous as any in history.*[5]

In mid-March the Allied forces advanced toward an island located only 350 miles off the coast of Japan—Okinawa. With plateau-like terrain ideal for airfields, its position was aptly suited for a base to launch an invasion. Only weeks after Pearl Harbor, an invasion of Japan had been discussed. It was then the Allies agreed they had to defeat Germany first—then the Japanese. It seemed as if the time had now come for an invasion. Nearly one hundred thousand trained troops awaited the Allied forces. Over 2,000 Kamikazes were called out in force to defend Okinawa. American naval forces destroyed the last of Japan's warships. Japan knew she was defeated, but was determined to fight to the last. All that remained were her entrenched, equipped, and eager homeland forces—ready for combat. The question of invasion by the Allies lay open. A final decision would have to wait.

During the final months of the war in Europe, Prime Minister Churchill lived day and night in the secret War Room at the Ministry of Defence in London. With each advance of the Allied line, he moved with great relish, the Allied position on the great map of Europe.[6] Since November of 1944, preparations along the western frontier had been ongoing as the Anglo-American armies made their way toward their ultimate objective. Imminent was the final Allied offensive to subdue Germany and end the long nightmare of death, destruction, and darkness that was the Third Reich.

The western boundary of Germany ran through the Rhine Valley. Stretching hundreds of miles, it formed the western front. By the first day of spring, March 21, 1945, the Allies controlled the entire borderland and ultimately the defense of the famed valley and its heart, the Rhine River.[D] The Germans lost all hope of defending their ground along the west bank of the ancient waterway. Immense Allied forces prepared to converge to cross the boundary that had not been crossed since Napoleon in 1805.[7] To hinder any attempts at crossing the Rhine River, the Nazi armies had successfully destroyed most bridges along its banks. Holding open a route of their own, the Germans failed to destroy the bridge at Remagen—a bridge they now needed for evacuation. By misjudging the swiftness of the Allied advance, they delayed too long. One of the most exciting episodes in the war occurred on the Bridge at Remagen. As the Allies approached, the Germans hastily set off demolition charges. Their efforts only slightly damaged the bridge. Capitalizing on the enemy's blunder, hundreds of American riflemen charged across. In mere minutes, the Allied forces had their first secure position on German soil. A surprised Supreme Commander, General Eisenhower acted quickly. Only days after the Americans crossed the Rhine River at Remagen, infantry and armored divisions plunged deep into enemy territory. The Germans launched several attacks. The last of the *Luftwaffe* attempted to destroy the vital link to their homeland, but to no avail.

Appointed by General Eisenhower and in command of the Allied forces in Western Europe, American General Omar Bradley[E] advanced from the south toward the western front. Britain's Commander-in-Chief, Field Marshal Montgomery, advanced from the north. Along a twenty-mile stretch on the west bank, ten temporary Allied headquarters were set up with an advance guard of 80,000 men—and millions more behind them.[8] The combined forces made ready to drive the enemy across the famed river and charge straight into his heartland.

At dawn on March 23, 1945, Britain's 21st Army, commanded by General Montgomery, arrived at the banks of the great river north of Cologne.[F] Prime Minister Winston Churchill was on the spot as time for the actual crossing of his country's forces approached. Two British airborne divisions prepared to provide a fifty-mile long smokescreen to protect two infantry divisions and the cream of British commando units. Just across the river, the Germans lay waiting—armed and ready. Everything seemed to pause as Britain's wartime leader delivered a most stirring address to His Majesty's forces as all awaited to fight the last Battle of the Rhine. It was reported that his mere presence had an effect on the British troops too dramatic for words. During his remarks about "this noble adventure" the men let out a resounding roar: "Good Old Winnie!" As he ended, cheers rang out as he gave his famous "V" for victory sign.[9] Affectionate waves of admiration and appreciation arose, for the man who never doubted this day would come.

Throughout the night, the attacking divisions poured across. At dawn, all could see the bridgehead had held with the Commandos firmly in control. The honor of leading the charge was given to the 51st and 15th British divisions and the 30th and 79th U.S. divisions. Air power was immense—in Churchill's words, *"second only to that of D-*

DAY in Normandy."[10] General Montgomery arranged the perfect point from which the Prime Minister could observe the entire spectacle. In the early morning hours from atop a green and rolling hill, the King's First Minister, who desired so much to lead in battle, witnessed "the great fly-in." The intense roar of 2,000 aircraft carrying over 20,000 British and American paratroopers filled the skies. In less than an hour, "tiny specks which came floating to earth" could be seen against the horizon as they descended upon the enemy. The largest airborne drop in history saturated the once impenetrable defense lines of the Third Reich. The vast Allied forces fanned out and crisscrossed the countryside as they prepared for the grueling and dangerous task of house-to-house fighting.

As the great battle ensued across the entire front, Mr. Churchill was taken by automobile to each staging point along the river. By evening he returned and was given the full picture of the battle from Montgomery. It was here Winston Churchill bestowed the greatest measure of praise for his Commander-in-Chief. He compared Montgomery's leadership and his operation to that of Marlborough. Churchill's ardent love for the strategy of war was coupled with his understanding of the great responsibilities of victory:

> *In the 18th century, the commander in chief acted through his lieutenant-generals who knew his mind and in whom he had full trust and confidence. They had no troops, but merely acted as extensions of their commander. Then Marlborough simply sat on his horse and directed by word of mouth the battle over a six mile front which ended in a day and settled the fortunes of great nations, sometimes for generations to come.*[11]

The next day, and with Germany in full view, Churchill and Montgomery lunched with General Eisenhower at a small table near the flowing waters of the Rhine. With delight, Churchill recalled the Supreme Allied Commander suggesting Britain's military leaders go across "where a fine view of the river and the opposite bank could be obtained." After lunch, Churchill remarked to his top commander,

"Why don't we go across and have a look at the other side?" To his surprise, Montgomery replied, "Why not?" After five long years of the ravages of war, the scene of the last major battle in Europe was serene by comparison. For unlike the Channel crossing on D-DAY, the crossing of the Rhine held little danger for Britain's Prime Minister. He remembered that he and Montgomery "crossed with several armed American officers and landed in brilliant sunshine and perfect peace on the German shore and walked about for half an hour or so unmolested."[12]

Success at the Rhine signaled all Allied forces in Western Europe to begin the victory march. At record-breaking speed, the Allied armies blanketed Germany with a triumph greater than their push across France. White flags of surrender were seen from houses and buildings in every town throughout Germany. Within the Allied forces, the morale was high and the mood was confident. Within the German ranks, desperation and fear ruled. With untiring efficiency, the Allies pushed the Nazis back over their own frontier. The last place the Germans firmly held on in the west was, in Churchill's words, "the renowned and dreaded" Siegfried Line. It only took a few days for the Allies to break through this heretofore impenetrable wall. As Churchill later recorded: *The Germans were forced steadily eastward and harassed continually from the air. It was the enemy's final offensive of the war.*[13] Little was left to conquer save the capital city of Berlin.

Allied bombers were now in command of German airspace. The bombing was relentless. With few divisions left to fight the Allies, Nazi soldiers simply gave up. Incomprehensibly, as the Nazis retreated, the erstwhile guarantor of Germany's sacred homeland, Adolf Hitler, ordered every house, building, factory, railroad, and bridge still standing be burned or destroyed. With no concern for the vast destruction and devastation of his country, Hitler then ordered Berlin's subway tunnels flooded to drown the thousands of Berliners who had fled to the safety of the underground.[14] Maniac to the end, astounding to the rational mind, and horrible by even his standards, Adolf Hitler told his remaining aides, "If Germany doesn't deserve to win, it deserves to disappear."[15] His evil genius had brought disaster to

Germany and irreparable damage to Europe. What a tragic lesson in misjudgment by the people of a nation in choosing their leader.

By early April, complete encirclement of Germany was achieved. The Anglo-American armies reached the Elbe River—only fifty miles from Berlin. Across its banks, the Red Army arrived a mere thirty miles from the capital. Victory would come as an avalanche. The vast armies linked forces, and with steady resolve, prepared to finish the job. The ring was closed:

> *Germany's Western front had collapsed...All organized resistance came to an end... Six weeks of successive battles along a front of over two hundred and fifty miles had driven the enemy across the Rhine with irreplaceable losses of men and material...Thus ended the last great German stand in the West.*[16]

On April 12, 1945, the world received the news: President Roosevelt was dead. Churchill later wrote of his reaction to the sad news of the death of his friend: *"It was as if I had been struck a physical blow."* In later remarks to Parliament he said of Franklin Roosevelt: *"He was the greatest American friend we have ever known."* With eloquent imagery, Winston Churchill sent his condolences via telegram to Mrs. Roosevelt:

> *Accept my most profound sympathy in your grievous loss, which is also the loss of the British nation and of the cause of freedom in every land...As for myself, I have lost a dear and cherished friendship which was forged in the fire of war. I trust you may find consolation in the magnitude of his work and the glory of his name.*[17]

By mid-April, the Red Army encircled the outskirts of the capital city. It was obvious the Allied and Soviet armies were about to split Germany in two. General Bradley advised that the cost of American lives would be too great and the need to accommodate political concerns would be prudent if the Allies took part. For these reasons Eisenhower decided that Stalin should take Berlin.[G] Portents of possible future conflict over post-war Europe predicted by Winston Churchill loomed large. In the next few years, he would be proven right again.

By April 22, Berlin was under direct attack by Stalin's unstoppable forces. Adolf Hitler was fifty feet underground in his bunker. The end of the malignant tyrant was near. Almost all his top officials were either killed or captured. Only Josef Goebbels remained by his side. When word came that Mussolini and his mistress had been shot, mutilated, and strung upside down in Milan Square, the Fuehrer-god of the evaporating Third Reich lashed into a violent frenzy.[18]

Delusional and drugged, his reality gone, Adolf Hitler fully expected his army to appear. In his last appearance, he briefly emerged to greet his "army" of a few young boys and old men. On April 29, he married his long-time mistress Eva Braun after they each signed a paper declaring they were of "true Aryan descent." Lest they be taken by the Soviets, a few hours later Eva took cyanide poison and died instantly. Hitler reportedly bit into a lethal capsule then put his pistol next to his right temple and fired. He had ordered his and Eva's bodies be wrapped in blankets, carried to the rooftop, covered in gasoline, and burned to ashes. Cheating the justice of an outraged and violated world, the end came ignobly to one of the most evil men in all of history.

In just seventeen days, Germany's capital city was razed by over two million Soviet soldiers. With great relish the Reds fired rockets against the Reich Chancellery[II] destroying it. The last German officer surrendered, raising a white flag from his bunker. Russian troops discovered the shallow graves with the bodies of Hitler and Eva. The Red flag was hoisted over the *Reichstag*.[19] Stalin was now its ruler. The Battle of Berlin was over.

In the last months of the war in Europe, a third of a million Nazi soldiers were killed or captured. The German war machine disintegrated. All Nazi opposition was crushed. At the end, the top leaders of this race of "supermen" showed the world the lowest form of cowardice. Instead of facing the consequences that were to be meted out by a desecrated civilized world, they each died by their own hand.

The day after Adolf Hitler was gone, Josef Goebbels, master of propaganda, chose to die in the same way as his Fuerher. He took his wife and six children with him. Heinrich Himmler, who had built the horrible and hated *SS* into a virtual state within a state, had replaced Hermann Goring as Hitler's second-in-command before the war's end. As the Allies closed in, Hitler's right hand man tried to save his own skin. Himmler informed on the whereabouts of Hitler and then dressed in the uniform of an enlisted man to avoid recognition by his captors. When discovered, he ingested a cyanide capsule and died within minutes. The mastermind of the ghastly "Final Solution" passed into infamy. Hermann Goring and several others were captured and prepared to stand trial at Nuremburg. At the end of the trial and before sentence was passed, the master of the once mighty *Luftwaffe* committed suicide in his cell.[20]

The Allies now began the grim work of liberating those in the Nazi concentration camps. Not until then did anyone truly realize the depth of the abysmal horrors of the Nazi regime. Those still alive were walking skeletons. Mass graves of mind-altering proportions were uncovered. Piles of human beings stacked twenty to thirty high outside buildings which housed soot-covered ovens were the gruesome reminders of atrocities and barbarities too inconceivable for words. The world was horrified. The cry was, "Never again!" General Eisenhower ordered the troops to bring German citizens "by point of bayonet if necessary" to see what had been committed by their leader and to solemnly bury the evidence of a diseased mentality. He ordered his top generals to see the camps "so that no one can ever say this did not happen."[21]

For the modern world, the decade of the 1930s provides a laboratory for the study of how tyranny can rise and succeed. Adolf Hitler not only created the times, the times created him. In the aftermath of the First World War, Germany was in desperate need of a strong leader. They found one who had unequalled ability to exploit and then shape events to his own ends. The power Hitler wielded was unprecedented both in its scope and in its technological resources. But, in the end, he made no lasting contribution—either moral or material—to mankind. His sordid legacy remains of one who committed crimes unparalleled in history and who broke down the whole structure of the world in which he lived, leaving behind a Germany and a Europe that remained divided for the next half-century.

President Harry S. Truman, America's new Commander-in-Chief, made it clear to the remnants of the Third Reich that there would be no negotiations and that surrender would be unconditional.General Eisenhower, Supreme Allied Commander, assured the Russians that no surrender by the Germans would take place unless it be to both Allied and Soviet generals. When Churchill heard of Germany's proposal for surrender to the Western Allies, but not to the Russians, the Prime Minister blurted out, *"It's all or none!"*[22]

On May 7, 1945, one week after the death of Adolf Hitler, Germany surrendered unconditionally.[1] Hitler's unrelenting war of purification had obliterated populations and destroyed cultures. But his spell was finally broken. His Third Reich was beaten, vanquished, finished. Of Hitler's two views of the world, one did break asunder—but at what cost? The boastful thousand year reign of the Third Reich lasted but a dozen years. Adolf Hitler had promised national renewal. What he left was a continent in ruins and the total defeat, devastation, and degradation of a nation that was stripped and shattered. Twenty million buildings were rubble, five million German citizens were dead or missing, eight million were homeless—a high price to pay for one man's fanatical and homicidal vision.[23] When news came to Winston Churchill of the deaths of Mussolini and Hitler, he did not gloat. When he heard of the fate of Hitler's henchman Heinrich Himmler, whom he once called *"the maggot in the Nazi apple,"* he quietly said, *"Justice has been done."*[24]

Only a remnant of the captured German officers remained. Brought to Allied headquarters, they were seated in two rows as they awaited the arrival of the Supreme Allied Commander. Allied officers lined the walls of a small room furnished only by a wooden table and a few chairs. The vanquished leaders expected a discussion of terms among gentlemen over handshakes and coffee. General Eisenhower entered. The Nazi generals stood and bowed in humility. Ike offered no handshake, but curtly asked, "Do you understand the terms of surrender?" The delegation replied, "Yes." Eisenhower abruptly turned and walked out.[25] Hitler's former commanders were stunned to be treated like the war criminals they were. General Eisenhower did exactly what he should have done. Considering to whom these men had sworn the oath of allegiance and whose crimes they carried out, Ike would have no appeasement with evil, preferring to make a point of the heavy cost of human life required to liberate the globe.

The next day was one of most glorious the world had ever known. No one who suffered and survived the scourge of malevolent destruction that had held civilization in its grip could have dreamed the darkness could end so brilliantly. Flags of freedom flew across a continent as the lights of liberty came on all over Europe. Jubilant masses joined in one of the greatest celebrations in history. It was "Victory in Europe Day," forever known as "V-E Day." President Truman addressed his nation by radio: "The end has finally come!" Precisely at 3:00 PM on May 8, 1945, church bells rang all across Great Britain. Almost five years to the day he became Prime Minister, a triumphant Winston Churchill did what he had done so many times throughout the war—he delivered a BBC world broadcast. The unshakable hope consistently supplied to war-torn Europe during its darkest hours gave way to glories and gratitude. The strong voice that for so long defied tyranny now broke with emotion:

> *The ceasefire began yesterday to be sounded all along the front…the German war is at an end…Almost the whole world was combined against the evil-doers who are now prostrate before us. Our gratitude to our splendid Allies goes forth from all our hearts in this Island and throughout the British Empire. This is Victory in Europe Day. Advance Britannia! Long live the cause of freedom! God save the King!* [26]

For many who lived through those times, "V-E Day" was not only a day of celebration, it was a day of reflection. As he waited that day for the Prime Minister to enter a Parliament filled to overflowing, biographer Guy Eden could not help but remember what had transpired exactly five years before:

> *On that sunny day when the cloud of war descended on the world and a shaken Neville Chamberlain stood in front of his peers, all looked intently at the Prime Minister. But, I looked at Winston Churchill sitting on the back bench seat he had occupied for ten long years of the wilderness. That night, the political storm had burst. That night, the nation found its Man of Destiny in Winston Spencer Churchill.[27]*

An eternity seemed to pass in a moment as Mr. Churchill entered the House. The world's most dignified deliberative body of democracy erupted into cheers. Members totally forgot themselves and leapt onto the benches, waving wildly. The Prime Minister smiled broadly with tears in his eyes and down his cheeks as he proudly proclaimed to his peers:

> *This is the greatest victory British arms has ever achieved... Thank you! In all our long history, we have never seen a greater day than this![28]*

Outside, crowds filled the streets of London chanting: "Churchill! Churchill! Churchill! We want Churchill!" In response, a grateful Prime Minister emerged onto the balcony of Buckingham Palace with the King and Queen and their young daughters.[j] He humbly stood before thousands of his uncontrollably jubilant countrymen and then called out to them:

> *My dear friends, this is your hour! This is not a victory of a party or of a class—it is a victory of the great British nation as a whole. We were the first, on this ancient island, to draw the sword against tyranny. There we stood alone. . .God bless you all! This is your victory! It is the victory of the cause of freedom in every land![29]*

The Spirit of Churchill, V-E Day, May 8, 1945.
Mrs. Churchill looks on. (The Broadwater Collection)

Twice during the evening, the Prime Minister came out on the balcony to address the vast sea of men, women, and children celebrating ***"the greatest outburst of joy in the history of mankind."*** Flashing his famous "V" for victory sign, he shouted to the ecstatic throng from the balcony: ***"Did anyone want to give in?"*** The crowd roared, *"No!"* ***"Were we downhearted?"*** Again, the crowd shouted, *"No!"* Then, in a simple and touching tribute to the man who had for so long inspired and comforted them with heroic language from another age, the endless crowd sang in one voice, "For He's A Jolly Good Fellow."[30]

Across five summers, Winston Churchill led his nation through its darkest hours. His spirit became the embodiment of the character of a people. His spirit sustained the "Fighting Forties." At the beginning of his matchless memoirs of the Second World War, Mr. Churchill reminds the world why men fight for liberty and recalls the worth of the half-decade struggle in three powerful sentences:

The road across these five years was long, hard, and perilous.
Those who perished upon it did not give their lives in vain.
Those who marched forward to the end will always be proud
to have trodden it with honour. [31]

The famous hymn of dedication to Sir Winston Churchill's most distinguished ancestor the first Duke of Marlborough, is a fitting tribute to his valiant wartime leadership. Two hundred years have not diminished its relevance to the leadership of Britain's Prime Minister during the Second World War. Its lyrical lines, by one of England's most celebrated poets, was said to be George Washington's favorite. The prose and the sentiment are as applicable to the hero of the Battle of Blenheim, whose destiny was to free a continent and thus prepare his nation to rise to historic heights of greatness, as they are to his adoring ancestor, who led in the liberation of the same continent, thereby preserving again the freedom of the nation. Two lives, two careers, two parallel destinies. Each directed the storm of sacrifice and each rode the whirlwind of war:

Me thinks I hear the drum's tumultuous sound,
The victor's shouts and dying groans confound;
The dreadful burst of cannon rend the skies,
And all the thunder of battle rise.

In peaceful thought the field of death surveyed,
To fainting squadrons sent the timely aid;
Inspired repulsed battalions to engage
And taught the doubtful battle where to rage.

So when an angel, by divine command,
With rising tempests shakes a guilty land,
Such of late o'er pale Britannia passed,
Calm and serene drives the furious blast;

And, pleased the Almighty's orders to perform,
Rides the whirlwind and directs the storm. [32]

A   Son of a general and a graduate of West Point, General Douglas MacArthur became one of America's most famous military leaders. He served as superintendent of West Point and rose through the ranks to become Chief of Staff of the United States Army in the 1930s. Recalled to active duty at the out break of World War II, he led the U.S. forces in the Philippines until the Japanese overran the islands in 1942. He was made commander of American forces in the South Pacific and directed the recapture of the strategic islands. He is best remembered for his famous "I shall return" in which he promised to liberate the Philippines. In 1944 he did. Later, he stood watch as the Japanese Foreign Minister signed the official papers of unconditional surrender aboard the USS *Missouri* on September 2, 1945.

B   Admiral William "Bull" Halsey was one of the most courageous commanders of the United States Navy. A graduate of the U.S. Naval Academy in Annapolis, he commanded a destroyer in World War I and later became an accomplished naval aviator. After the attack on Pearl Harbor and America's entrance in the war, Admiral Halsey's battleship was the only American naval presence in all the Pacific. Known for his daring and creative campaigns, he carried out several surprise attacks against the Japanese throughout the world's largest ocean. His fleet and his leadership were the keys to victory at Guadalcanal in 1942.

C   Admiral Kurita was commander of the Japanese Center Force and of the flag ship of the main Japanese fleet, the *Musashi*.

D   The Rhine River is 700 miles long and flows swiftly through the most densely populated area of Western Europe. The Rhine Valley is one of the most ancient areas of civilization on the European continent and its famed river the chief waterway for over two thousand years. Rich in history, the Rhine has been an integral part of shaping Europe's culture. Many sites along its river banks and up its fertile mountains were founded by the Romans.

E   A graduate of West Point, General Bradley was director of the U.S. army's school of infantry at the start of World War II. In 1943, he commanded American forces in North Africa in their victory at Tunisia. He helped plan D-DAY and was present at the liberation of France. Omar Bradley commanded the largest American force under one general, the U.S. 12th Army and oversaw European operations until Germany surrendered. At the end of the war, he became the first Chairman of the Joint Chiefs of Staff.

F   This ancient city, called "jewel of the Rhineland," was founded by the Romans and is home to one of the world's most spectacular cathedrals which Allied bombers were meticulously careful not to harm.

G   At this point, Churchill was more concerned than Roosevelt or Eisenhower about post-war Europe, but lacked the military or political strength to act with out the Americans. With the war on Japan unfinished, the Americans could not afford a breach with Stalin. With the Red Army racing toward Berlin, there was little else Churchill could do. Because of this decision, Stalin had a green light in controlling the fate of Berlin. His grip on the city formed the core reason it was divided with half remaining under communist rule for the next 45 years.

H   The Reich Chancellery was the official residence of the Fuehrer.

I   President Roosevelt adamantly insisted upon unconditional surrender. And considering the emotions of the time, this was perfectly understandable and in many quarters, justified. Churchill accepted this, as there was precious little else he could do. However, the decision proved not the wisest, for it allowed no Germans any concessions—even the non-Nazi factions. And the decision proved quite harmful to the peace and stability of post-war Europe in that it created a vacuum in Germany that was quickly filled by Stalin and the Communists in Eastern Europe.

J   The eldest daughter of King George VI and Queen Elizabeth is Her Majesty Queen Elizabeth II, Great Britain's reigning monarch for the past half-century.

[The chapter title is taken from the motto of the Wallace clan of Scotland. According to Winston Churchill in *A History of the English-Speaking Peoples*, Sir William Wallace, Scottish patriot and martyr, is considered the first person in European history to have embodied the spirit of nationalism, having given his life not for land, title, riches, or King, but for his country alone—a century before one who embodied the same, Joan of Arc of France.]

Chapter 15

BACK TO THE FUTURE

We cannot say "the past is the past" without surrendering the future.
Sir Winston Spencer Churchill

Peace, at long last, came to Europe. Relegated to the tragic pages of history, the infamous Third Reich was gone. Exultant celebrations in Europe gave way to reality as, in Churchill's view, only half the war was won. There was little time to rest as the Allied leaders mustered forces in a final push to win the war in the Pacific. In just twelve weeks, the Empire of Japan would surrender unconditionally. But an ominous barrier between erstwhile allies had begun to form. The seeds of a new kind of war had been sown. A harvest of tension and conflict was but a year away.

In mid-summer of 1945 the last wartime conference was convened to determine how the peace of post-war Europe would be secured. From July 17 to August 2, a summit of the three Allied leaders met in the city of Potsdam, Germany.[A] Gone was Roosevelt. President Harry S Truman,[B] Prime Minister Winston Churchill, and Premier Stalin met at the Potsdam Conference to discuss the next step in the war with Japan and the redrawing of the boundaries of the European states.

The first meetings were amiable, with Truman expressing his desire for the Anglo-American friendship to continue as strong as ever, Churchill expressing to Stalin, *"a welcome to Russia as a Great Power on the sea,"* and Stalin ready to talk trade with Great Britain. The stage was set and the mood captured by powerful Churchillian understatement:

> *The three Powers gathered round the table were the strongest the world had ever seen, and it was their task to maintain the peace of the world.[1]*

But the inevitable was inevitable. Conflict soon arose when Stalin adamantly refused to allow the Western powers to interfere with his control of Eastern Europe. Britain's Prime Minister recalled in retrospect: *"Frustration was the fate of this final Conference of the Three."* As always, Winston Churchill possessed the far more realistic view of the Russians than did Roosevelt or his successor.[2]

As he surveyed the situation during the last days of the war, he lamented of Stalin's Red Army: *"The more they fought the Nazis, the heavier our debt became."* The Soviets felt—and rightly so—that the West did owe them for what they had done. Winston Churchill knew full well the dilemma as he summed up the situation: *"Communist Russia is becoming a danger to the free world."*[3]

Churchill admired the new President as *"a man of exceptional character and ability, simple and direct methods of speech, and a great deal of self confidence and resolution."*[4] But as the talks proceeded, he opposed Truman's agreement with Stalin for the massive withdrawal of all Allied presence in Eastern Europe. With great reluctance, knowing full well that Poland would become a "satellite" of the Soviet Union, and because he could do little else, Churchill agreed to "Polish administration" of German territory in the Soviet zone. These unfortunate decisions were at the time understandable for they allowed Soviet forces to occupy and eventually control half a continent, which came to be known as "the Eastern Bloc."[c] How differently would post-war Europe have looked, what divisions might have been avoided, what conflicts quelled, and what suffering by millions under the heel of communism been unnecessary had his words been heeded.

On the first day of the Potsdam Conference *"world-shaking news arrived."* The first atomic bomb had been tested over the deserts of New Mexico. Churchill had hoped, *"The Japanese people, whose courage I had always admired, might find the apparition of this almost supernatural weapon an excuse which would save Japan's honour and release them from their obligation of being killed to the last man…Here then was a speedy end to the Second World War, and perhaps to much else besides."*[5]

Knowing full well the devastating potential of the atomic bomb, Winston Churchill never wavered in his support of the necessary use of the best available weapons to save Allied lives.[6] Even in considering the most powerful armament yet devised, he applied his philosophy of war and peace—a philosophy captured best in the four memorable lines he used at the beginning of each volume of *The Second World War*. Pithy and to the point, he described this litany as "The Moral of the Work:"

IN WAR: Resolution
IN DEFEAT: Defiance
IN VICTORY: Magnanimity
IN PEACE: Goodwill

As preparations were finalized to end the war with Japan, elections in Britain were underway. The war not quite over and the work at Potsdam unfinished, Mr. Churchill flew to England to await election results from his home district and across the nation. Accompanied by his daughter Mary,^D they landed at Northolt where Mrs. Churchill waited at the airfield for their arrival. The three had a quiet evening together. By noon the next day, it was clear the direction the elections were taking. His beloved wife, ever at his side with support and comfort, told him: "It may well be a blessing in disguise." His terse reply: "At the moment, it seems quite effectively disguised."[7]

When the final count was in, Winston Churchill decisively won his constituency and retained his seat, but his Tory Party lost overwhelmingly. His Government was swept out of office in a landslide. It was the most brutal blow of his career and one of the most dramatic reversals in the life of a political figure in the history of democratic nations. Even members of the opposition were astounded. There seemed no need in time of peace for an old man of war. It was said at the time that the nation—and the world—was shocked: "No one dreamed the English people would be so ungrateful." It was as if his beloved country was saying: "You cannot administer the new world, you could only rescue the old."[8] Stunned and resentful, the outgoing Prime Minister refused the King's offer of the highest order of knighthood in the realm, the Order of the Garter.^E Always descriptive of the situation, he was quoted as saying, "How can I accept the Garter when the people have just given me the Boot?"[9]

The election of 1945 and its timing may never be fully understood. Was it due to party rivalries and union demands both suppressed by years of war? Was it, understandably, an exhausted people merely desirous of stability and security after years of suffering and sacrifice? Was it the belief that the nation did not require the leadership of an impulsive lover-of-war unfit for a time of peace? Was it a lingering mistrust of a political opportunist who changed sides at will and who could not make up his mind about communism? After blood, toil, tears, and sweat, did Britons simply yearn for higher wages and shorter hours? Whatever the reasons, a mere eleven weeks after the end of the war in Europe and before the end of the war itself, it seemed that Winston Churchill was simply cast aside. With a tinge of bitterness, he recorded the fervency of his emotions this way:

> *The power to shape the future would be denied me. The knowledge and experience I had gathered, the authority and goodwill I had gained in so many countries, would vanish . . .the verdict of the electors had been so overwhelmingly expressed that I did not wish to remain even for an hour responsible for their affairs.*[10]

Never far from his view of responsibility to the future, Mr. Churchill later recorded that in the summer of 1945 he had prepared for "a show-down" over the question of Poland and Austria and would not hesitate at the end of the conference to make "a public break if necessary" with his Allied partners.[11] But it was not to be. History had taken a hand. He did not return to office—or to Potsdam. Five years that changed a century ended in a day. A nation in peril had turned to him. A nation in peace had turned him out. These inevitable moments in time wedded him to his destiny—a destiny which seemed eerily to fulfill the motto emblazoned on the coat of arms of the Churchill family: *Faithful but Unfortunate.*

In time and upon reflection, Winston Churchill would articulate the dichotomy of democracy—that the true strength of rule by the people is often found in their freedom to subjugate to oblivion leaders who have served them well. In his account of the war years, the redoubtable statesman applied words penned centuries before by Plutarch, one of the greatest philosophers of ancient Greece: *"Ingratitude towards their great men is the mark of strong peoples."*

The House of Churchill is represented by a lion couchant guardant argent supporting a banner with coupled hand. The House of Spencer is represented by the head of a griffin with wings expanded rising from a coronet. The ancient family motto of the Churchill family was adopted by the first Sir Winston, father of John Churchill, the 1st Duke of Marlborough. Its Spanish inscription *fiel pero desdichado* translates: "faithful, but unfortunate." (John Forster, Librarian, Blenheim Palace)

Winston Churchill understood his time on the world stage was a fulfillment of his destiny, and he willingly played his part. The day after the loss of his position and power, he issued his "Message to the Nation." In his final wartime address, the out-going Prime Minister eloquently expressed his bow to the irresistible force of history. Reflecting upon his call as servant-leader, he chose to end his voluminous memoirs with these lines:

> *The decision of the British people has been recorded in the votes counted today. I have therefore laid down the charge which was placed upon me in darker times...It only remains for me to express to the British people, for whom I have acted in these perilous years, my profound gratitude for the unflinching, unswerving support which they have given me during my task, and for the many expressions of kindness which they have shown towards their servant.[12]*

The vital work of the last summit of the war carried on. Britain's new Prime Minister, Clement Atlee, assumed the mantle as one of "the Three." An invasion of Japan was discussed, but it was not to be. The Americans were not about to risk untold thousands more of her fighting men and engage in brutal combat over many months or perhaps years in an effort to take Japan. With sober understanding of the ramifications of the atomic bomb and its breathtaking power to devastate, the Allies issued their pronouncement from Potsdam: "Japan must agree to unconditional surrender of all armed forces."[13] The Empire immediately replied: "Not acceptable." The conference adjourned on August 2, 1945. Sometime within the next 72 hours, Franklin Roosevelt's successor, President Harry S Truman gave the go-ahead to launch the weapon to end all weapons. Four days later, the world changed forever—1,600 feet above Japan. On August 6, 1945, the first atomic bomb in history was dropped over the city of Hiroshima.[F] The target: the main bridge in the heart of the city. [G] In the Enola Gay, a specially equipped B-29 named for the commander's mother, Lt. Col. Paul W. Tibbetts and his crew left the evening of August 5, flew all night, and approached the coast of Japan in the shrouded silence of the dawn hours of August 6, 1945. At 8:15 AM, Japanese time, the atomic age began.

A weapon was unleashed that would end a world at war. Over 100,000 human beings were instantly incinerated. The entire city of five square miles was laid bare. A beautiful city, gleaming in the sun, was in a moment covered in ash. Astonishingly, the word came from the obdurate Japanese War Council: "No surrender." Three days later, a second atomic bomb was unleashed over the city of Nagasaki. Unconditional surrender by Japan was no longer in question. The Emperor could do nothing else but agree. But according to the terms of the Potsdam agreement, it was too late. Japan now had to agree to *unconditional* surrender and be subordinate to the Allied powers and agree to free elections by her people. The Emperor declared "yes." On September 2, 1945, Japan's foreign minister, under the watchful eye of General Douglas MacArthur, signed the surrender aboard the USS *Missouri* as she lay anchored in the tranquil waters of Tokyo Bay. To the assembled company, MacArthur declared: "Freedom, justice, tolerance." The Second World War was over.

Reflecting the feeling of his countrymen that the United States did not start the war but they were bound to finish it, President Truman solemnly but firmly declared: ***"This action taken by the United States ended the war and saved thousands of American lives."*** Years before, and motivated by the interests of peace and not war, the world-renowned scientist Dr. Albert Einstein, in a 1939 letter to President Roosevelt, suggested the development of so powerful a weapon. In his memoirs of the war years, Winston Churchill reflected on the significance of such a weapon of apocalyptic proportions. An unwavering advocate of the doctrine of peace through strength, [11] he believed such power should always remain in the hands of the free world: ***"It** [the atomic bomb] **kept Stalin out of Western Europe. It became a weapon of diplomacy."***[14] Six decades after the advent of the atomic age, the unanswerable, two-sided question still remains: have nuclear weapons made war more or less likely? Civilized man must continue to possess the hope that such a question should always remain for *discussion only*.

Every great leader of a free people understands that the strength and resolve of his nation's military—those who perform the ultimate unselfish sacrifice by fighting and winning the wars—is to whom the debt of liberty and peace is owed. Just two generations after the 20th century's greatest conflict and greatest achievement, another in the long line of stalwart British Prime Ministers expressed this truth as he eloquently called on the past as sentinel to the future. On March 20, 2003, Prime Minister Tony Blair delivered an apposite address to his nation following his order for the deployment of British military land, sea, and air forces to liberate the nation of Iraq:

> *The threat today is not that of my father's generation. War between big powers is unlikely. Europe is at peace. The Cold War is a memory. But this new world faces a new threat of disorder and chaos from either brutal states or extreme terrorist groups. Both hate our way of life, our freedom, our democracy...That is why I have asked our troops to go into action tonight. As so often before, on the courage and deter- mination of British men and women, serving our country, the fate of many nations rests.*

On May 1, 2003, at the conclusion of the liberation phase of the Iraqi War, President George W. Bush[I] also employed the indelible imagery of freedom's finest hour in his address to the American nation. One hundred miles off the coast of California, in the sunlit evening of a calm and shining sea, the officers and crew of the USS *Abraham Lincoln*[J] gathered on the deck to hear the President's stirring address broadcast to the nation and around the world. In celebration of the lib- eration of Iraq[K] from tyranny, the Commander-in-Chief thanked the armed forces, the American people, and the free nations in partner- ship in "a noble cause." He hearkened back to the greatest triumph of freedom over tyranny in the history of man. His message began and ended in cheers and tears and left no doubt as to the motive and mis- sion of the free world: to never conquer—to only liberate:

> *The character of our military throughout history—the daring of Normandy, the fierce courage of Iwo Jima, the decency and ideology that turned enemies into allies—is preserved in this generation. . . In defeating Nazi Germany and Imperial Japan,*

244

Allied forces destroyed entire cities while enemy leaders who started the conflict were safe until the final days . . . Military power was used to end a regime by breaking a nation. Today, we have the great power to free a nation by breaking a dangerous and aggressive regime. . . No device of man can remove the tragedy from war, yet it is a great advance when the guilty have far more to fear from war than do the innocent. . . Everywhere that freedom arrives, humanity rejoices. Everywhere that freedom stirs, let tyrants fear . . . We stand for human liberty.

It has been well-said that the essence of leadership is possessed by those with the ability to see further down the road than those around them can.[15] However, just seeing is often not enough. Leadership during history's most crucial times requires unflinching courage to act upon what is seen. Such pivotal points in the life of a nation depend upon leaders with the ability to see triumph in the face of tragedy with the sheer stubbornness to persevere—leaders with downright grit. In his portrait in pen, Churchill biographer Guy Eden put it well. Describing Churchill's ability to persevere, Eden referred to his prescience:

His mind, so resourceful and original as that which away back in the dark days, saw, afar off, the certainty of victory when others saw only the nearness of defeat.[16]

It could be rightly said that Winston Churchill was never fully understood nor fully appreciated by his contemporaries even though history has validated again and again the truth of his belief in the axiom that too often nations must take up arms for the sake of liberty and peace. His firm reliance on the past, guardianship of the present, and faith in the future yet unseen, secures him an unimpeachable place among the greatest of statesmen.

Although the monumental events of the 1940s had come to a close, Winston Churchill would not allow himself "to fall below the level of events." Accordingly, he chose the most fitting of titles for the last volume of his account of the Second World War. Poignant and potent, *Triumph and Tragedy* describes the man himself and the tenor of his transitional times. Optimistic? Most assuredly. Realistic? Without question. Global war was now over and peace was a reality. Yet portents of tragic events lay in the wake of shattered Russian promises, for unfettered freedom would not be experienced by millions of Europeans for half a century more. In the defeat of fascism, there was triumph. With the spread of communism, there would be tragedy.

But the war-weary world was in no mood to hear of possible dangers in its era of peace. The task of sentinel fell once again on the shoulders of a statesman well-acquainted with rejection and dismissal, a statesman familiar with the special courage of conflict, and a statesman unafraid to state hard truth. The task fell on Winston Churchill. In his memoirs of both the First and Second World Wars, Mr. Churchill argued that tragedy awaits nations that do not heed the lessons of history. In the immediate post-war world of the 1940s, he described the unfortunate but predictable path taken by the victorious nations. Once again Winston Churchill donned the mantle of vindicated prophet:

> *How the great Democracies Triumphed and so were able to Resume the Follies which had so nearly Cost them their Life.*[17]

In the summer of 1945, the curtain of events had gone down on one of the most important acts ever played out on the world stage. As one looks back on those days, the incomparable words of John Milton, second only to Shakespeare in England's long litany of literary giants, speak to a time in Churchill's life that had become all too familiar to him. In the wilderness once again, Winston Churchill could only wait for the world to come to him. It would. In the last line of Milton's autobiographical and powerful poem, *On His Blindness,* the poet pens the definitive statement on duty with its most challenging aspects—patience and trust. Milton's memorable and often quoted words are applicable to the totality of the life and career of one of Britain's greatest sons: *"He also serves who only stands and waits."*

On March 5, 1946, in a small college town nestled in the shadow of the gentle hills of the American Midwest, with conviction and courage, one man would once again leave his indelible mark on the future—and on history. Within eight months of the end of the war in Europe, Winston Churchill looked back to the future in his warning to the West to be ever on guard against tyranny and totalitarianism— dangers looming large and poised to threaten again the peace of the Free World. On a windswept hill on the campus of Westminster College in Fulton, Missouri, Winston Spencer Churchill would once again wield the sword of the spoken word. Because he knew an iron curtain was descending across Europe, he prepared to brandish his rhetorical rapier. In one phrase, and with one stroke, he would divide the world into the symmetry of two ideologies. In one thrust, he would set the course of nations headed down two separate paths. Winston Spencer Churchill was about to shake a complacent world and strengthen those things which remain.

A Located southwest of Berlin, Potsdam is the capital of Brandenburg, Germany. It was once the royal residence of the King of Prussia and the military and intellectual center of that once mighty empire. By the 20th century, it was a suburb of Berlin.

B In the 1944 elections, US Senator from Missouri, Harry S. Truman, was chosen to be President Roosevelt's running mate on the Democratic ticket. After Mr. Roosevelt was sworn in for an unprecedented fourth term as President, his Vice-President served only 83 days. Upon the death of FDR, Mr. Truman became the 32nd President of the United States. One month later, Germany surrendered. In 1946, the new President established an aid program to prevent the spread of communism in Europe and Asia known as "The Truman Doctrine."

C President Truman was under pressure to win the war in the Pacific and keen to persuade the Soviets to enter that theater of war. Europe was devastated and public opinion in Britain and America would have had enormous difficulty understanding a new conflict with our Russian ally. Besides, the reality of Red Army domination of Eastern Europe, meant that it was probably too late to fight an effective battle for Poland. Churchill felt this keenly, after all Britain had gone to war over Poland, but there was little he and Truman could do at Potsdam save try to draw up working agreements with Stalin for Poland and Germany. In due course, when Stalin began to break these agreements, they were then in a stronger political and moral position to mount an effective challenge and carry public opinion with them.

D Mary Churchill is currently The Lady Soames DBE (Dame of the British Empire)

E The Most Noble Order of the Garter was established in 1348 by King Edward III and is the highest order of chivalry in the British Empire. It is named for the patron saint of England, St. George, a Roman soldier executed for his Christian faith. The motto of a Knight of the Garter is "shame on he who evil thinks." Its origins are traced to an incident when King Edward picked up the dropped garter of the Countess of Salisbury and tied it round his own leg. That the Sovereign should do this humble deed was an act of ultimate chivalry. Its distinctions are many, but first and foremost, it is bestowed as a personal gift of the Sovereign. This most elite honor in Britain is held by the Monarch and the Prince of Wales and only 24 other individuals at any time. Pomp and pageantry accompany its ancient induction ceremony held at magnificent Windsor Castle. In 1953 at the request of HM Queen Elizabeth II, Rt. Hon. Winston Churchill humbly and gratefully received from her hand this highest honor in the ancient and sceptered isle.

F In one of the best-kept secrets of the war, a team of top scientists worked on the euphemistically named "Manhattan Project." From heavy water experiments conducted early in the war, they developed a uranium bomb of tremendous power over many months and tested it over the deserts of New

Mexico. For "good results," the bomb had to be detonated exactly 1,600 feet over its intended target.

G   Four cities had been selected as sites. Only the weather forecast determined the unfortunate target. Of the four target cities, Hiroshima, Nagasaki, Niaguta, and Kokurra, only Hiroshima was predicted to have clear skies and unlimited visibility.

H   President George Washington, in his 1st Inaugural Address on January 8, 1790, stated: "To be prepared for war is one of the most effectual means of preserving peace." Two hundred years later, the phrase "peace through strength" became a staple of President Ronald Reagan's foreign policy—especially in negotiations with the Soviet Union during the height of the Cold War.

I   Dressed in full flight gear, Mr. Bush, a trained National Guard pilot, became the first President in United States history to land a fighter jet aboard a moving aircraft carrier at sea.

J   The USS *Abraham Lincoln* is a Nimitz-class carrier. This class of battleships is the largest class of ships in the United States Navy and named for Admiral Chester A. Nimitz, the Supreme Allied Commander in the Pacific during World War II.

K   At this writing, the war against terrorism is ongoing and the post-liberation efforts to bring democracy to Iraq are continuing.

Chapter 16

A FIXED POINT

Here we are and here we stand—a veritable rock of
salvation in an ever-changing world.
Prime Minister Winston Churchill
Annual Speech, Guildhall in London, November, 1942

At the close of the Second World War Winston Churchill retrospectively remarked:

I leave the judgment of our action, with confidence,
to the world—and to history.[1]

The world—and history—still judges. In his 1949 article in *The Atlantic Monthly*, historian Isaiah Berlin declared: "Winston Churchill is the largest human being of our time, a gigantic historical figure whose work and person will remain the object of scrutiny and judgment to many generations." Such was the strong emotion felt by those who lived during the life and times of Britain's iconic wartime leader. In May of 1940, the turning point of his career became the turning point of his nation. In March of 1946, the expected end of his career became the unlikely beginning of an era. Six decades have not altered this perception:

In 1940, Churchill's noble rhetoric—with some help from
the RAF—sustained the cause of Western liberty when Britain
stood alone against the Nazi juggernaut . . . In 1946, he
warned a tired and complacent America about the threat
to liberal values and world peace posed by an aggressive
communist tyranny in charge of the destiny of half of Europe.[2]

Those who have written the record of those times and those who have since lived in the post-war world have acknowledged that few in history have been pressed into service at the most pivotal times in the life of their nation. Throughout the unparalleled life and career of Winston Churchill there was a continuum of courage, a plumb line of confidence: ***Never give up! Never lose heart! Do your duty!*** Perhaps best illustrated on a wartime poster which adorned British factory walls, his message seemed to capture the morale-building mood of those days. The poster was a take-off of the famous American image of "Uncle Sam" in patriotic regalia, resolute countenance, and index finger pointing outward with commanding message: I WANT YOU! The British version featured a defiant Churchill adorned with requisite bowtie, glaring outward with the stern admonition: "DESERVE VICTORY!"[3]

It has been well said that Winston Churchill was a true man of "the West." This all-encompassing term transcends the finite, a belief system defined by a view of the world buttressed by a specific set of ideas, defined principles, and enduring values. The West: a confident declaration that the individual is always of infinite value and therefore must take preeminence over any system or government. The West: the essence of the Free World. To Churchill, the West was ***"...beyond politics and geography...the human desire for freedom and the courage to bear it."[4]*** Borderless and boundless, the West is a world and life view, a universal idea applicable in any time or place, and wonderfully expressed two centuries ago by American patriot and statesman, Benjamin Franklin: ***"Where liberty dwells, there is my country."[5]***

Throughout history few individuals have typified a life that is relevant for all times, all eras, all seasons. Such individuals never really leave the world, and the world never really leaves them. When the whole world seems to be turning in a thousand different directions, these individuals seem to never move, never vary, never change. It is in those times of turning, times of great uncertainty, the world and history is fortunate to encounter remarkable individuals who possess the surety of what has been thoughtfully described as "large-souled greatness."[6] Several decades ago, political philosopher Leo Strauss applied this concept to Winston Churchill: "A man like Churchill proves that possibility of ***megalofuxia*** [greatness of soul] exists today exactly as it did in 5th century B.C."[A]

In Robert Bolt's incomparable play and later Academy Award winning film, ***A Man for All Seasons***,[B] he paints a portrait of Sir Thomas More, the respected and trusted adviser of King Henry VIII. A masterful study of the politics and intrigue of the 16th century, the play and film are noted for the beauty and craftsmanship of the actors' lines, flawlessly delivered against the lavish backdrop of the production. Yet the vehicle of storytelling never takes precedence over the principal player. A humble and devoutly religious man, Thomas More did not crave power, trust in royal favors, or seek the trappings of high office, yet the king gave him the highest lay position in all England—Lord Chancellor. The king called Thomas "my friend," an honor, above all, that overwhelmed him. In his time at the pinnacle of power in all England, Sir Thomas never wavered in his faith or his convictions. When earthly power conflicted with his convictions regarding eternal power, he followed his conscience—even to the executioner's block. When all the world seemed to move in Henry's direction, Thomas stood alone. One of the most memorable lines in the play describes him best. He was "a fixed point in a world of turning." Sir Thomas could serve the king or follow his conscience, but he could not do both. His last words captured for all time the cosmic conflict: "I die the King's good servant—but God's first."

It has been said that Thomas More embodied the character of a true patriot: one who is loyal both to King and God, but fears only God. Perhaps in this unique quality lies the most enduring element of statesmanship. In its final analysis, such a posture eliminates earthly fear and assures an individual complete freedom to put the interests of his conscience—and his country—first. At the end of the play, Sir Thomas is alone in his room of imprisonment in the Tower of London. Through his tiny window to the world he witnessed the changes in the four seasons during his year of captivity. His trial is imminent. His family, finally allowed to visit him, knows they have seen him for the last time. These final words spoken by Sir Thomas to his beloved daughter Margaret powerfully, yet humbly, illuminate the reality of the limitations of human intellect as they remind the hearer that the essence of duty to God, family, and country may ultimately lie in the giving of one's life. Sir Thomas tells his heartbroken Meg, "Finally, it is not a matter of reason, it is a matter of love."

A man for all seasons. A man for all ages. A man who, in an earthly sense, remains immortal. The world will always turn and change, but the lasting values and principles—and those who hold, defend, and preserve them—are fixed points in a world of turning. Unmindful of its great need for such individuals, the world never clamors for them. Often obscured in the times in which they live, the world finally and always recognizes, and yes, reveres them. Times and eras change, but transcendent truths change not. Civilization depends upon courageous men and women who understand that there are, and always must be, those things worth living for and those things worth dying for.

In the short span of years between the end of the Second World War and the beginning of a "cold" war that would last half a century, the world witnessed a clash of civilizations. Over the next five decades, the world was confronted by a stark choice between the two. It would take a statesman who had faced difficulty and peril with dedication and purpose to bring a sense of moral clarity to the conflict; a steady statesman with courage to proclaim that it is not enough to fight and *defend* against an enemy, but to fight and *vanquish* the enemy; a statesman so rare, even without a formal platform or position, he could master the events of an era; a statesman motivated by principle and conviction, not politics or convenience, to stand fast upon what he knew was good and right and true and lasting.

It has been rightly said that many observers of Winston Churchill believed his objectives—and his principles—were often obscured.[7] Was Winston Churchill a man of war or a man of peace? Few doubt the former; many have questioned the latter. At the end of the Second World War, the question was certainly open-ended. One thing is clear—he understood that true freedom was possible only when people and nations were not conquered, but liberated—people and nations rooted in and guided by principles:

> *Principles are eternal. They can be read in history. Eternal principles such as courage and honor are the moral equivalent of certain laws throughout the universe...They can be neglected, but cannot be lost. They can be thrown down, but they cannot be broken.*[8]

During a lifetime that spanned the age of cavalry to the age of rockets, Winston Churchill understood that wars are fought for many reasons—but never for "peace." Through first-hand experience he knew that peace does not come through just desire for it or from appeasement to it. He knew that refusing to stand up to evil could mean peace, but only temporarily, for he knew that genuine peace comes from the total victory of freedom. Winston Churchill was consistently compelled to speak about the harsh reality that peace is not just the absence of war, but often and tragically the presence of tyrannies so strong as to allow no resistance—tyrannies so powerful as to prevent liberty from triumph.

Perhaps the dichotomy is best summed up in a statement he made during the height of the greatest conflict of the 20th century. This statement supports a view he maintained throughout his long life and career, that only freedom makes peace possible—not the other way around:

> *Unless we win the war, we need not plan for the peace, for there will be none!*[9]

Consistency of conviction remained an integral component in the character of Winston Churchill. In or out of a definitive leadership role made no difference to him. One year before Britain declared war on Germany and three years before the United States entered the fight, Mr. Churchill broadcast an impassioned appeal for greater involvement in the European conflict directly to the United States. His plea went right to the root of the matter as he gave credence to his conviction, that in the final analysis, what sustains men and nations is not the might of force and weapons, but the enduring power of what they believe and why they believe it:

> *Britain must arm...But arms are not sufficient by themselves. We must add to them the power of ideas... It is the very conflict of spiritual and moral ideas which gives the free countries a great part of their strength.*[10]

What Winston Churchill said in the 1930s when Adolf Hitler was gobbling up Europe and exporting totalitarian fascism was applicable to the unpredictable war years of the 1940s. What he stood for through the valleys and victories of the Second World War was applicable to the tension-filled Cold War years of the 1950s. What he maintained is still relevant to the struggles and triumphs of liberty in the 21st century. There had been peace in Hitler's occupied countries, "peace" enforced by intimidation, fear, brutality, barbarity, and death—a peace *imposed* on enslaved populations who clamored for liberation. In the immediate years following the Second World War, and for a quarter of a century, the Soviet Union had peace. A "peace" enforced from Siberia to Moscow, from the Ukraine to the Urals. Peace, but not freedom.

The "consistency of aim" attributed to Churchill was never more clouded than when applied to his stance on communism. He never truly lost his zeal in opposing this menace perhaps because he had witnessed the chaos of the Bolshevik Revolution in 1917 with its subsequent creation of the iron-fisted Soviet Union. To political allies and opponents alike he not only appeared inconsistent but opportunistic as his position seemed to change with the circumstances. No cloudiness was in his mind—he had been most consistent. As each system was totalitarian in its own right, he resolved that each had to be opposed—one at a time if necessary. During the Second World War he put aside his aversion to the oppressive system of communism to deal with the immediate threat of fascism.[11] Within a year of the war's end, he would again proclaim the dangers of Stalinism to Western Europe for he looked upon his opposition to both tyrannies as his duty to strengthen the West's faith in the moral superiority of democracy and the inevitability of its triumph.[12] Allen Packwood recalls this era and cites the consistency of conviction in the life of Winston Churchill:

> *To Churchill, Britain was not just a European power. She was a global power…His view of Britain as a European Great Power and a guarantor of the Continent's stability meant that he was not prepared to support appeasement*

and allow a revived Germany to upset the balance of power. His Victorian education, his romantic view of history, his experiences in the First World War, his awareness of his ancestry, and his own sense of destiny impelled him to speak out...To Churchill, the only hope for war ravaged Europe was closer union which would also serve as a check to the expansion of Soviet communism. Through the whole of his life and career, Winston Churchill was broadly consistent in his approach to the world.[13]

Euphoric days following the end of the war gave way to uneasiness in Europe and America as emerging divisions in the newly liberated continent became apparent. The times created the leader and the leader created the times for the post-war role of Winston Churchill as both herald and prophet is one history has held securely for him and no other. The grand old man marked these uncertain days by his uncanny ability to foresee potential threat to freedom and democracy. Consistent to himself and to his principles, Winston Churchill was too "Churchillian" to remain quiet for long. Compelled to communicate strong realities, Churchill found that opportunity presented itself for him to once more stand on the world stage. Resurrected again from political oblivion, he delivered a peacetime speech that advocated the continued strength of the Anglo-American Alliance and friendship, even as it persuasively hearkened the nations of the West to contemplate the unthinkable:

Winston Churchill used his high profile platform to comment on the structures that he felt were necessary to prevent a Third World War...During much of the speech, he stresses the need for the continuance of strong Anglo-American alliance and friendship...even as he challenges the world to safeguard the Continent from the tyranny of totalitarianism or the tragedy of another war.[14]

Perhaps second only to "our finest hour," the best-remembered words of Winston Churchill were spoken not in his beloved homeland, but delivered in the geographic center of the United States.

Without a global stage from which to proclaim his premonitions, Mr. Churchill accepted a handwritten invitation from President Truman to speak in the home state of the American leader. As "a private visitor" he considered it an honor to be introduced by the President of the United States and was grateful for "the opportunity of addressing this kindred nation, as well as my own countrymen across the ocean, and perhaps some other countries, too." Self-effacing in his time out of power, and therefore not constrained by the dictates of international diplomacy, he declared, "I speak only for myself. There is nothing here but what you see."[15]

As President Truman sits near, former Prime Minister Winston Churchill delivers the speech that shook the world. Just months later Truman told him, "Your prophecy has come true." (The Winston Churchill Memorial and Library, Fulton, Missouri)

After five winters of war, spring at long last arrived. On March 5, 1946, Winston Churchill traveled to Westminster College in Fulton, Missouri.[c] From a small college town in the heartland of America, he electrified the world in cadences of carefully chosen oratory and declared that the firm and tough tendons which supply strength and power to the body—the sinews—must be applied to the hard-won peace of the Free World. Even as he unabashedly warned the Western world of Russian expansion in Eastern Europe, he made firm his desire and hope the peace would hold. Therefore, with optimism, he chose the title for his speech, *The Sinews of Peace*. But optimism would not overshadow truth or reality. Realizing the last thing war-weary populations wanted to hear from their leaders was the possibility of a new threat to their hard-won freedom and peace, Mr. Churchill pressed forward. While he gloried in the well-deserved peace, he pictured the possibility of a new menace poised to at best, de-stabilize, at worst, strike. Stirring words wedded to an enthralling speaking style combined to bequeath a speech that has endured. Ironies abound in its lines, for its premise about peace is remembered for launching a war—even if only a "cold" one. Unpopular abroad, dismissed at home, tolerated in America, it reverberated around the world.[D]

The intervening years have confirmed *The Sinews of Peace* marked a defining moment during the half-century of shadowy subterfuge between superpowers. Russian historians note its debut as the moment of schism between East and West. In an era of simmering tensions and often open hostilities, the bold words of Winston Churchill defined the geopolitics of the atomic generation. One phrase emerged which became the opening salvo of the Cold War. That phrase, of course, was *iron curtain*.[E]

Winston Churchill could see what caused war and created freedom. He could see tyrants coming while others could not. He knew what to do while others did not. Throughout the progression of time and the turning of seasons, this is what has set him apart. His quintessential speech on freedom versus peace called on the Western powers to form an alliance of defense against Russia by seeking a doctrine of *peace through strength*.[F] Immediately denounced as a warmonger, Winston Churchill did not have to wait long for history to justify him—the Cold War years did that. Within the intense prose of what would be called "the iron curtain speech," the many points he postulated became a part of Western policy and polity during the fifty-year superpower standoff.

At the dawn of the 21st century, the forces of freedom and justice can look back to the previous century with confidence. From the glorious triumphs in two World Wars and the stunning victory in the Cold War, to the challenges and commitments ahead in the winning of the Terror War, the "iron curtain speech" by Winston Churchill is one of the most important set of words he left in his vast legacy. They speak certainty and comfort to an uncertain and anxious world. As the world faces a new global enemy, the parallels personify the ongoing struggles of mankind: how to balance liberty with order and peace with security. From the pronouncements of one of history's greatest champions of liberty and representative government, subsequent generations can understand that the perpetual work of freedom, justice, and the rule of law must continue. From the reference to the special bond between Britain and America he so relished, Winston Churchill reaffirmed the foundation—and responsibility—of the free nations of the world.

Spoken a half-century ago to a menace now marginalized, the words spoken by Mr. Churchill in *The Sinews of Peace* were as amazingly prescient as they were keenly prophetic. As such, they shall always seem pertinent, for they still speak to any era threatened by a new enemy and to a world engaged in war. Applicable to every age, Winston Churchill not only understood his times, but all the times yet to come. As if six decades have been swept from the shadows of time, one can almost hear the unmistakable growl and glow of one of history's fixed points in a world of turning:

> *Ladies and gentlemen, the United States stands at this time at the pinnacle of world power. It is a solemn moment for American Democracy. For with primacy in power is also joined an awe-inspiring accountability to the future. If you look around you, you must feel not only the sense of duty done but also you must feel anxiety lest you fall below the level of achievement. Opportunity is here now, clear and shining for both our countries. To reject it or ignore it or fritter it away will bring upon us all the long reproaches of the after-time...*

> *When the designs of wicked men or the aggressive urge of mighty States dissolve over large areas the frame of civilized society, humble folk are confronted with difficulties with which they cannot cope...We must be certain that our temple is built, not upon shifting sands, but upon the*

rock. Anyone can see with his eyes open that our path will be difficult and also long, but if we persevere together as we did in the two world wars—though not, alas, in the interval between them—I cannot doubt that we shall achieve our common purpose in the end...

We cannot be blind to the fact that the liberties enjoyed by individual citizens through-out the United States and throughout the British Empire are not valid in a considerable number of countries, some of which are very powerful. ...We must never cease to proclaim in fearless tones the great principles of freedom and the rights of man which are the joint inheritance of the English-speaking world and which through Magna Carta, *the* Bill of Rights, *the* Habeus Corpus, *trial by jury, and the English common law find their most famous expression in the American* Declaration of Independence. *All this means that the people of any country have the right, and should have the power by constitutional action, by free unfettered elections, with secret ballot, to choose or change the character or form of government under which they dwell; that freedom of speech and thought should reign; that courts of justice, independent of the executive, unbiased by any party, should administer laws which have received the broad assent of large majorities or are consecrated by time and custom. Here are the title deeds of freedom... Here is the message of the British and American peoples to mankind. Let us preach what we practice—let us practice what we preach.[16]*

At this point, Churchill prepared to issue his warning to the West. He prefaced his stern admonition with his sincere desire that "the Temple of Peace" continue with all partners working together. He then put forth his firm belief that the best course of action for any nation lay in the preventing of war by wise use of strong and resolute pre-emption. In this, Winston Churchill has lessons for today. In this, Winston Churchill has lessons for tomorrow. Not only relevant to the immediate post-war world of the late 1940s, Mr. Churchill's caveat to the Free World is astonishingly applicable to the Terror War of the 21st century. By commandeering historical descriptives like "the dark ages" and "the Stone Age," Mr. Churchill prepared the world for its future:

> *The dark ages may return, the Stone Age may return on the gleaming wings of science, and what might now shower immeasurable material blessings upon mankind, may even bring about its total destruction. Beware, I say: time may be short. Do not let us take the course of allowing events to drift along until it is too late...There is the path of wisdom. Prevention is better than cure.*

It is not known if the modern heirs of the Anglo-American alliance and friendship, President George W. Bush and Prime Minister Tony Blair, consulted *The Sinews of Peace*, but their strategy of offense in taking the Terror War to the terrorists as a preemptive strike seems to be lifted from its pages. What is known is that the direct action taken by the 21st century guarantors of peace and freedom made relevant the words of wisdom spoken decades ago by Winston Churchill. As if a macabre appointment had been kept, sixty years later a ruthless and barbaric enemy indeed rose from the recesses of the dark ages of the 7th century. With prophetic precision, one man predicted the possibility a malevolent enemy with access to apocalyptic weapons could crash on to the world stage. It did. The Stone Age indeed returned on September 11, 2001, riding on "the gleaming wings of science."

In March of 2003, on the eve of the Iraqi War, the grandson and namesake of Sir Winston Churchill expressed his views in an editorial in *The Wall Street Journal*. Winston S. Churchill reflected on parallels he believed his grandfather most probably would have drawn between the widening war on global terror to the global war against fascist totalitarianism in which his grandfather engaged and directed. As America, Britain, and their allies reached the gates of Iraq, several comparisons were notable. With a touch of his grandfather's blunt assessment, Mr. Churchill the younger compared "the fecklessness" of the victorious post-World War I nations who allowed the emerging Axis powers to "flout the resolutions" of the League of Nations, to several modern nations of the 21st century. He goes on to declare that such nations embody a "feebleness of spirit, an unwillingness to face the realities of the world we live in, and a determination to place corrupt self-interest before the common good." Here he applies the warnings from his grandfather's precise post-war speech to the war on global terror:

> *As thunderclouds gather over the Middle East, America and Britain stand once again shoulder to shoulder preparing to draw the sword in defense of freedom, democracy, and human rights. A line has been drawn in the sand as President Bush and Prime Minister Blair intend today in the case of Iraq, Winston Churchill in 1948 favored the threat—and if need be the reality—of a pre-emptive strike to safeguard the interests of the Free World. Aware of the dangers ahead, Churchill believed that the United States— while it still had a monopoly of atomic power should require the Soviet Union to abandon the development of these weapons, if need be by threatening their use. The Truman Administration chose not to heed his advice. The result was the Cold War...* [17]

Even before the post-war years of the 1950s began, Winston Churchill still stood astride the geopolitical landscape like a colossus. His "iron curtain speech" drew the line between belief systems—ideologies of freedom and tyranny with their inevitable and respective consequences. As splitting the atom marked the advent of the nuclear age, so splitting these ideologies marked the advent of the atomic generation. Prefaced with cordial gestures toward the Soviet Union and Marshall Stalin, Mr. Churchill's speech extended friendship and a sincere desire for peace before issuing his immortal affirmation. Immortal, because the redoubtable statesman's words foreshadowed what *did* happen in Europe over the next generation. Within its lines was a warning. Within the warning was a painful reminder that his previous pronouncements regarding the situation in Europe had fallen on deaf ears. He now prompted his audience—and the world—to remember that no matter how discomforting and disquieting the message may be, the messenger must not be dismissed again:

A shadow has fallen upon the scenes so lately lighted by the Allied victory. Nobody knows what Soviet Russia and its Communist international organizations intends to do in the immediate future, or what are the limits...We aim at nothing but mutual assistance and collaboration with Russia...We welcome Russia to her rightful place among the leading nations of the world. Above all, we welcome, or should welcome, constant, frequent and growing contacts between the Russian people and our own people on both sides of the Atlantic... It is my duty, however, to place before you certain facts about the present position in Europe. **From Stettin in the Baltic to Trieste in the Adriatic an IRON CURTAIN has descended across the Continent.** *Behind that line lie all the capitals of the ancient states of Central and Eastern Europe.... all these famous cities and the populations around them lie in what I must call the Soviet sphere...*

These are somber facts for anyone to have to recite on the morrow of a victory gained by so much splendid comradeship in arms and in the cause of freedom and democracy; but we should be most unwise not to face them squarely while time remains...I have, however, felt bound to portray the shadow which, alike in the west and in the east, falls upon the world...On the other hand, I repulse the idea that a new war is inevitable; still more that it is imminent. It is because I am sure that our fortunes are still in our own hands and that we hold the power to save the future, that I feel the duty to speak out now that I have the occasion and the opportunity to do so...Our difficulties and dangers will not be removed by closing our eyes to them. They will not be removed by mere waiting to see what happens, nor will they

*be removed by a policy of appeasement. . .Last time I saw it
all coming and I cried aloud to my own fellow-countrymen
and to the world, but no one paid any attention. . .There
never was a war in history easier to prevent by timely action
than the one which has just desolated such great areas of the
globe. It could have been prevented in my belief without the
firing of a single shot. . . Ladies and gentlemen, I put it to
you, surely, we must not let that happen again.*[18]

The Sinews of Peace traveled a step beyond the themes of inspiration and motivation inextricably woven throughout the classic collection of the wartime speeches of Winston Churchill. There is no questioning the familiar Churchillian elements within its lines, but its heart belies the mission of a sentinel. It is a blueprint for the calling up of courage in the doing of the difficult things, the right things, even when one must stand alone. It is a voice from the past which speaks clearly to the present and blazes a trail to the future. Bristling and blunt, it embodies a spirit which was needed in his time and is needed in ours: truth, optimism, duty, bravery, and hope.

Why do the words and pronouncements of Winston Churchill not only survive, but still speak? Was it his considerable talents in crafting the English language? Was it his amazing ability to create a symbiotic relationship between the written and spoken word? Was it because he wrote his speeches not merely as prose, but for effective delivery? Or did the secret lie not in stylized rhetoric, but in substantive realities communicated? There is little argument Mr. Churchill's flair for fine-tuning the English language has few rivals. Many have cited the beauty and resonance of his often-appropriated "Psalm-form" with its mono-syllabic phrases and hard, rolling cadences. His technique was to write, in the modern sense, in "sound bites," making masterful use of rhetorical questions he answered himself.[19] His ornamental oratory, rhythmic and moving, would not have been important during domestic debates but was absolutely critical to the survival of his nation during time of war. At a time when words changed history, his visual style of speaking lifted a nation's morale, strengthened its resolve, and gave it hope. Once described as "verbal pomp and emotional circumstance," his words were not only emotional, they were essential.[20] His speeches were not only lyrical, they were life-supporting. Therefore, we remember him as much for *what* he said as *how* he said it. At the core of the grand themes he employed—ancient notions of duty, honor, patriotism, and devotion—lay the unshakable, time-tested, and history-proven truths that ideas have consequences and ideas rule the world.

No matter how turbulent and tempest-tossed the times become, the speech that shook the world recalls the fixed and fundamental truths of life validated by human history. No matter what challenges lie ahead for liberty and democracy, *The Sinews of Peace* reassures Britain and America their strong bond of alliance and friendship must, and will, endure. With firm faith, its uplifting finish never doubts the continuance of the great heritage of a stalwart people:

> *Do not suppose that half a century from now you will not see 70 or 80 millions of Britons spread about the world united in defense of our traditions, and our way of life, and of the world causes which you and we espouse. . .*
>
> *If all British moral and material forces and convictions are joined with your own in fraternal association, the high roads of the future will be clear, not only for us but for all, not only for our time, but for a century to come.*[21]

A   The reference to the 5th century BC individual is undoubtedly Pericles.
    Considered the greatest leader of ancient Greece, Pericles brought democracy
    to its fullest measure and unified his nation. A statesman of the first order,
    Pericles is remembered primarily as "the leading citizen of Athens" who
    presided over that ancient land's finest hour: "the Golden Age of Greece."

B   *A Man for All Seasons* swept the major categories at the 1966 Academy Awards
    including: Best Picture, Best Director, Best Screenplay, and Best Actor.

C   To commemorate the historic visit and speech by Winston Churchill,
    Westminster College re-constructed the Church of St. Mary the Virgin,
    Aldermanbury, a 12th century London church designed by Britain's most
    celebrated architect and designer of magnificent St. Paul's Cathedral in London,
    Sir Christopher Wren. The church was dismantled stone by stone and erected
    on the Westminster campus and dedicated in 1969. The beautiful edifice
    is the only authentic Wren building in the United States.

D   In the days that followed, President Truman distanced himself from Churchill,
    as did Britain and the world. As the Cold War escalated and communism spilled
    out from the borders of Russia, Truman later told the British Lion, "Your
    prophecy has come true."

E   Winston Churchill did not invent or initiate the metaphor "iron curtain."
    The phrase cropped up during the war and had been used in German
    communiqués later discovered. The origin is most likely from Josef Goebbels
    in messages describing how the advancing Red Army formed a curtain of
    iron and literally shut down Nazi armies as they attempted to invade Russia.
    Churchill was using the term in telegrams before the end of the war.

F   In the victory over the repressive system of communism and its dismantlement
    in the former Soviet Union, this foreign policy doctrine was well-applied a half-
    century later by one of Mr. Churchill's notable successors, British Prime Minister
    Margaret Thatcher, and her American counterpart and friend, President Ronald
    Reagan. The peace through strength doctrine was the lynchpin principle
    advocated in the winning of the Cold War.

Chapter 17

FORGE AND ANVIL

Now, at last they were beginning chapter one of the great story,
which no one on earth had read—which goes on forever—
in which every chapter is better than before.

C.S. Lewis
The Last Battle

What is the measure of a man? What shapes and molds him? What unique character qualities might he possess that change a world? The English word **character** is derived from Latin and means "to stamp and engrave through pressure." In times of great testing the true mettle of a man is laid bare. In those most difficult times character is revealed. The essence of greatness is often not readily seen but most often discovered in the simplicity of qualities stamped and engraved through pressure, qualities forged on the anvil of days. When the long life and career of Winston Churchill is examined, qualities of character that mold individual greatness must come to mind: *vision*—ability to see and understand what is ahead; *conviction*—steadfast belief in a cause or a goal; *courage*—boldness to act on what one believes; *determination*—resolve to persist in spite of challenges, circumstances, difficulties or defeats; *optimism*—confident and cheerful belief for the best possible outcome; *endurance*—to continue under pain and hardship without being overcome; *responsibility*—will to preserve the trust and guard the duty one has been given.[1]

One of the most encouraging aspects of the life of Winston Churchill is certainly his amazing longevity. But, more than living an abundance of years, each generation can take heart from how well he spent his near-century of life on earth. It is what he did with his life that captivates. It is his example of sheer perseverance that instructs. In May of 1940 when the preservation of the civilized world was at stake, the man met the moment and the moment met the man. At the age of sixty-five, when most are entering their retirement years, Winston Churchill rose to heights of historic greatness, not just as Prime Minister of Great Britain, but as a symbol of defiance in the face of tyranny, a symbol of dedication in the fight for freedom. He did not just say, "Never give in!" He lived it. In March of 1946, at the ripe old age of seventy, Winston Churchill did not relinquish his vaunted place at the heights of historic greatness. Just months after the climax of one of civilization's greatest struggles, once again the man met the moment and the moment met the man. With a sense of duty, he assessed the post-war situation. With decisiveness, he evaluated a course of action. With courage, he warned the world of what might come. With responsibility, he prepared the world for what *did* come.

The spirit of Churchill at age six. His "chubby defiance" would define him in history and preserve his world.
(The Broadwater Collection)

What life lessons can be modeled by the example of Winston Churchill? Reminiscent of the words of King Solomon written three millennia ago, the life and legacy of Winston Churchill is a model of inspiration, perseverance, and hope: *"Sow your seed in the morning and at evening let not your hands be idle, for you do not know which will succeed, whether this or that, or whether both will do equally well."*[2] At the dawn of his public life, Winston Churchill burst onto the world stage to defend King and Country armed with but a single pistol. At the seeming twilight of his life, Winston Churchill dominated an era and shaped a world.

In "Savior of the West," Assumption College Professor Daniel Mahoney explains this incomparable individual's indelible impact on his times and our history:

> *It was precisely Churchill's old-fashioned engagement with the dramatic aspects of human history that allowed him to articulate perfectly what was at stake in the great conflict between National Socialism and what he did not hesitate to call 'liberal and Christian civilization.' Churchill's magnificent speeches during the Battle of Britain reminded the beleaguered citizens of Great Britain that they were fighting for enduring principles and allowed them to rise above their mortal selves...In 1946, at Fulton, Missouri, he warned a tired and complacent America about the threat to liberal values and world peace posed by an aggressive Communist tyranny in charge of the destiny of half of Europe. . . These remarkable successes in the twilight of his life were made possible by a lifetime of action and reflection that prepared him for participation in a monumental drama. That life still inspires, because—despite its limitations—it embodied genuine human greatness.*[3]

It only took a matter of months from the "iron curtain speech" for Mr. Churchill's blunt assessment to blossom into reality. The Second World War was over and Berlin laid waste by Stalin's Red Army, conditions were critical for a take-over by an occupying power. The consequences of a single decision would be felt for the next half-century. The Allies agreed to Soviet occupation and allowed Germany and its once proud capital to be divided in two: East and West. In the West, France controlled the north, the United States controlled the south, and Great Britain controlled the center. In the East, the Soviet Union controlled it all. From this point, the Soviet Premier took every measure to prevent any contact with the Western allies by East Germany or the eastern sector of her beleaguered capital city. A philosophical, metaphorical, and literal line was drawn: communist Germany in the East and democratic Germany in the West. Over the next 36 months, tensions heightened. A Soviet noose tightened around East Berlin. Preparing for the inevitable arrival of American and British forces, Stalin set up "the Russian zone." Determined to destroy the remnants of his former foes, Stalin closed off East Germany to the outside world. A curtain of iron descended across the West. Churchill had been right.

In June of 1948, ingredients for a "cold" war were brewing. The Soviets firmly held their grip on their European territory and imposed a blockade of Berlin. Stalin used the infamous Hitler ploy, "Let's see what the West will do..." with a strategy to force the United States, Britain, and France out of Germany. The Americans were determined to act. The blockade was countered with one of the most dramatic rescues in history—the Berlin airlift. Over twenty thousand U.S. troops surrounded by a half million Red soldiers passed through a hundred miles of now Soviet territory.[A] United States Navy convoys shipped tons of fuel, and Navy pilots dropped over 7,000 tons of cargo—vital supplies of food and medicine—to the trapped and starving Berliners. The deliverance of Berlin beat the Russians without firing a shot. Stalin knew now what the West could do. He backed off and backed down. An uneasy peace set in as "war in the shadows began."[4]

Shifting from uneasy ally, the Soviet Union was now a looming threat. Within a dozen years after the iron curtain clanged shut on nations the Western allies sacrificed to liberate, Josef Stalin's successor, Nikita Khrushchev "cut Berlin in half." The building of *Die Mauer* or "The Wall" began. On August 12, 1961, East German workers began digging postholes and pouring concrete all along one of the major streets of Berlin, *Friedrich Strasse.* In the early morning hours of August 13 the workers brought out huge spools of barbed wire and began stringing miles of the material along the thoroughfare. The people knew the gateway to freedom was closing fast. The "wall" literally tore families apart. From the Eastern sector of Berlin, fathers would leave in the morning for their work in the Western sector and be unable to return home that evening. Children would visit their grandparents in one sector, and be barred from returning to their parents or their home. Erected at intervals all along the barricade were watchtowers manned by heavily armed East German border guards. Over the many months and years to follow, thousands were shot and killed attempting to escape to freedom. By autumn of 1961, tons of concrete and miles of barbed wire were in place. By February of 1962, the permanent concrete wall[B] was completed. It was said that West Berlin became "an isolated island of freedom deep inside the communist block."[5]

The Free World began a decades-long standoff with the Communists behind the "iron curtain."[C] The memorable metaphor forever attributed to Winston Churchill became the all-encompassing term to describe the divisions of Europe and a continent divided between tyranny and liberty. The Berlin Wall was not only a concrete barrier, it became a symbol of communist oppression in the 20th century. The "wall" became the stark reality of the "iron curtain." The infamous barrier became the embodiment of one of Winston Churchill's harshest statements about the ideology of communism. A statement proved, once again, to be prophetic, for nothing would be settled with Russia until everything was settled forty years later at the complete fall of the Berlin Wall and the Soviet Union:

> *Of all the tyrannies in history, the Bolshevist tyranny is the worst, the most destructive, the most degrading. . . It would be a mistake to assume that nothing can be settled with Soviet Russia unless or until everything is settled.*[6]

As the world faced the challenges of the nuclear age, the iron curtain, with all its ramifications and consequences, became the dividing line between two belief systems. In an effort to quell the ever-present tensions, America's new and young President John F. Kennedy declared in 1961: "Better a wall than a war."[D] In June of 1963, mere months before his assassination, JFK arrived in West Berlin. Greeted by "a sea of people," he addressed the people of East Berlin, and by extension, all those enslaved by the tyranny of communism. His words shook the world—both East and West:

> *Freedom has many difficulties and democracy is not perfect, but we have never had to put up a wall to keep our people in! All free men, wherever they may live, are citizens of Berlin. So, therefore as a free man, I take pride in the words* **Ich Bin Ein Berliner!**[E]

It has been well said that "the courage of great men outlives them to become the courage of their people and the peoples of the world."[7] In June of 1987, West Berlin welcomed another President of the United States. Forty years after the brutal Berlin blockade and succeeding triumphant airlift, President Ronald Reagan stood on a specially built dais in front of the most famous access point through the Berlin Wall, Brandenburg Gate. His speech was the death knell for the infamous wall, a divided Europe, and the totalitarianism of the Communist states. President Reagan issued a challenge to Soviet President Mikhail Gorbachev, a challenge that reverberated around the world: *"Mr. Gorbachev, open this gate...Mr. Gorbachev, tear down this wall!"* Mr. Reagan's courageous contention marked the beginning of the end of communism's grip in Eastern Europe and became the staging point for the fall of the Soviet Union. Within 24 months, as border guards simply stood by and watched, Germans tore the wall down themselves and thousands poured across the forbidden zone. The Cold War was over, Eastern Europe was free, and the Soviet Union became Russia again.

The world witnessed once again the effect from a single speech by a courageous statesman. One speech foretold the Cold War, one speech finished it. At the advent of the Cold War, Winston Churchill warned of "an iron curtain descending across the Continent." At the demise of communism in half of Europe and a third of Asia, Ronald Reagan hastened the end of the Cold War with his intrepid call to freedom. When the Berlin Wall came down, so did the "iron curtain."

Through most of the life of Winston Churchill, what seemed to be a twilight was just one more dawn. One more campaign to wage, one more book to write, one more wrong to right: he was undaunted. Physically, mentally, and politically he seemed indestructible. His principles and convictions were inextricably woven into an elegant tapestry that was his life, a tapestry as colorful, as artistic, as intricate as the magnificent tapestries adorning the walls of his birthplace, Blenheim Palace. Majestic tapestries, visual and lasting reminders of the heritage of two valiant warriors bearing the same immortal name: CHURCHILL.

Perhaps the greatest living monument to the legacy of Winston Churchill is the enduring alliance and friendship between Great Britain and the United States. The white-hot fires of the Second World War forged a strong bond between the President of the United States and the Prime Minister of Great Britain, a bond that held fast and firm, a bond as vital and real today as it was sixty years ago. Differences in political affiliations have not separated it. Winds of war have buffeted, but not shaken it. It is resilient and resolute. In his second address to a Joint Session of the United States Congress at the height of the war, Prime Minister Churchill reaffirmed the insoluble bond between two nations:

> *The experiences of a long life and the promptings of my blood have wrought in me the conviction that there is nothing more important for the future of the world than the fraternal association of our two peoples in righteous work both in war and peace.*[8]

As the act of forging fashions metal by heating and hammering on the anvil, agreements are forged and fashioned from shared values, shared history, shared purpose. Forging also means to move ahead steadily and gradually toward a goal or destination. To move toward freedom and democracy, unencumbered bonds of alliance are vital for victory over the enemies of civilization. Inscribed for posterity on the wall of the Imperial War Museum and Cabinet War Rooms in London is a lasting tribute to a friendship forged in trials and in triumphs:

> *The alliance forged between Britain and the United States in that dark age of Nazi and Japanese tyranny stands to this day despite the passing of over half a century.*[9]

In an article entitled "In the Footsteps of Giants" best-selling author Jon Meacham draws fitting parallels between Franklin Roosevelt and Winston Churchill to the modern-day heirs of the Anglo-American Alliance, George W. Bush and Tony Blair:

> *Bush and Blair inherited an awesome legacy—a friendship that saved the world . . . They were brought together by, and together shaped, epic events . . . The Roosevelt-Churchill connection set the tone for a series of relationships between ensuing American Presidents and British Prime Ministers— Reagan and Thatcher, Bush and Blair—who were brought together by common interests and shared values . . . Bush and Blair—men of roughly the same generation, linked by common religious faith and a certitude that the war on terror requires steely resolve no matter what some European nations or the press might think—write their own chapter in the long story of Anglo-American relations. They, too, are held together by a shared sense of mission. As the wars of the 21st century take shape, George W. Bush and Tony Blair are working in the shadow and style the Great Men of World War II.*[10]

Recalling the special relationship and enduring role of the Transatlantic Alliance, Sir Winston's grandson, Winston S. Churchill, penned an article for the *Wall Street Journal* on the eve of the Iraq War. His words reaffirmed the basis of a strong and lasting union:

Like President Reagan before him, George W. Bush has what my grandfather would have called 'the root of the matter' in him. He is able to discern the most important issues of the day and to stand firm by his beliefs. Likewise, Tony Blair. On Iraq and the Anglo-American alliance, the British Prime Minister has got it absolutely right: he is pursuing the true national interest of Great Britain, which is to stand at the side of the Great Republic, as my grandfather was fond of calling the land of his mother's birth.[11]

In November of 2003, six months after the initial phase of the war of liberation in Iraq, George W. Bush traveled to London with the First Lady and top members of his Cabinet. Mr. Bush became the first American president welcomed by the Prime Minister to speak at Whitehall Palace[F] and the first President since Woodrow Wilson invited to stay with the royal family at Buckingham Palace. The President was honored on his official state visit to Whitehall by the attendance of Her Majesty, Queen Elizabeth II and His Royal Highness, Prince Philip. On the eve of the President's visit, Prime Minister Tony Blair reaffirmed the special bond between nations and friends:

Much has been said about the Anglo-American Alliance. Let me be perfectly clear. This is not merely an alliance between Britain and America that exists because of our historical relationship or one of a shared history. Our alliance exists because of shared values. Our alliance exists to address the struggles in the 21st century.

At Whitehall, the name synonymous with the center of the Government of the United Kingdom, President George W. Bush laid down the principles behind the War on Terror, affirmed his commitment to forge ahead, and repaid the Prime Minister's compliment in his address to the people of America and Great Britain:

There remains a bit of England in every American. So much of our national character comes from you—and we're glad for it. The fellowship of generations is the cause for common beliefs. . . More than an alliance through security and commerce, the British and American people have an alliance of values. . . So much good has come from our Alliance of conviction and might. So much now depends on the strength of this Alliance as we go forward. The United States and Great Britain share a mission in the world beyond the balance of power or the simple pursuit of interest. We seek the advance of freedom and the peace that freedom brings. Together, our nations are standing and sacrificing for this high goal, in a distant land, at this very hour. And America honors the idealism and the bravery of the sons and daughters of Britain.

History holds securely the place of Franklin Roosevelt and Winston Churchill as two of the world's most decisive and powerful leaders, statesmen who influenced the outcome of one of civilization's most deadly conflicts. Yet, they could enjoy the most simple of life's pleasures. In 1943, at the height of the war, the President invited his friend for a weekend of rest and relaxation at his rural retreat in the shadow of the mountains of Pennsylvania. Not far from the famous Civil War battlefield of Gettysburg was Mr. Roosevelt's northern Maryland getaway he affectionately called Shangri-La. The world now knows it as Camp David.[6] A charming story is recounted about these contemporaries sitting side by side in canvas chairs on the banks of the tranquil waters of an old iron ore pit at the base of the rocky streams of the Catoctin Mountains. Mr. Roosevelt loved to fish while Mr. Churchill enjoyed just sitting by his friend relishing his favorite cigar. What vital strategies might have been mapped, what important decisions might have been made by an American and an Englishman relaxing on the banks of a quiet fishing hole. The historical irony of this little spot could hardly have escaped either man, for it lies not far from where American colonists extracted iron ore to make cannon balls used against the British in the War for Independence.[12]

Certainly one of the greatest strengths possessed by Winston Churchill was his indefatigable inspiration. He fulfilled a destiny as few had done before. He was dismissed many times as an anachronism—out of time and place. Yet he was, of all leaders, most needed in his own time. And, as history has continued to reveal, his particular brand of conviction, courage, and commitment has been the model for leaders of any generation. When the inspiration of history itself was needed most, he was resolute. He called up the courage of his countrymen—the courage he knew was there—and they answered. In this, he inspired not only his nation, but the world. In this, he still inspires all who are wise enough to hear his voice. And in this, history has bestowed upon him immortality.

In the Cabinet Room of 10 Downing Street, the Prime Minister of Great Britain, 1940-1945. (Imperial War Museum, MH-26392)

From a survey published in 2001 naming Sir Winston Churchill one of the greatest Britons of all time, he is remembered for moving the emotions of a people and a nation:

> *Every setback was countered with resolve—every success with words of inspiration. Winston Churchill was the consummate English bulldog who refused to come to heel! Britain was on the brink of defeat and Europe under Hitler's feet. His rhetoric and force of personality made Britain believe in victory! His speeches have stood the test of time. They still stir the emotions and reach the heart.*[13]

In the final days of the life of Winston Churchill, Sir Bernard Law Montgomery, the Supreme Commander of British forces in the Second World War, remembered the great man this way:

> *Never has any land found any leader who so matched the hour as did Sir Winston Churchill. When he spoke—in words that rang and thundered like the Psalms—we all said 'that is how we feel and that is how we shall bear ourselves.' He gave us the sense of being a dedicated people with a high purpose and an inevitable destiny. There was a moral magnificence about him which transforms the lead of lesser men into gold. He inspired us all.*[14]

Winston Churchill will also be remembered for his quickness in handling words and ideas, his talent for making clever remarks. In a word—wit. His unbeatable combination of irascible wit and irrepressible humor was never lost—especially on his adversaries. Blenheim Palace Librarian John Forster tells a wonderful story illustrating how even his barbs could display warmth. Before the opening night on the London stage of his acclaimed masterpiece, *Pygmalion,*" famed playwright and author George Bernard Shaw sent an invitation to an up and coming young political firebrand named Winston Churchill:

Dear Churchill,

Enclosed please find two tickets to the opening of my new play on the London stage. Come, bring a friend—if you have one.

Shaw

Never one to be upstaged, Churchill wrote back immediately:

Dear Shaw,

Thank you for the kind offer of tickets to your new play. I regret I am unable to attend the first night. However, I shall attempt to attend the second night—if there is one.

Churchill

In the years which followed his glory days, Mr. Churchill remained in Parliament. Not the most effective of opponents to the post-war Labour Government, he turned from politics to writing. It was said that on occasion he would rise to his feet in the House of Commons "to defend the historical continuity of our Island life." But now he was mostly content to feed his goldfish at Chartwell and pursue his passion for painting. He became quite the prodigious author, turning out his four-volume *A History of the English-Speaking Peoples* and his six-volume *The Second World War.* Both were incredible and incredibly successful. He and his beloved wife, Clementine, traveled the globe where in country after country he was greeted as "the Free World's honored guide and counselor." He took up horse-racing and achieved Churchillian success with his horse, *Colonist II,* which won a dozen races, most notably in 1951 at the *Winston Churchill Stakes.*[15] An active rider well into his 60s, he once remarked: *"There is nothing better for the inside of man than the outside of a horse."*

After living three-quarters of a century, at the age of 76, Winston Churchill was recalled a final time to lead his nation as Prime Minister. But, this time, it was in an era of peace. He had come full circle. At last he was acknowledged as a man for *all* seasons. He declared, "The last prize I seek to win is as the architect of a lasting peace." In 1952 he addressed a Joint Session of the United States Congress for a third and final time. Here he forcefully declared, "We must not lose hope!"[16]

The year 1953 was especially fulfilling for the grand old man as the well-deserved honors poured in, honors so wondrous there seemed no more left to gain. The newly crowned Queen Elizabeth II persuaded him to finally accept the Knight of the Garter. In the great solemnity of the ancient ritual, the grateful and faithful servant of his Sovereign, Winston Churchill accepted from her hand Britain's highest order of knighthood. Following the ceremony, *Sir* Winston Churchill walked directly behind the honor guard. Resplendent in the velvet robes and plumed hat of the Order, the incomparable statesman was the focus of the magnificent processional which wound through the throng gathered in the immense courtyard of Windsor Castle. That same year, Sir Winston was awarded one of the world's most coveted honors—the Nobel Prize. In the category of Literature, Winston Churchill was honored for his achievements as author and orator. Simply stated, he was feted for his excellent accomplishments "of the written and spoken word."[17]

In 1954, Mr. Churchill celebrated his 80th birthday. As he entered the revered chamber of the House of Commons, a lone drummer beat in Morse code the famous wartime message: "V-for-victory." The Prime Minister addressed his countrymen in the House he so loved: "I am now nearing the end of my journey." Four months later, he stepped down from his nation's highest office and left the world he spent his life to build. It was said that "he was almost beyond criticism as he was adequate in praise."[18] Re-elected at age 85 to Parliament, he returned to the place he had known for two-thirds of a century, the place where he had served during the reign of six sovereigns of the British Empire. This time he took a place on the back benches of Parliament. In the days which followed, Sir Winston opposed accepting a Lordship. He had no desire to be addressed as "Lord" for it would have taken him out of his beloved House of Commons and lost him the title he cherished most, "Mr. Churchill."

Time and again his colleagues in the House waited to hear him speak out as he had always done, but he kept still. In the evening of his life, he was content to just sit and listen to the lively debate between the leaders of his nation. A career unparalleled in history was winding down.

Always held by Americans in the highest regard and special esteem, in 1963 Winston Spencer Churchill was made an honorary citizen of the United States. He became the first individual so honored by America since the General Marquis de Lafayette. The first honorary citizen helped America fight against the British in the American War for Independence. The second was a British subject who fought with America to ensure the freedom of the world. In his remarks at the ceremony to confer the honorary citizenship, President John F. Kennedy beautifully stated what all present knew so well:

> *We meet to honor a man whose honor requires no meeting— for he is the most honored and honorable man to walk the stage of human history in the time in which we live. Whenever and wherever tyranny threatened, he always championed liberty. Facing firmly toward the future, he has never forgotten the past.[19]*

On January 24, 1965, two months after his 90th birthday, Winston Spencer Churchill passed into legend. Finally, ultimately, irrevocably the entity which had been known simply as "the voice" was forever stilled. Stricken by a stroke, for nine days a grieving public held vigil. For nine days the pages of history waited. At 8:00 AM on a Sunday morning the great bell of St. Paul's Cathedral tolled the mournful message—he was gone. For three days and nights his body lay in state in the place reserved only for Kings, ancient Westminster Hall.[1] Contemporary writers noted: "In sorrow, but more in pride, the British paid their last tribute to the man who had touched them with greatness."[20] In the bitter cold of a London winter, a third of a million Britons lined up for hours to silently pass by his coffin. Ceremoniously draped by his nation's distinctive flag,[3] the coffin which bore his earthy remains also displayed

With casket draped in the Union Jack, the body of Sir Winston Churchill lies in state. In Westminster Hall, lines of mourners pass by. At the four corners of the coffin, four Life Guards in full dress stand with heads bowed and swords at rest. (© The Associated Press)

his nation's highest honor. Resting on a black velvet pillow atop his country's colors lay the insignia of the Order of the Garter.

The body of Winston Churchill was borne by the Royal Navy Gun Crew on a gun carriage reserved for royalty. Tens of thousands grieving countrymen lined the streets of London and watched in silence as Lady Churchill rode by in the Queen's own horse-drawn coach. Flanked by Her Majesty's personal guards regaled in scarlet coats, the splendid processional proceeded to the most fitting place for the funeral of the man who led his nation through its darkest days. The last rites for Winston Churchill would be given in the magnificent edifice still standing after the Blitz—St. Paul's Cathedral. One of the world's largest cities, usually bustling and busy, was hushed. The processional seemed to tell Mr. Churchill's life story.

From St. Margaret's Church where he and Clementine were married, the cortège passed by the many government offices associated with him: Treasury, where he served as Chancellor of the Exchequer; Ministry of Munitions, where his idea of the land tank was developed; the Colonial Office, reminding the nation of his firm belief in the civilizing merits of colonialism; the War Office, a fitting place for a valiant soldier from the trenches of World War I; 10 Downing Street, where he walked across the street and into history; the Admiralty, from where he commanded the Royal Navy in two World Wars; and Trafalgar Square with its imposing statue of Lord Nelson.[K] The great Nelson, like Churchill, saved his nation and preserved freedom across the globe because he dared to take impossible risks.[21] At last he arrived at St. Paul's. Standing still on the great stone steps, the Queen of England awaited him.[L]

Under the grand dome of St. Paul's Cathedral, with every pew filled to capacity, the casket was regally borne up the great aisle. The magnificent choir sang *"Who would true valour see, Let him come hither..."* Monarchs and ministers, commoners and peers, all stood. Lady Churchill in long, black veil was accompanied by her only son, Randolph. The casket placed atop the catafalque was fittingly flanked by the tombs of the nation's greatest soldier, The Duke of Wellington, and the nation's greatest sailor, Lord Nelson. Interred in the corner directly across, Dr. Samuel Johnson,[M] literary titan of the 18th century, seemed to provide the perfect epitaph: *"A man's words live on long after him."*[22]

Amid the breathtaking beauty of one of the world's most spectacular houses of worship, amid the royalty of many nations and leaders from around the world, the simple elegance of the Anglican burial service was conducted. The Dean of St. Paul's opened with the simplicity of true words: "Brethren, we are assembled here on occasion of the burial of a great man who has rendered memorable service to his country and to the cause of freedom."[23]

At the close of the service, all stood to sing the final song, Mr. Churchill's personal favorite, the majestic anthem of the American Civil War, *Battle Hymn of the Republic.* Its spirited strains resounded through the cathedral and evoked once again the strong alliance that had preserved the Free World. When the glorious reverberations ceased, all remained standing, silent and still to the stirring notes from a single trumpet. As if the sky had been pierced, *Reveille* recalled the eternal morning awaiting. Final notes rang in solemn refrain as *The Last Post* reminded all present the day was done. The last call had been given. Winston Spencer Churchill had passed into the ages.

One last duty remained, the trip to his final resting place. As the grieving family departed the service, behind them walked the Heralds of Britain's College of Arms, one bearing a standard with the brilliant colors of the Churchill family coat of arms. RAF jets soared overhead in memory of the man who gave grateful tribute to "the few" who once served in their ranks, the gallant fighter pilots who, against all odds, defeated the greatest air armada in history. Eight Grenadier guards in somber silence bore his remains aboard the launch for his final ride across the Thames. Following the route used for the last ride of Lord Nelson, the Navy skimmer crossed the famed river. Lining both sides of the Thames were the huge cranes and derricks of a modern industrial city, bent down halfway as if to bow in homage.[24] London seemed to stop as only the crack of cannon and the drone of bagpipes could be heard along one of the world's busiest waterways.

With family by his side, the mortal remains of Winston Churchill were placed on a special train at Waterloo Station. The unused rail line was reopened for his final trip home to rest in the shadow of his birthplace. With Blenheim Palace gleaming in the distance, his body was carried to the private burial in the simplicity of rustic Bladon Churchyard, exactly one mile from the place which helped shape his destiny. Now he would rest in peace, as he wished, with his ancestors.

Beautifully said of him at the time of his passing was "the indomitable spirit outlives the clay." It has. Announcing to the world the news of his death, the BBC broadcast a simple statement followed by the three dots, one dash tones for the letter "V" in Morse code. The unmistakable notes recalled the introduction to Beethoven's *Fifth Symphony* that precluded Mr. Churchill's wartime broadcasts and became a signal code to the European resistance fighters. Now, they reminded the world of a fighting spirit left to history. All over the United Kingdom, from the Houses of Parliament to every ship in the

Royal Navy, the Union Jack flew at half-staff. The *Times of London*, for the first time ever, printed no advertisements on its front page, just a tribute to "the greatest Englishman of his time." Famed Lloyds of London, renowned for insuring the great ships on the world's oceans, tolled its giant bell only once at the stroke of noon as it had always done when a great ship, long overdue to port, had been lost at sea.[25] In a specially convened memorial session held in the House of Commons, tributes by friends and former foes were heard in a chamber filled to overflowing. The most powerful image was one vacant seat, the seat that for decades was always for Mr. Churchill.[26]

Winston Spencer Churchill was the rarest of statesmen. He mastered events. At his passing, former President Harry S Truman said: *"Winston Churchill's mortal remains have passed on, but his spirit will live for centuries. He typified man's resolution to be free and man's courage to face and overcome those who would threaten his liberties and free institutions."*[27] Oxford scholar, author, and Churchill contemporary Isaiah Berlin said of him: *"His world is built upon the supreme value of action, of the battle between simple good and simple evil, between life and death—but above all, battle. He always fought. To the demoralized French in 1940: 'we shall fight on forever and ever!' and under this sign his whole life has been lived."*[28]

Former President Dwight D. Eisenhower remembered "that moving winter day when his soul was committed to the hands of God amid stately pageantry." The Supreme Commander of Allied forces in World War II reflected upon the unimpeachable place in history occupied by his friend, Sir Winston Churchill. As Mr. Eisenhower lamented the loss to the world, he cautioned his countrymen to protect the future by guarding the past:

Winston Churchill typified the valor and stamina of his great nation. With unequaled eloquence and indomitable will, he rallied his people. In their desperate plight he gave them morale—and in warfare, morale is everything. As Prime Minister of Great Britain, Sir Winston Churchill fought tyranny with words that sang like the Psalms and with deeds that defied surrender. . . As I knelt at St. Paul's, around me were old shields, old flags, and old prayers—all the evidence of Britain's long continuity—and I wondered if we in the United States with our devotion to the new at the expense of the old, to the future at the expense of the past, are not forsaking something precious. For only a nation steeped in history and pride could produce a Churchill.[29]

Winston Spencer Churchill: troubled child, young soldier, man of action, adventurous historian, matchless orator, resolute leader, world hero, man of his century, towering champion of Western civilization. Winston Spencer Churchill: unabashed Victorian, unapologetic patriot,.dweller of the past, ready for the future.

Sir Winston Churchill forged for his nation and the Western world the understanding of why we fight. He lived in view of his mortality. In time of terror, his indomitable spirit lives on in immortality. The world shall forever be fortunate to follow a brand of leadership he fashioned for himself and his nation in its finest hour.

What through the radiance which was once so bright
Be now forever taken from sight,
Though nothing can bring back the hour
Of splendour in the grass, of glory in the flower;
We will grieve not, rather find strength in what remains behind.
William Wordsworth, *Intimations of Immortality*

A   American troops, tanks, and armored divisions followed along the famed Fulba Gap, the ancient path taken by the barbarians who, in AD 410, poured over the borders of the Roman Empire and sacked its capital city—Rome.

B   There was actually a west wall and an east wall. In the middle was a ribbon of ground that formed a corridor and came to be called "the death strip." It was "a killing zone" fortified by miles of barbed wire, machine gun fortified watchtowers, and walking patrols accompanied by attack dogs. There was no doubt as to its purpose—to keep East Berliners captive.

C   The "iron curtain" became the political, military, and ideological barrier erected by the Soviet Union to seal off itself and its communist-controlled satellite countries of Eastern Europe from open contact with the free nations of the world.

D.   It has been said Ronald Reagan believed President Kennedy's stance to be an act of appeasement and that Reagan cited this statement crucial to his decision to leave the Democrat Party to join the Republican Party. Both Kennedy and Reagan were life-long ardent anti-communists. Historians have stated Mr. Reagan's metamorphosis a natural progression of events in his life.

E.   John F. Kennedy's famous words translate: "I am a Berliner!" This bold affirmation declared that all free people were as one, no matter in which nation across the globe they lived.

F.   Once the regal residence of the Archbishops of York, Whitehall Palace was the main home of the British monarchs from 1530 to 1698. Once called York Palace, it was inhabited by the highest churchman in the reign of King Henry VIII, Cardinal Wolsey. Fallen from favor and stripped of his power during the turbulent time of the King's dramatic divorce, Wolsey's home was relinquished to Henry who built it into the largest palace in Europe. During Churchill's time at the helm in the Fighting Forties, Whitehall was at the hub of action as it housed the Ministry of Defence. Today, the Cabinet offices of the British government are located at Whitehall. Considering the often rough-and-tumble debate in the House of Commons, perhaps it is fitting that built on the site of King Henry VIII's cockfighting pit is the residence of the Prime Minister of Great Britain, 10 Downing Street.

G.   President Truman made the location an official residence. President Eisenhower renamed FDR's hideaway "Camp David" after his grandson, David Eisenhower. It is still the primary place of rest and relaxation used by the President of the United States. Camp David has been the scene of many high-level Presidential conferences and international summits with invited foreign heads of state.

H.   *Pygmalion* opened at the Park Theatre in London on October 12, 1914. This unforgettable story has been performed countless times all over the world. Made into a musical motion picture in 1965, it has become the adored classic film, *My Fair Lady*.

^I   Westminster Hall adjoins the House of Commons. Its stone walls were erected in 1097 by the son of William, the Conqueror, King Rufus.

^J   The flag of the United Kingdom is called the Union Jack. It is comprised of layered red, white, and blue crosses: the red vertical and horizontal cross of St. George for England, the white "X" cross on a blue field of St. Andrew for Scotland, and the red "X" cross on a white field of St. Patrick for Ireland.

^K   In honoring Sir Winston Churchill, Queen Elizabeth broke royal precedent by attending the funeral of a commoner. She also made history by waiving her right to enter the cathedral last.

^L   Lord Horatio Nelson was one of history's most brilliant military tacticians and most daring of commanders. Britain's premier Admiral during the Napoleonic Wars, Lord Nelson won a spectacular victory in the decisive Battle of Trafalgar. France and Spain had formed an alliance to crush England. On October 21, 1805, off the coast of Spain, Nelson lined his fleet up against the enemy. In a stunning act of courage on the high seas, Nelson's flagship, *Victory*, broke through the French line and soundly defeated the enemy vessels. Not one British ship was lost, and Napoleon abandoned his plan to invade England. Nearing the end of the battle, Lord Nelson was felled by a French sniper. Carried below deck, he lived long enough to know of the victory. His last words were, "Thank God I have done my duty." His legacy was to make the high seas free for all nations and ensure British naval supremacy for a century.

^M   Dr. Samuel Johnson has been considered 18th century England's most outstanding personage. His monumental work, Dictionary of the English Language, published in 1755 was a milestone. His edition on Shakespeare with its acclaimed Preface, placed the playwright at the pinnacle of literary giants.

A RENDEZVOUS

Many men are great, but few capture the imagination and the spirit of the times. The ones who do are unforgettable.
Ronald Reagan

Winston Churchill had a rendezvous with history. He kept it. Those of us in the civilized world know how *well* he kept it. Today, at Westminster Abbey, history keeps a rendezvous with him. As each new generation turns to the past for the strength and inspiration to face the future, men and women are encouraged by the lives and testimonies of great individuals. There, inscribed on a simple plaque are the words: REMEMBER WINSTON CHURCHILL.

The visual qualities of Churchill the man are indelibly impressed in our memories. The newsreel footage, photographs from that dark and triumphant era, his unique physicality, all create a vivid picture: his look of "a scowling cherub" as he reluctantly stood for his most famous portrait; the English bulldog features with trademark cigar clenched tightly in his teeth; the derby hat either placed firmly atop his sparsely planted scalp, or held aloft by his cane as he made his way through cheering crowds madly scrambling to catch a glimpse of him; and the famous "V" for victory sign, his very own expression which became a symbol of courage, determination, and hope. His very image has become, in modern times, the very embodiment of the indomitable British spirit:

Trust the people! I shall tell them the worst,
they won't let the Old Country down!'

The last Sovereign Mr. Churchill gratefully served was Her Majesty, Queen Elizabeth II. At his passing, Britain's reigning monarch succinctly summarized what this one life had meant to her cherished realm:

The survival of this country and the sister nations of the Commonwealth in the face of the greatest danger that has ever threatened them will be a perpetual memorial to his leadership, his vision, and his indomitable courage.[2]

In Guy Eden's post-war chronicle, *Portrait of Churchill*, he closed with the following admonition to every generation that will live in the shadow of a giant of history:

The name of Winston Churchill runs like a thread through the history of this century. He has made his indelible mark on the story of our times—on the history of all time. We of this generation ought to know our Winston Churchill. Unless we can get in our minds a clear picture of him, we shall not get a clear picture of the history of our own times.

After Winston Churchill passed into immortality, eloquent statements were made the world over from kings and queens, Presidents and Prime Ministers. The most impressive by far came from an unlikely and humble source, the old lion's bodyguard, Sgt. Edmund Murray of Scotland Yard. With simple clarity Mr. Murray reminded the world of its loss and history of its gain:

Well, he's gone now. When the king is dead we say, "The King is dead. Long live the King." What do we say now? Who is there to talk of?[3]

During a time that shaped Winston Churchill as few others, a stern yet tender poem was penned by a World War I Canadian medical officer. Crumpled copies, sometimes smeared with blood, were found in the pockets of fallen Allied soldiers lain across the battlefields of France—deathless warriors who had a rendezvous with history—and kept it. The doleful refrains remind as long as heroes live, the torch of liberty will never be extinguished. Though it fall to the ground, it must only wait for dedicated and determined hands to take it up again, dutiful hands ready and willing to pass it to those who come after. This spirit of the continuity of liberty cannot die. This spirit of duty and honor survives:

In Flanders fields the poppies blow
Between the crosses, row on row.
That mark our place, and in the sky
The larks still bravely singing, fly
Scarce heard amid the guns below.

We are the Dead. Short days ago
We lived, felt dawn, saw sunset glow,
Loved and were loved, and now we lie
In Flanders Fields.

Take up our quarrel with the foe:
To you from failing hands we throw
The torch; be yours to hold it high.
If ye break faith with us who die,
We shall not sleep, though poppies grow
In Flanders Fields.

[*In Flanders Fields* was reprinted in America and used as a recruitment incentive. For two generations, American schoolchildren read it in their textbooks. Flanders Field is a United States military cemetery in Flanders, Belgium, where hundreds of Allied soldiers lie peacefully under rows of white crosses.]

Addendum

More Wit and Wisdom from Sir Winston

Churchill on politics:
> *Politics are almost as exciting as war and quite as dangerous, although in war you can be killed only once, in politics many times.*

Churchill on party politics:
> *Some men change their party for the sake of their principles; others their principles for the sake of their party.*

Churchill on political reality:
> *We have no lasting friends, no lasting enemies, only lasting interests.*

Churchill observing a political neophyte:
> *He's the only bull I know who carries his china shop around with him.*

Churchill on power:
> *Power, for the sake of lording it over fellow-creatures or adding to personal pomp is rightly judged base. But power in a national crisis, when a man believes he knows what orders should be given, is a blessing.*

Churchill on democracy:
> *Democracy is the worst form of government except for all those other forms that have been tried from time to time.*

Churchill on war and peace:
> *I have always urged fighting wars and other contentions with might and main till overwhelming victory, and then offering the hand of friendship to the vanquished.*

Churchill on socialism:
> *There are only two places where socialism will work: Heaven, where it's not needed, and Hell, where they already have it.*

Churchill, the philosopher:

> *If you're not a liberal at 20 you have no heart. If you're still a liberal at 30 you have no brain.*

Churchill on the Anglo-American union:

> *My mother was American and my ancestors were officers in Washington's army. I am an English-speaking union.*

Churchill on outlook:

> *The pessimist sees the difficulty in every opportunity. The optimist sees the opportunity in every difficulty.*

Churchill on book writing:

> *Writing a book is an adventure. To begin with it is a toy and an amusement. Then it becomes a mistress, then it becomes a master, then it becomes a tyrant.*

Churchill on true friendship:

> *In describing Lord Beaverbrook, he remarked, "Max is a foul-weather friend."*

Churchill on duty:

> *Deserve victory.*

Churchill on eternity:

> *I am prepared to meet my Maker, whether my Maker is prepared for the great ordeal of meeting me is another matter.*

Churchill on legacy:

> *The span of mortals is short, the end universal. Noble spirits yield themselves willingly to the successively failing shades which carry them to a better world or to oblivion.*

SUGGESTED CLASSIC FILMS FROM THE WORLD WAR II ERA

The Mortal Storm   1940

Set in 1933, this powerful film is based on the novel by the same name which chronicles the tragic results of the rise of Hitler and Nazism on a German family. It examines the cost of convictions and choices on both sides of the struggle and unforgettably portrays the ultimate price of freedom. Adolf Hitler was so outraged by its message, that he had it and all MGM productions banned from Germany and "the Third Reich."

The Sea Hawk   1940

One of Winston Churchill's favorite films, this exciting Errol Flynn swashbuckler personifies the patriotism and courage of Sir Francis Drake during the reign of Elizabeth I prior to the planned invasion of England by the Spanish Armada. The last speech, delivered by one of the best portrayals of Queen Elizabeth on film, was actually written for the movie-goers of the day and directed not at Philip of Spain, but at Adolf Hitler and his planned invasion of Britain.

Mrs. Miniver   1942

This story of a typical British family and their indomitable spirit during WWII garnered five major Academy Awards including Best Picture. The film's last speech by the town minister is so compelling, FDR had it printed and given to Allied troops. Winston Churchill said of Mrs. Miniver: "It has done more for the British war effort than a fleet of battleships."

Casablanca   1942

The definitive World War II film and considered one of the greatest motion pictures ever produced. Intrigue, love and hate; Nazis and a European freedom fighter; courage, country, duty, and honor; denial of self and the price of liberty—all at Rick's Café.

Edge of Darkness   1943

Critics agree that this is one of the best films about WWII made during the war. It is a story of the underground resistance fighters in Nazi-occupied Norway with application to the freedom-fighters from the captured countries of the day. An underlying theme illustrates what can happen to a nation when tyranny threatens and its people are without the ability to defend themselves.

Watch on the Rhine   1943

A German resistance leader visits pre-Pearl Harbor America and is faced with the dilemma of killing a Nazi spy or allowing his resistance friends in Germany to be murdered. Because the United States had not yet entered the war, the questions evoked become: is this murder or an act of war, and is there a universal law above the laws of nations that a civilization must adhere to if it is to survive?

In Our Time   1943

Set in Poland before the Nazis invade on September 1, 1939 and Britain declares war on Germany, this film chronicles the struggles within an aristocratic family whose members experience the disintegration of their world and their choice between appeasement and dishonor or death and deathless glory. The valor of the Polish resistance set against the might of the armies of the Third Reich makes for an unforgettable climax.

BIBLIOGRAPHY

PROLOGUE
1. Realm, January/February 2002
2. Time for Truth, Os Guinness, Baker Books, Grand Rapids © 2000
3. The Weekly Standard, March 29, 2004

ONE   THE WAY AHEAD
1. The Immortal Battalion, G.C.F. Productions © 1943 (narrator: Quentin Reynolds)
2. Dr. Kenneth Setton, National Geographic, Volume 130, 1966, "The 900th Anniversary of the Norman Conquest"
3. Life Magazine, February 5, 1965, Vol. 58, No. 5 [Churchill Funeral Edition] "The Last Honors" by Alan Moorehead
4. NPR "All Things Considered," February 11, 2005
5. "Defending Churchill's Legacy," University of Colorado Professor James Hume, NewsMax Magazine, July 2002
6. "Statesmanship and Its Betrayal," Mark Helprin, The Wall Street Journal, July 2, 1998
7. The Weekly Standard, January 10, 2000, "The Very Model of a Democratic Statesman," Christopher Matthews
8. "Britain's Bulldog," Neil Jones, Realm, December 2002, Vol. 107
9. National Geographic, "Be Ye Men of Valour," 1965 Churchill Funeral Edition
10. Readers Digest, "People I Have Loved, Known, or Admired" by Leo Rosten, Vol. 4 © 1971
11. The Great Republic by Sir Winston Churchill, edited by Winston S. Churchill, Random House, New York, © 1999
12. LOOK , January 12, 1965; Vol. 29, No. 1(Churchill Funeral Editon)
13. Sir Winston Churchill "The Final Tribute," Carolyn Bennett Patterson, National Geographic August 1965
14. LOOK, Vol. 29, No. 1, January 1965 (Churchill Funeral Editon)
15. The Wit and Wisdom of Sir Winston, Adam Sykes and Iain Sproat, Leslie Frewin Publishers, Ltd., London © 1965
16. "Blair's Finest Hour" by Paul Greenberg, The Washington Times, October, 2001
17. The Second World War, Volume 2 (Their Finest Hour), Houghton Mifflin Co.© 1948
18. The Second World War, Volume 6 (Closing the Ring), Houghton Mifflin Co.© 1948
19. The Second World War, Volume 1 (The Gathering Storm), Houghton Mifflin Co.©1948
20. Stephen Mansfield, Never Give In, Highland Books © 1995
21. Churchill: The Life Triumphant, United Press International , American Heritage Publishing Co, Inc. © 1965 [Definitions of character qualities from Character Sketches, Advanced Training Institute, Bill Gothard, Oakbrook, IL]

TWO   THEN AND NOW
1. The History of Britain, "The Two Winstons," Simon Schama, Volume VI, BBC Productions © 2001
2. "Winston is Back," Larry P. Arnn, Claremont Review of Books, Spring 2002 [reviews of Churchill: A Biography by Roy Jenkins and Churchill: A Study of Greatness by Geoffrey Best]
3. Charles Colson, Breakpoint, June 2002
4. Samuel Huntington, "The Clash of Civilizations," Foreign Affairs (Summer 1993)
5. Ibid.
6. "Fighting Fanaticism," Stephen Hayward, The Weekly Standard, 10-29-01
7. Christopher Hitchens, Atlantic Monthly, June 2004
8. "Fighting Fanaticism," Stephen Hayward, The Weekly Standard, 10-29-01
9. The River War: An Account of the Re-Conquest of the Sudan, Winston Churchill; Carroll & Graff Publishers
10. Ibid.

11. Ibid.
12. Ibid.
13. George W. Bush, White House Press Conference, March 19, 2004 [1st anniversary of Iraqi War]
14. Prime Minister Tony Blair, Annual Conference of Britain's Labour Party, September 30, 2003
15. Whitehall Palace, November 20, 2003; President George W. Bush, September 11, 2001
16. Ibid.
17. Winston S. Churchill, "The Cost of Freedom," Fox News Channel, March 19, 2003
18. President George W. Bush, Address to the United Nations General Assembly, September 21, 2003
19. The Lord of the Rings, Return of the King, New Line Cinema Productions,© 2004
20. Lend Me Your Ears: Great Speeches in History, William Safire, W.W. Norton & Co., New York; London, ©1992
21. Winston Churchill, 1948 speech to the Congress of Europe; the Hague, Brussels, Belgium

THREE   RECONNAISSANCE
1. The Apostle Paul's first letter to the Corinthians, New King James Version
2. Death of the Reich: The Last Days of World War II, The History Channel, 2003
3. The Second World War, Volume I (The Gathering Storm), Houghton Mifflin Co. © 1948
4. Why We Fight, Volume 2, "The Nazis Strike," U.S. War Department & Frank Capra Productions © 1943
5. The Seventh Cross, MGM (Metro Goldwyn Mayer) Productions, ©1944

FOUR   WOLF AT THE DOOR
1. The Second World War, Volume I (The Gathering Storm), Houghton Mifflin Co.© 1948
2. Ibid.
3. "Churchill and Goring," David Wolper Presents, The History Channel, 2002
4. "Churchill and Hitler" David Wolper Presents, The History Channel, 2002
5. The Second World War, Volume I (The Gathering Storm), Houghton Mifflin Co. © 1948
6. Our Century, The History Channel © 2003
7. Ibid.
8. Churchill: The Life Triumphant, United Press International , American Heritage Publishing Co, Inc. © 1965
9. Adolf Hitler, The History Channel © 2002
10. Ibid.

FIVE   IN THE WILDERNESS
1. Churchill Exhibit, Blenheim Palace (courtesy of the 11th Duke of Marlborough)
2. John Forster, Librarian, Blenheim Palace, Oxfordshire, England (interview, February, 2002)
3. Ibid.
4. Ibid.
5. Ibid.
6. Ibid.
7. William Shakespeare, The Tempest, Act 2, Scene 1
8. Churchill: The Life Triumphant, United Press International , American Heritage Publishing Co, Inc. © 1965
9. John Forster, Librarian, Blenheim Palace, Oxfordshire, England (interview, February, 2002)
10. Ibid.
11. The Blenheim Papers, Blenheim Palace (courtesy of the 11th Duke of Marlborough)
12. Churchill: The Life Triumphant, United Press International , American Heritage Publishing Co, Inc. © 1965
13. Ibid.
14. Allen Packwood, Director, Churchill Archives Centre, Cambridge University (interview, February, 2002)
15. Ibid.
16. Ibid.
17. Ibid.
18. The Wit of Sir Winston, Adam Sykes and Iain Sproat, Leslie Frewin Publishers, Ltd., London © 1965
19. Imprimis, Hillsdale College, Hillsdale, Michigan, January 2001

20. Allen Packwood, Director, Churchill Archives Centre, Cambridge University (interview, February, 2002)
21. Portrait of Churchill, Guy Eden; Hutchinson & Co., Ltd., London © 1945
22. The Second World War, Volume I, (The Gathering Storm), Houghton Mifflin Co.© 1948
23. Speech to the House of Commons, 1935 (Churchill: The Life Triumphant)
24. Churchill: The Life Triumphant, United Press International , American Heritage Publishing Co, Inc. © 1965
25. Churchill: The Unruly Giant, Norman Rose, The Free Press, NY & London, 1994
26. Imprimis, Hillsdale College, Hillsdale, Michigan, January 2001
27. "Thinking Things Over," The Wall Street Journal, Robert L. Bartley, March 17, 2003
28. Men and Nations, Anatole G. Mazour and John M. Peoples, Harcourt Brace, NY, 1971
29. Kingdoms in Conflict, "The Roots of War," Charles Colson, Zondervan Publishing House, 1987
30. Allen Packwood, Director, Churchill Archives Centre, Cambridge University (interview, February, 2002)
31. Lend Me Your Ears: Great Speeches in History, William Safire, W.W. Norton & Co., New York; London, ©1992

SIX   VINDICATED PROPHET
1. Churchill: The Life Triumphant, United Press International , American Heritage Publishing Co, Inc. © 1965
2. The Second World War, Volume 1, (The Gathering Storm), Houghton Mifflin Co.© 1948
3. Ibid.
4. Ibid.
5. Portrait of Churchill, Guy Eden; Hutchinson & Co., Ltd., London © 1945
6. The Second World War, Volume 1 (The Gathering Storm), Houghton Mifflin Co. © 1948
7. Ibid.
8. Churchill: The Life Triumphant, United Press International , American Heritage Publishing Co, Inc. © 1965
9 Ibid.
10. John Forster, Librarian, Blenheim Palace, Oxfordshire, England (interview, February, 2002)
11. "The Nuremberg Laws," PBS Broadcast, May 23, 2003   (Simon Wiesenthal Center Production)
12. Echoes from the Holocaust, Mira Kimmelman, University of Tennessee Press © 1997
13. "War Crimes," The Weekly Standard, June 2002
14. Adolf Hitler, The History Channel, 2002
15. Echoes from the Holocaust, Mira Kimmelman, University of Tennessee Press © 1997
16. The Second World War, Volume 1 (The Gathering Storm), Houghton Mifflin Co. © 1948
17. Never Again: A History of the Holocaust, Sir Martin Gilbert, Harper-Collins © 2000
18. The Second World War, Volume 1, (The Gathering Storm), Houghton Mifflin Co.© 1948
19. Why We Fight, Volume 2, "The Nazis Strike," U.S. War Department & Frank Capra Productions © 1943
20. Portrait of Churchill, Guy Eden; Hutchinson & Co., Ltd., London © 1945
21. Kingdoms in Conflict, "The Roots of War," Charles Colson, Zondervan Publishing House, 1987
22. Churchill: The Life Triumphant, United Press International , American Heritage Publishing Co, Inc. © 1965
23. The Second World War, Volume 1, (The Gathering Storm), Houghton Mifflin Co. © 1948
24. Ibid.
25. Why We Fight, Volume 2, "The Nazis Strike," U.S. War Department & Frank Capra Productions © 1943
26. Dr. Thomas Sowell, Human Events, Eagle Publishing Corporation, Washington, DC, 2002
27. Winston Churchill, First Lord of the Admiralty; Speech at Free Trade Hall, January 27, 1940

SEVEN   "VERY WELL, ALONE!"
1. The Second World War, Volume 2, (Their Finest Hour), Houghton Mifflin Co. © 1948
2. Churchill: The Life Triumphant, United Press International , American Heritage Publishing Co, Inc. © 1965
3. The Second World War, Volume 2, (Their Finest Hour), Houghton Mifflin Co. © 1948
4. Portrait of Churchill, Guy Eden; Hutchinson & Co., Ltd., London © 1945
5. The Second World War, Volume 2, (Their Finest Hour), Houghton Mifflin Co. © 1948
6. Portrait of Churchill, Guy Eden; Hutchinson & Co., Ltd., London © 1945
7. Allen Packwood, Director, Churchill Archives Centre, Cambridge University (interview, February, 2002)
8. The Second World War, Volume 2, (Their Finest Hour), Houghton Mifflin Co. © 1948

9. Churchill: The Life Triumphant, United Press International , American Heritage Publishing Co, Inc. © 1965
10. Five Days in London, John Lukacs, Yale University Press, © 1999.
11. Churchill: The Life Triumphant, United Press International , American Heritage Publishing Co, Inc. © 1965
12. Portrait of Churchill, Guy Eden; Hutchinson & Co., Ltd., London © 1945
13. Churchill: The Life Triumphant, United Press International , American Heritage Publishing Co, Inc. © 1965
14. Portrait of Churchill, Guy Eden; Hutchinson & Co., Ltd., London © 1945
15. The Second World War, Volume 2, (Their Finest Hour), Houghton Mifflin Co. © 1948
16. Churchill: The Life Triumphant, United Press International , American Heritage Publishing Co, Inc. © 1965
17. Ibid.
18. Ibid.
19. The Second World War, Volume 2, (Their Finest Hour), Houghton Mifflin Co. © 1948
20. Winston Churchill, The History Channel, 2002
21. The Second World War, Volume 2, (Their Finest Hour), Houghton Mifflin Co. © 1948

EIGHT   FIRE OVER ENGLAND
1. The Second World War, Volume 2, (Their Finest Hour), Houghton Mifflin Co. © 1948
2. Ibid.
3. Why We Fight, Volume 2, "The Nazis Strike," U.S. War Department & Frank Capra Productions © 1943
4. Portrait of Churchill, Guy Eden; Hutchinson & Co., Ltd., London © 1945
5. Why We Fight, Volume 4, "The Battle of Britain," U.S. War Department & Frank Capra Productions © 1943
6. "Churchill and Goring," David Wolper Presents, The History Channel, 2002
7. Adventures in English Literature, Rewey Belle Inglis and Josephine Spear, Harcourt, Brace & Co., New York ©1958
8. The Second World War, Volume 2, "The Wizard War," (Their Finest Hour), Houghton Mifflin Co. © 1948
9. "Churchill and Goring," David Wolper Presents, The History Channel, 2002
10. C. H. Davis interview, October, 2001 (The author's father, a veteran of the U. S. Navy during WWII, taught classes to Navy pilots in the use of RADAR and SONAR.)
11. "Winston Churchill," The History Channel, 2002
12. The Second World War, Volume 2, (Their Finest Hour), Houghton Mifflin Co. © 1948
13. Why We Fight, Volume 4, "The Battle of Britain," U.S. War Department & Frank Capra Productions © 1943
14. The Second World War, Volume 2, (Their Finest Hour), Houghton Mifflin Co. © 1948
15. Churchill: The Life Triumphant, United Press International , American Heritage Publishing Co, Inc. © 1965
16. Why We Fight, Volume 4, "The Battle of Britain," U.S. War Department & Frank Capra Productions © 1943
17. The Second World War, Volume 2, (Their Finest Hour), Houghton Mifflin Co. © 1948
18. "Modern Marvels: RADAR," The History Channel, 2003
19. Realm, March-April issue, 2001
20. Churchill: The Life Triumphant, United Press International , American Heritage Publishing Co, Inc. © 1965
21. Ibid.
22. Ibid.
23. Portrait of Churchill, Guy Eden; Hutchinson & Co., Ltd., London © 1945
24. John Forster, Librarian, Blenheim Palace, Oxfordshire, England (interview, February 2002)
25. Churchill: The Life Triumphant, United Press International , American Heritage Publishing Co, Inc. © 1965
26. Ibid.
27. Portrait of Churchill, Guy Eden; Hutchinson & Co., Ltd., London © 1945
28. Churchill: The Life Triumphant, United Press International , American Heritage Publishing Co, Inc. © 1965
29. Portrait of Churchill, Guy Eden; Hutchinson & Co., Ltd., London © 1945
30. Ibid.
31. Why We Fight, Volume 4, "The Battle of Britain," U.S. War Department & Frank Capra Productions © 1943
32. Mrs. Miniver, Metro-Goldwyn-Mayer Productions, ©1942
33. Ibid.

NINE   ENGLISH BULLDOG

1. Churchill: The Life Triumphant, United Press International , American Heritage Publishing Co, Inc. © 1965
2. Portrait of Churchill, Guy Eden; Hutchinson & Co., Ltd., London © 1945
3. The Second World War, Volume 3, (The Grand Alliance), Houghton Mifflin Co. © 1948
4. The Second World War, Volume 2, (Their Finest Hour), Houghton Mifflin Co. © 1948
5. National Geographic, "Be Ye Men of Valor," Volume 128, No. 2, August, 1965 (Churchill Funeral Edition)
6. The Second World War, Volume 2, (Their Finest Hour), Houghton Mifflin Co. © 1948
7. National Geographic, "Be Ye Men of Valor," Volume 128, No. 2, August, 1965 (Churchill Funeral Edition)
8. The Second World War, Volume 3, (The Grand Alliance), Houghton Mifflin Co. © 1948
9. The Second World War, Volume 2, (Their Finest Hour), Houghton Mifflin Co. © 1948
10. Churchill: The Life Triumphant, United Press International , American Heritage Publishing Co, Inc. © 1965
11. The Second World War, Volume 3, (The Grand Alliance), Houghton Mifflin Co. © 1948
12. Portrait of Churchill, Guy Eden; Hutchinson & Co., Ltd., London © 1945
13. The Second World War, Volume 3, (The Grand Alliance), Houghton Mifflin Co. © 1948
14. Ibid.
15. Portrait of Churchill, Guy Eden; Hutchinson & Co., Ltd., London © 1945
16. National Geographic, "Be Ye Men of Valor," Volume 128, No. 2, August, 1965 (Churchill Funeral Edition)
17. The Second World War, Volume 3, (The Grand Alliance), Houghton Mifflin Co. © 1948
18. Portrait of Churchill, Guy Eden; Hutchinson & Co., Ltd., London © 1945
19. The Second World War, Volume 3, (The Grand Alliance), Houghton Mifflin Co. © 1948
20. Ibid.
21. Churchill: The Life Triumphant, United Press International , American Heritage Publishing Co, Inc. © 1965
22. Why We Fight, Volume 7, "War Comes to America," U.S. War Department & Frank Capra Productions © 1943
23. The Second World War, Volume 3, (The Grand Alliance), Houghton Mifflin Co. © 1948
24. Portrait of Churchill, Guy Eden; Hutchinson & Co., Ltd., London © 1945
25. The Second World War, Volume 3, (The Grand Alliance), Houghton Mifflin Co. © 1948
26. Churchill: The Life Triumphant, United Press International , American Heritage Publishing Co, Inc. © 1965
27. The Second World War, Volume 3, (The Grand Alliance), Houghton Mifflin Co. © 1948
28. National Geographic, "Be Ye Men of Valor," Volume 128, No. 2, August, 1965 (Churchill Funeral Edition)
29. The Second World War, Volume 3, (The Grand Alliance), Houghton Mifflin Co. © 1948
30. Churchill: The Life Triumphant, United Press International , American Heritage Publishing Co, Inc. © 1965
31. The Second World War, Volume 3, (The Grand Alliance), Houghton Mifflin Co. © 1948
32. Ibid.
33. Portrait of Churchill, Guy Eden; Hutchinson & Co., Ltd., London © 1945
34. The Second World War, Volume 3, (The Grand Alliance), Houghton Mifflin Co. © 1948
35. "O, God Our Help in Ages Past," Isaac Watts, 1719
36. The Second World War, Volume 3, (The Grand Alliance), Houghton Mifflin Co. © 1948
37. The Great Republic, Sir Winston Churchill, edited by Winston S. Churchill, Random House, New York © 1999
38. BBC World Broadcast, August 24, 1941

TEN   TO MAKE MEN FREE

1. The Second World War, Volume 3, (The Grand Alliance), Houghton Mifflin Co. © 1948
2. John Forster, Librarian, Blenheim Palace, Oxfordshire, England (February 2002)
3. Allen Packwood, Director, Churchill Archives Centre, Cambridge University (interview, February 2002)
4. The Second World War, Volume 3, (The Grand Alliance), Houghton Mifflin Co. © 1948
5. Allen Packwood, Director, Churchill Archives Centre, Cambridge University (interview, February, 2002)
6. National Geographic, "Be Ye Men of Valor," Volume 128, No. 2, August, 1965 (Churchill Funeral Edition)
7. Churchill: The Life Triumphant, United Press International , American Heritage Publishing Co, Inc. © 1965
8. The Second World War, Volume 3, (The Grand Alliance), Houghton Mifflin Co. © 1948
9. National Geographic, "Be Ye Men of Valor," Volume 128, No. 2, August, 1965 (Churchill Funeral Edition)
10. Why We Fight, Volume 5, "The Battle of Russia," U.S. War Department & Frank Capra Productions © 1943

11. Portrait of Churchill, Guy Eden; Hutchinson & Co., Ltd., London © 1945
12. Why We Fight, Volume 1, "Prelude to War," U.S. War Department & Frank Capra Productions © 1943
13. Portrait of Churchill, Guy Eden; Hutchinson & Co., Ltd., London © 1945
14. Why We Fight, Volume 7, "War Comes to America," U.S. War Department & Frank Capra Productions © 1943
15. Ibid.
16. The Second World War, Volume 3, (The Grand Alliance), Houghton Mifflin Co. © 1948
17. Days of '41: Pearl Harbor Remembered, Ed Sheehan, Kapa Associates, Ltd., Honolulu ©1977
18. The Second World War, Volume 3, (The Grand Alliance), Houghton Mifflin Co. © 1948
19. Ibid.
20. Portrait of Churchill, Guy Eden; Hutchinson & Co., Ltd., London © 1945
21. The Second World War, Volume 3, (The Grand Alliance), Houghton Mifflin Co. © 1948
22. "Secrets of the Axis Revealed," The History Channel, 2002
23. The Second World War, Volume 3, (The Grand Alliance), Houghton Mifflin Co. © 1948
24. National Geographic, "Be Ye Men of Valor," Volume 128, No. 2, August, 1965 (Churchill Funeral Edition)
25. Ibid.
26. The Great Republic, Sir Winston Churchill, edited by Winston S. Churchill, Random House, New York © 1999
27. Newsweek, September 27, 2001
28. President George W. Bush, Speech to a Joint Session of the Congress, September 2001
29. PBS NewsHour with Jim Lehrer, October 2, 2001
30. The Guardian, October 7, 2001
31. The Great Republic, Sir Winston Churchill, edited by Winston S. Churchill, Random House, New York © 1999

ELEVEN   INTO THE BREACH

1. The Second World War, Volume 3, (The Grand Alliance), Houghton Mifflin Co. © 1948
2. Winston Churchill, Second Address to a Joint Session of Congress, May 19, 1943
3. The Second World War, Volume 3, (The Grand Alliance), Houghton Mifflin Co. © 1948
4. Why We Fight, "War Comes to America," Volume 7, U.S. War Department & Frank Capra Productions © 1943
5. The Second World War, Volume 3, (The Grand Alliance), Houghton Mifflin Co. © 1948
6. Portrait of Churchill, Guy Eden; Hutchinson & Co., Ltd., London © 1945
7. Crusade for Europe, Dwight D. Eisenhower, Doubleday & Company, Inc., New York © 1948
8. The Second World War, Volume 3, (The Grand Alliance), Houghton Mifflin Co. © 1948
9. Ibid.
10. Ibid.
11. The Second World War, Volume 3, (The Grand Alliance), Houghton Mifflin Co. © 1948
12. The Second World War, Volume 4, (The Hinge of Fate), Houghton Mifflin Co. © 1948
13. Ibid.
14. National Geographic Vol. 128, No. 2, August 1965
15. The Second World War, Volume 3, (The Grand Alliance), Houghton Mifflin Co. © 1948
16. Ibid.
17. Portrait of Churchill, Guy Eden; Hutchinson & Co., Ltd., London © 1945
18. "Great Britons," Realm, June 2000
19. The History Channel, 2002, "Winston Churchill"
20. "Great Britons," Realm, June 2003
21. The Second World War, Volume 3, (The Grand Alliance), Houghton Mifflin Co. © 1948
22. Ibid.
23. Portrait of Churchill, Guy Eden; Hutchinson & Co., Ltd., London © 1945
24. The Great Republic, Sir Winston Churchill, edited by Winston S. Churchill, Random House, New York © 1999
25. The Second World War, Volume 4, (The Hinge of Fate), Houghton Mifflin Co. © 1948
26. The Second World War, Volume 3, (The Grand Alliance), Houghton Mifflin Co. © 1948

27. The Second World War, Volume 4, (The Hinge of Fate), Houghton Mifflin Co. © 1948
28. Portrait of Churchill, Guy Eden; Hutchinson & Co., Ltd., London © 1945
29. The History Channel, "Winston Churchill," 2000
30. The Second World War, Volume 4, (The Hinge of Fate), Houghton Mifflin Co. © 1948
31. Rt. Honorable Winston Churchill, First Speech to a Joint Session of Congress, December 26, 1941
32. "10 Downing Street" (official website of the Prime Minister of Great Britain) (excerpts of speeches in 2002)
33. Sketches from English History, Arthur M. Wheeler (Professor of History, Yale College), Chautauqua Press © 1886
34. William Shakespeare, Henry V, Act III, Scenes i and ii

TWELVE   THE NOBLEST WORK
1. Churchill: The Life Triumphant, United Press International , American Heritage Publishing Co, Inc. © 1965
2. The Second World War, Volume 3, (The Grand Alliance), Houghton Mifflin Co. © 1948
3. Ibid.
4. Flags of Our Fathers, James Bradley, Bantam Books, New York © 2001
5. The Second World War, Volume 3, (The Grand Alliance), Houghton Mifflin Co. © 1948
6. Allen Packwood, Director, Churchill Archives Centre, Cambridge University (interview, February, 2002)
7. Churchill: The Life Triumphant, United Press International, American Heritage Publishing Co, Inc. © 1965
8. The Second War, Volume 4 (The Hinge of Fate), Houghton Mifflin Co. © 1948
9. Allen Packwood, Director, Churchill Archives Centre, Cambridge University (interview, February, 2002)
10. The Second World War, Volume 3, (The Grand Alliance), Houghton Mifflin Co. © 1948
11. Ibid.
12. Ibid.
13. Why We Fight, "War Comes to America," Volume 7, U.S. War Department & Frank Capra Productions © 1943
14. "Secrets of the Axis Revealed," The History Channel, 2002
15. Why We Fight, "War Comes to America," Volume 7, U.S. War Department & Frank Capra Productions © 1943
16. The Second World War, Volume 3, (The Grand Alliance), Houghton Mifflin Co. © 1948
17. "Secrets of the Axis Revealed," The History Channel, 2002
18 Why We Fight, "War Comes to America," Volume 7, U.S. War Department & Frank Capra Productions © 1943
19. Portrait of Churchill, Guy Eden; Hutchinson & Co., Ltd., London © 1945
20. The Second World War, Volume 4 (The Hinge of Fate), Houghton Mifflin Co. © 1948
21. Adolf Hitler, The History Channel, 2000
22. Winston Churchill, Second Address to Joint Session of Congress, May 19, 1943
23. The Second World War, Volume 4 (The Hinge of Fate), Houghton Mifflin Co. © 1948
24. Portrait of Churchill, Guy Eden; Hutchinson & Co., Ltd., London © 1945
25. The Second World War, Volume 4 (The Hinge of Fate), Houghton Mifflin Co. © 1948
26. Allen Packwood, Director, Churchill Archives Centre, Cambridge University (interview, February, 2002)
27. The Second World War, Volume 4 (The Hinge of Fate), Houghton Mifflin Co. © 1948
28. Ibid.
29. John Forster, Librarian, Blenheim Palace, Oxfordshire, England (interview, February 2002)
30. National Geographic, Volume 128, No. 2, August, 1965 (Churchill Funeral Edition)
31. Churchill: The Life Triumphant, United Press International , American Heritage Publishing Co, Inc. © 1965
32. The Second World War, Volume 4 (The Hinge of Fate), Houghton Mifflin Co. © 1948
33. Ibid.
34. Ibid.
35. Winston Churchill, Speech at Harvard University, September 6, 1943
36. The Second World War, Volume 4 (The Hinge of Fate), Houghton Mifflin Co. © 1948
37. Ibid.
38. Churchill: The Life Triumphant, United Press International , American Heritage Publishing Co, Inc. © 1965
39. Ibid.
40. National Geographic, "Be Ye Men of Valor," Volume 128, No. 2, August, 1965 (Churchill Funeral Edition)
41. The War Cabinet Rooms (official tour guide information)

42. The Second World War, Volume 4 (The Hinge of Fate), Houghton Mifflin Co. © 1948
43. "D-Day: The Total Story," The History Channel, 2003
44. The Second World War, Volume 4 (The Hinge of Fate), Houghton Mifflin Co. © 1948
45. World at War: D-Day, G. C. Skipper, Regensteiner Publishing, Chicago © 1982
46. "Modern Marvels," The History Channel, 2003
47. "D-Day, the Total Story," The History Channel, 2002
48. Portrait of Churchill, Guy Eden; Hutchinson & Co., Ltd., London © 1945
49. "Heavy Metal," The History Channel, 2003
50. Churchill: The Life Triumphant, United Press International , American Heritage Publishing Co, Inc. © 1965
51. "Heavy Metal," The History Channel, 2003
52. The Second World War, Volume 4 (The Hinge of Fate), Houghton Mifflin Co. © 1948
53. "Heavy Metal," The History Channel, 2003
54. Ibid.
55. "Heavy Metal," The History Channel, 2003
56. Ibid.
57. Portrait of Churchill, Guy Eden; Hutchinson & Co., Ltd., London © 1945
58. The Second World War, Volume 4 (The Hinge of Fate), Houghton Mifflin Co. © 1948
59. "D-Day: The Total Story," The History Channel, 2002
60. Portrait of Churchill, Guy Eden; Hutchinson & Co., Ltd., London © 1945
61. Crusade for Europe, Dwight D. Eisenhower, Doubleday & Company, Inc., New York © 1948
62. The Second World War, Volume 4 (The Hinge of Fate), Houghton Mifflin Co. © 1948
63. "Heavy Metal," The History Channel, 2003
64. World at War: D-Day, G. C. Skipper, Regensteiner Publishing, Chicago © 1982
65. Ibid.
66. "D-Day: The Total Story," The History Channel, 2002
67. Portrait of Churchill, Guy Eden; Hutchinson & Co., Ltd., London © 1945
68. Ibid.
69. The Second World War, Volume 4 (The Hinge of Fate), Houghton Mifflin Co. © 1948
70. The Great Republic, Sir Winston Churchill, edited by Winston S. Churchill, Random House, New York © 1999
71. "D-Day: The Total Story," The History Channel, 2002
72. Henry V, by William Shakespeare, Act IV, Scene iii

THIRTEEN   ON THE RAMPARTS

1. The Great Republic, Sir Winston Churchill, edited by Winston S. Churchill, Random House, New York © 1999
2. The Second World War, Volume 5 (Closing the Ring), Houghton Mifflin Co. © 1948
3. "Heavy Metal," The History Channel, 2002
4. John Forster, Librarian, Blenheim Palace, Oxfordshire, England (interview, February 2002)
5. The Second World War, Volume 4 (The Hinge of Fate), Houghton Mifflin Co. © 1948
6. Ibid.
7. D-Day: The Total Story, The History Channel, 2002
8. Stephen Ambrose, "D-Day: The Total Story," The History Channel, 2002
9. Ibid.
10. The Second World War, Volume 5 (Closing the Ring), Houghton Mifflin Co. © 1948
11. "Modern Marvels: Sherman Tanks," The History Channel, 2003
12. Invasion: 1944, Winston Churchill, Regnery Publications © 1946
13. The Second World War, Volume 5 (Closing the Ring), Houghton Mifflin Co. © 1948
14. Ibid.
15. "Modern Marvels: Sherman Tanks," The History Channel, 2003
16. The Second World War, Volume 5 (Closing the Ring), Houghton Mifflin Co. © 1948
17. Ibid.

18. "Heavy Metal: Tanks," The History Channel, 2003
19. The Second World War, Volume 5 (Closing the Ring), Houghton Mifflin Co. © 1948
20. Ibid.
21. The Second World War, Volume 4 (The Hinge of Fate), Houghton Mifflin Co. © 1948
22. The Second World War, Volume 5 (Closing the Ring), Houghton Mifflin Co. © 1948
23. Ibid.
24. The Second World War, Volume 6 (Triumph and Tragedy), Houghton Mifflin Co. © 1948
25. The Second World War, Volume 5 (Closing the Ring), Houghton Mifflin Co. © 1948
26. The Second World War, Volume 3 (The Grand Alliance), Houghton Mifflin Co. © 1948
27. The Second World War, Volume 5 (Closing the Ring), Houghton Mifflin Co. © 1948
28. The Wit of Sir Winston, Adam Sykes and Iain Sproat, Leslie Frewin Publishers, Ltd., London © 1965
29. The Second World War, Volume 6 (Triumph and Tragedy), Houghton Mifflin Co. © 1948
30. Churchill: Forging An Alliance for Freedom, Allen Packwood, Speech at the Heritage Foundation, February 2004
31. The Second World War, Volume 6 (Triumph and Tragedy), Houghton Mifflin Co. © 1948
32. "Allah Mode," The Weekly Standard, July 15, 2002
33. The Second World War, Volume 6 (Triumph and Tragedy), Houghton Mifflin Co. © 1948
34. Churchill: The Life Triumphant, United Press International , American Heritage Publishing Co, Inc. © 1965
35. Ibid.
36. The Wall Street Journal, Prime Minister Tony Blair, Address to Joint Session of Congress, July 17, 2003
37. The Weekly Standard, April 7, 2003 (quoted from The Mail on Sunday)
38. "Statesmanship and Its Betrayal," by Mark Helprin, The Wall Street Journal, July 2, 1998

FOURTEEN   FOR LIBERTY
1. The Second World War, Volume 6 (Triumph and Tragedy), Houghton Mifflin Co. © 1948
2. Ibid.
3. Ibid.
4. Ibid.
5. Ibid.
6. Portrait of Churchill, Guy Eden; Hutchinson & Co., Ltd., London © 1945
7. "Last Days of World War II," The History Channel, 2003
8. The Second World War, Volume 6 (Triumph and Tragedy), Houghton Mifflin Co. © 1948
9. Portrait of Churchill, Guy Eden; Hutchinson & Co., Ltd., London © 1945
10. The Second World War, Volume 6 (Triumph and Tragedy), Houghton Mifflin Co. © 1948
11. Ibid.
12. Ibid.
13. Ibid.
14. "Last Days of World War II," The History Channel, 2003.
15. "Hitler and the Occult," The History Channel, 2002 (quoted by Manfred Rommel, son of "the Desert Fox")
16. The Second World War, Volume 6 (Triumph and Tragedy), Houghton Mifflin Co. © 1948
17. Ibid.
18. Adolf Hitler, The History Channel, 2001
19. Death of the Reich: The Last Days of WWII, The History Channel, 2003
20. Justice at Nuremberg: The Last Days of WWII, The History Channel, 2003
21. Death of the Reich: The Last Days of WWII, The History Channel, 2003
22. Portrait of Churchill, Guy Eden; Hutchinson & Co., Ltd., London © 1945
23. Adolf Hitler, The History Channel, 2001
24. Portrait of Churchill, Guy Eden; Hutchinson & Co., Ltd., London © 1945
25. Justice at Nuremberg: The Last Days of WWII, The History Channel, 2003
26. Winston Churchill: The Private War, Round Hill Productions, Home Box Office (HBO) © 1980
27. Winston Churchill, The History Channel, 2000
28. Portrait of Churchill, Guy Eden; Hutchinson & Co., Ltd., London © 1945

29. Winston Churchill, The History Channel, 2000
30. Winston Churchill: The Private War, Round Hill Productions, Home Box Office (HBO) © 1980
31. The Second World War, Volume 1 (The Gathering Storm), Houghton Mifflin Co. © 1948
32. Joseph Addison, 1672-1719 (quoted in Churchill: The Life Triumphant)

FIFTEEN   BACK TO THE FUTURE
1. The Second World War, Volume 6 (Triumph and Tragedy), Houghton Mifflin Co. © 1948
2. Ibid.
3. Ibid.
4. Ibid.
5. Ibid.
6. Allen Packwood, Churchill Archives Centre, Cambridge University (interview, February, 2002)
7. The Second World War, Volume 6 (Triumph and Tragedy), Houghton Mifflin Co. © 1948
8. Anatole Grunwald, Churchill: The Life Triumphant, American Heritage Publishing Co, Inc. © 1965
9. "People I Have Loved, Known, or Admired," Leo Rosten, Readers Digest, 1971
10. The Second World War, Volume 6 (Triumph and Tragedy), Houghton Mifflin Co. © 1948
11. Ibid.
12. Message to the Nation from the Prime Minister, July 26, 1945 (The Second World War, Volume 6)
13. "The Potsdam Declaration," July 26, 1945
14. The Second World War, Volume 6 (Triumph and Tragedy), Houghton Mifflin Co. © 1948
15. Advanced Training Institute of America, Bill Gothard, Oakbrook, Illinios
16. Portrait of Churchill, Guy Eden; Hutchinson & Co., Ltd., London © 1945
17. The Second World War, Volume 6 (Triumph and Tragedy), Houghton Mifflin Co. © 1948

SIXTEEN   A FIXED POINT
1. The Second World War, Volume 6 (Triumph and Tragedy), Houghton Mifflin Co. © 1948
2. "Savior of the West," Professor Daniel Mahoney, Assumption College, National Review, December 31, 2001
3. Why We Fight, "War Comes to America," Volume 7, U.S. War Department & Frank Capra Productions © 1943
4. Anatole Grunwald, Introduction, Churchill: The Life Triumphant , American Heritage Publishing Co, Inc. © 1965
5. Benjamin Franklin, letter to Benjamin Vaughn, 1783; Great American Quotations by William Federer
6. "A Lion Like Churchill," Stephen Hayward, National Review, June 28, 2004.
7. Portrait of Churchill, Guy Eden; Hutchinson & Co., Ltd., London © 1945
8. "Statesmanship and Its Betrayal," Mark Helprin, The Wall Street Journal, July 2, 1998
9. Portrait of Churchill, Guy Eden; Hutchinson & Co., Ltd., London © 1945
10. Churchill: Forging An Alliance for Freedom, Allen Packwood, Speech at the Heritage Foundation, February 2004
11. Allen Packwood, Director, Churchill Archives Centre, Cambridge University (interview, February, 2002)
12. Churchill: The Life Triumphant, United Press International , American Heritage Publishing Co, Inc. © 1965
13. Churchill: Forging An Alliance for Freedom, Allen Packwood, Speech at the   Heritage Foundation, February 2004
14. Ibid.
15. Introduction to The Sinews of Peace, Westminster College Publications, Fulton, Missouri
16. Sir Winston Churchill, The Sinews of Peace, Westminster College Publications, Fulton, Missouri
17. "My Grandfather Invented Iraq" by Winston S. Churchill, The Wall Street Journal, March 16, 2003
18. Sir Winston Churchill, The Sinews of Peace, Westminster College Publications, Fulton, Missouri
19. John Forster, Librarian, Blenheim Palace, Oxfordshire, England (interview, February, 2002)
20. Churchill: The Life Triumphant, United Press International , American Heritage Publishing Co, Inc. © 1965
21. Sir Winston Churchill, The Sinews of Peace, Westminster College Publications, Fulton, Missouri

SEVENTEEN   FORGE AND ANVIL

1. Advanced Training Institute Publications, Oakbrook, Illinois; Webster's New Collegiate Dictionary © 1959
2. Ecclesiastes 11:6 (New International Version, NIV)
3. National Review, December 31, 2001 (book review of Churchill: A Study in Greatness by Geoffrey Best)
4. "Berlin: Frontline of the Cold War," War Stories with Oliver North, FoxNews Channel, 2004
5. Ibid.
6. The Second World War, Volume 6 (Triumph and Tragedy), Houghton Mifflin Co. © 1948
7. Archibald MacLeish, The Weekly Standard, November 5, 2004
8. Second Address to Joint Session of Congress, May 19, 1943
9. Realm, Volume 104, January-February, 2002
10. "In the Footsteps of Giants," Jon Meacham, Readers Digest, April 2004
11. Winston S. Churchill, "My Grandfather Invented Iraq," The Wall Street Journal, 2003
12. Catoctin History, "Shangri-La: A Mountain, A Vision, A Place in History," Tom McFadden, Fall issue, 2003
13. Realm, Volume 104, 2002
14. "The Man of the Century" (Churchill exhibit, Westminster College, Fulton, Missouri)
15. Churchill: The Life Triumphant, United Press International, American Heritage Publishing Co, Inc. © 1965
16. Ibid.
17. Allen Packwood, Director, Churchill Archives Centre, Cambridge University (interview, February, 2002)
18. Churchill: The Life Triumphant, United Press International , American Heritage Publishing Co, Inc. © 1965
19. President John F. Kennedy, April 9, 1963
20. Churchill: The Life Triumphant, United Press International , American Heritage Publishing Co, Inc. © 1965
21. "Inside the Twentieth Century," LOOK, January 12, 1965; Vol. 29, No. 1 (Churchill Funeral Edition)
22. Ibid.
23. "Be Ye Men of Valour," National Geographic, Vol. 128, No. 2, August 1965 (Churchill Funeral Edition)
24. "People I Have Known and Admired," Leo Rosten, Readers Digest, © 1971
25. LIFE, February 5, 1965, Vol. 58, No. 5 (Churchill Funeral Edition)
26. "An Empty Seat" by Lee Hall, Life Magazine, February 5, 1965, Vol. 58, No. 5
27. "The Man of the Century," Churchill exhibit ,Westminster College, Fulton, Missouri
28. "The Churchill I Knew," Dwight D. Eisenhower, National Geographic, Vol. 128, No. 2, August 1965
29. "Be Ye Men of Valour," National Geographic, Vol. 128, No. 2, August 1965 (Churchill Funeral Edition)

[Definitions of character qualities from Character Sketches, Advanced Training Institute, Bill Gothard, Oakbrook, IL]

(Churchill Archives Centre; Baroness Spencer-Churchill Papers)